Breaking the Sound Barrier:
Teaching Language Learners How to Listen

Gianfranco Conti and Steve Smith

Copyright © 2019 G. Conti and S. Smith

All rights reserved.

ISBN: 978-1-0969-7388-1

Imprint: Independently Published

Edited and formatted by Elspeth Jones

Dedico questo libro alla mia splendida bimba, Catrina Jade, ai miei impareggiabili genitori Mario e Ketty e alla mia dolce metà, Corynn.
Gianfranco

Dedicated to my dear wife Elspeth and son Joel.
Steve

ABOUT THE AUTHORS

Gianfranco Conti taught for 25 years at schools in Italy, the UK and in Kuala Lumpur, Malaysia. He has also been a university lecturer, holds a Masters degree in Applied Linguistics and a PhD in metacognitive strategies as applied to second language writing. He is now an author, independent educational consultant and active professional development provider. He has written over 1600 resources for the TES website, which awarded him the Best Resources Contributor in 2015. Gianfranco writes an influential blog on second language acquisition called The Language Gym, co-founded the interactive website language-gym.com and the Facebook professional group Global Innovative Language Teachers (GILT). He tweets as @gianfrancocont9 and can be reached at thelanguagegymcpd@gmail.com.

Steve Smith taught French for over 30 years in UK secondary schools, including 24 years as Head of Department at Ripon Grammar School. After graduating in French and Linguistics, he did a Masters degree focusing on second language learning and acquisition. He now produces resources for his widely used website frenchteacher.net, writes a blog on language teaching and is a professional development provider, working both independently and for the AQA examination awarding body. He is visiting lecturer and Lead Subject Tutor for the PGCE course at the University of Buckingham and is author of *Becoming an Outstanding Languages Teacher* (Routledge, 2017). Steve tweets as @spsmith45 and can be reached at spsmith45@aol.com.

ACKNOWLEDGEMENTS

We would like to acknowledge in particular Elspeth Jones, Emerita Professor at Leeds Beckett University, for her painstaking work editing and proof-reading the text.

We thank Professor Suzanne Graham at the University of Reading, for her generous contributions to the chapter on cognitive and metacognitive strategies. We are also grateful to Dr Adriana Perez Encinas, Dolly Predovic and Dr Tanja Reiffenrath for checking the accuracy of target language texts and to Wei Jean Liew for her cover artwork.

In addition we thank the many scholars, teacher educators and teaching colleagues who have helped us develop our thinking over the years.

CONTENTS

About the Authors
Acknowledgments
List of Figures
List of Infoboxes
List of Tables
Glossary of Terms

Introduction   1

1   How do we listen?   9

2   The principles of Listening-as-Modelling (LAM).   21

3   Teaching sounds: fun with phonology.   31

4   Teaching lexical retrieval through listening.   59

5   Teaching parsing, grammar and lexicogrammar.   95

6   Interpersonal listening.   121

7   Task-based listening.   149

8   LAM in action: three sample teaching sequences.   171

9   Making the most of songs.   189

10 Assessment and preparing for exams.   199

11 Cognitive and metacognitive strategies.   213

12 Planning for improvement.   225

    Conclusion   231

    Appendix: List of Activities   233
    Bibliography   237
    Index   249

LIST OF FIGURES

3.1	A framework for phonological instruction
3.2	The vocal tract
3.3	Phonics with pictures (French)
3.4	*Sentence stealer* game
4.1	A model of working memory (Baddeley, 2003)
4.2	The phonological loop structure (Baddeley et al, 2000)
4.3	*Climb the wall* game
4.4	A listening brain teaser for near-beginners
4.5	Example picture for *Listen and colour in*
4.6	*Listen and draw:* Our sitting room
4.7	Example of a *Spot the nonsense* task
4.8	Example of *Spot the missing detail* in Spanish
4.9	*No snakes, no ladders*
4.10	Re-ordering task using L1 sentences instead of pictures
5.1	*Listen and correct* (French)
5.2	*Spot the missing detail* task (Italian)
6.1	Present and imperfect contrasted
6.2	Picture for creative storytelling
8.1	Fluency card on talking about a past holiday
8.2	*Pyramid translation*
8.3	Source text for sequence 3: film review

LIST OF INFOBOXES

1	Skill theory
2	Comprehensible input (CI)
3	What is working memory?
4	What is PPP?
5	From Comprehensible input (CI) to Input processing (IP)
6	What is metacognition?
7	Phonetics, phonology and phonics
8	The mental lexicon
9	Human forgetting rates
10	Dual Coding Theory
11.	Cognitive Load Theory
12	Two types of grammatical knowledge
13	Pedagogical versus internalised grammar
14	Morphology and syntax
15	Parsing
16	Information gap activities
17	Should I correct students' errors?
18	The Comprehension Hypothesis
19	The Interaction Hypothesis
20	Narrow listening
21	Cognitive empathy

LIST OF TABLES

1.1	Top-down processing skills (adapted from Field, 2008)
1.2	A bottom-up processing model (Field, 2008)
3.1	Minimal pairs
4.1	Nation's (2013) three dimensions of knowing a word
4.2	Taxonomy of lexical chunks, adapted from Lewis (1997)
4.3	Learnability: how hard are words to learn? (adapted from Nation, 2007)
4.4	Sample narrow listening texts
4.5	Human forgetting rates (Ebbinghaus, 1885)
4.6	Example of an Italian sentence builder
4.7	*Same or different* cards
4.8	*Multi-choice match* task
4.9	*Listening slalom*
4.10	*Gapped parallel texts* (Spanish example)
4.11	*Bad translation* (Italian example)
4.12	*Listening grids*
4.13	Three texts designed for *Spot the Difference*
5.1	Clause types in English
5.2	Sentence builder
5.3	A parsing grid
5.4	*Spot and rewrite the pattern*
5.5	Sample *Either… or* task.
5.6	*Find the object*
5.7	Minimal pairs - structure recognition
5.8	A collocational grid used to practise French verb patterns
5.9	Beginner-level Italian narrow listening texts on the topic of leisure
5.10	*Word completion* (French)
5.11	*Morphology chart*
6.1	Hierarchy of question types
6.2	Modelling the imperfect tense through QA
7.1	Planning and running a task (based on J. Willis)
7.2	Role-play cards for *The two detectives*
8.1	The MARS-EARS pedagogical cycle
8.2	12 communicative functions and their sub-functions
8.3	Example of sub-functions and related lexicogrammar constructions
8.4	Communicative drill cards
8.5	L1 to L2 narrow translation texts
8.6	Spanish narrow listening / reading texts
9.1	Recommended French songs
9.2	Recommended German songs
9.3	Recommended Spanish songs
10.1	Question types to use in listening tests
10.2	Strategies students can use while doing tests
11.1	Cognitive and metacognitive strategies summarised (Vandergrift, 1997).
11.2	A pedagogical cycle for implementing strategies

GLOSSARY OF TERMS

ACTFL	American Council on the Teaching of Foreign Languages.
Assimilation	A sound change where some phonemes change through the influence of other nearby sounds.
CEFR	The Common European Framework of Reference for Languages, often referred to as CEFR, is an international standard for describing different competence levels within a language.
GCSE	High stakes exam taken at age 15-16 in England, Wales and Northern Ireland.
Input	Language which learners hear or read.
L1	The student's first language.
L2	The language being learned.
LAM	*Listening-as-Modelling gradually builds student expertise and self-efficacy through a process of explicitly taught exercises which target the specific skills required to be an effective listener* (see Chapter 2).
Lexicogrammar	Term is used to describe the continuity between grammar and vocabulary.
Lexis	Words and word units such as formulaic phrases.
Metacognition	'Thinking about thinking', becoming aware of and monitoring one's higher-order thinking skills.
Metalanguage	The language used to talk about language.
Micro-skill	A sub-skill which contributes to an overall skill.
Morpheme	A word or part of a word.
Morphology	The study of words, the parts that form them, and their relationship to other words in the same language.
Phoneme	A unit of sound that distinguishes one word from another in a particular language.
Phonics	A way to teach reading by focusing on the correspondence between the sounds (phonemes) of a language and the spelling patterns (graphemes) that represent them.
Phonology	The sounds and sound patterns of a particular language.
Phonotactics	A branch of phonology that deals with restrictions in a language on the permissible combinations of phonemes.
Syntax	The rules, principles, and processes that govern the structure of sentences, usually including word order.

x

INTRODUCTION

1.   The importance of listening

Thank you for reading our book which is aimed at pre-service teachers and others who wish to refine their craft of language teaching. We hope you will find it interesting and useful. Most readers will be teachers of Modern Foreign Languages (World Languages), but teachers of English as a Second Language will find much to interest them here too. As with *The Language Teacher Toolkit*, the handbook we wrote in 2016, this is not a scholarly work, but a book written for teachers, by teachers in an attempt to marry evidence and practice.

We decided to write this volume for two main reasons.

Firstly, our conversations with language teachers suggest that listening is a neglected area which students often find the hardest. Three factors explain why this seems to be the case:
- Listening places substantial demands on students' ability to decode and instantly make meaning from a continuous stream of sounds.
- In listening lessons students often feel they are being tested, not taught.
- In tests and exams students get no more than a couple of opportunities to hear texts, so panic can take hold and minds go blank.

Secondly, of all the language skills, we believe listening to be the most important for the development of second language proficiency. Our brains are wired to pick up language through listening. Young children essentially acquire their first language by this means. The literacy skills of reading and writing are not biologically primary, and many people struggle with them. Scholars of second language acquisition are of the view that the main way we acquire a new language is by receiving what is labelled *Comprehensible Input*, either through listening or reading, which we eventually convert into output when we write and speak. This emphasises the essential modelling role that listening has in language learning, a role which can be much further developed in classrooms than it currently is.

With these concerns in mind, we have written a book which will help you develop students' confidence and skills as listeners. Our guidance is partly based on one of the most up to date research models about how listening works. We attempt to match our proposed activities to this model and research in general.

The emphasis is on teaching **beginners up to intermediate level** (CEFR levels A1 to B1; ACTFL Novice to Intermediate High) in high schools (typically 11 to 16 year-olds). Lesson activities use English, Spanish, German and Italian, but can all be adapted easily to the language you teach. **The focus is firmly on practical lessons – over 200 separate tasks are listed**, which we hope will help students 'break the sound barrier'.

2. How to use this book

You could read through the whole book in order, since it is written with a clear narrative structure in mind. But equally you could dip into different chapters according to what interests you most. You might like to highlight the activities you find most appealing, or use the book as a reference when searching for something productive and enjoyable for a lesson. A page-referenced appendix provides a summary of the many tasks described. Have a look through the contents below.

Chapter 1 How do we listen?
We describe how listening works, referring to top-down and bottom-up processing skills, the five phases of listening as described by one scholar, John Field; the issues of *priming* and *chunking*; the key role of *Comprehensible Input* and the need to integrate listening with the other skills of speaking, reading and writing. This chapter shows that the listening lesson is about much more than just listening.

Chapter 2 The principles of Listening-as-Modelling.
The concept of *Listening as Modelling* (LAM) is laid out, which underpins much of the approach we describe. Aspects such as *input-flooding, thorough and extensive processing, scaffolding* and *interpersonal listening* are considered.

Chapter 3 Teaching sounds: fun with phonology
This chapter sets out a framework for ear training. How can we sensitise students to sound, and help them break up the stream of sound? A wide range of engaging, low-preparation activities based on phonology and phonics are described, along with suggestions of how they can be woven into lessons.

Chapter 4 Teaching lexical retrieval through listening
The vital role of vocabulary and how it is best acquired form the focus of this chapter. What does it mean to know words and phrases? How can we use listening as a means to build vocabulary knowledge and skill? Lots of vocabulary-based activities are described, which help vocabulary retrieval during listening.

Chapter 5 Teaching parsing, grammar and lexicogrammar
How can we develop students' ability to *parse* utterances, i.e. use their knowledge of grammar to make sense of utterances and thus make meaning? A rationale for teaching grammar and lexicogrammar through listening is described, and numerous examples given of easy activities with grammar at their core.

Chapter 6 Interpersonal listening
How can we build a more communicative, interpersonal approach into listening lessons, while keeping a focus on listening as modelling, not testing? The role of questioning and other interactions is explored, along with how to make language comprehensible. Examples of practical lesson ideas are offered, some teacher-led, some student-led.

Chapter 7 Task-based listening
The thinking behind task-based teaching and listening is discussed, followed by examples of how purposeful communicative tasks, including games, can be built into lessons as part of a listening programme.

Chapter 8 LAM in action: three sample teaching sequenecs
We walk the reader through three detailed sample teaching sequences illustrating the Listening-as-Modelling approach and how the other language skills can be integrated into listening-focused lessons.

Chapter 9 Making the most of songs
How can songs be exploited in the classroom to support listening skills? A detailed list of ways to make the most of a song is offered, along with examples of songs recommended by teachers for French, German and Spanish.

Chapter 10 Assessment and preparing for exams
This chapter considers how to assess listening and how to help students prepare for exams. Principles of effective assessment are provided, together with what that means for the classroom. Specific tips and advice are offered to help teachers and students prepare for exams.

Chapter 11 Cognitive and metacognitive strategies
What is the role of strategies in helping students develop their skills? To what extent can students make use of strategies to make the most of their existing knowledge and to compensate for any lack of knowledge? Specific research-supported techniques are suggested.

Chapter 12 Planning for improvement
We put forward ideas to help teachers and departments plot a way forward if they wish to improve their students' listening performance over time.

3. The Cinderella skill?

Decades of classroom second language acquisition research have highlighted the fact that listening is the skill language teachers:
- understand the least;
- usually have fewer resources for;
- feel the least confident teaching;
- neglect the most.

This is why listening is often referred to in the specialised literature as the 'Cinderella skill' (Vandergrift, 1997; Nunan, 1997). But why do many teachers report that teaching listening is an area they often neglect? What aspects of current practice might be holding some students back?

For various reasons including tradition, fashion and the influence of exams, many teachers use a mixture of grammar exercises, translation, verb conjugation, drills, question and answer, pair and group oral work, games, vocabulary apps and comprehension exercises based on the written or spoken word. If a lesson is observed, there is a tendency to want to show students *producing* language at all costs. This is understandable, given that it is much easier to evaluate something you can see or hear. There is therefore a temptation to avoid demonstrating tasks which involve the teacher talking a good deal from the front or students listening to recordings.

In addition, many teachers, especially those with weaker spoken fluency, may be tempted to limit themselves to the listening activities provided by the text book, without exploiting that material in depth or training students to discriminate really carefully (Chambers, 1996). There can be a tendency to work through familar routines without critically evaluating them (Field, 2008).

Other teachers may also underestimate the extent to which their own modelling of spoken target language (L2) is the most important source of tailor-made listening. Plenty of great work goes on in classrooms, in terms of exploiting audio and video recordings, teacher-student interaction and in the area of phonological training (which has seen something of a resurgence at primary and secondary level). But even so, lesson observers frequently report that L2 is underused. Give us more target language, they say!

Teachers sometimes report how difficult it can be to find the audio sources they would like to use which, added to their overloaded timetables, often means they fall back on the course book. With these points in mind, it may be better to read texts aloud than play audio recordings in the formative years of listening instruction. There is much to be said for 'talking to the eyes', as it were, modelling sounds clearly and making language more understandable, while engaging in two-way communication.

Far from being the Cinderella skill, we believe that listening needs to take centre stage in the language lesson.

4. From testing to modelling

Too often, listening exercises feel like tests. A recording is played two or more times, students perform a written task and the answers are corrected. Students get used to a regular diet of gap-filling, comprehension questions, multiple-choice, matching tasks and true/false exercises. So a listening activity becomes a test of comprehension which yields a *product*, i.e a set of answers. While this has a place (for example when preparing for the demands of an exam), students will become better listeners in the long run if we place a greater emphasis on the actual *process of listening*.

This means moving away from a culture of quizzing students, which often results in them making educated guesses, to one of *modelling*, where listening tasks are carried out with the aim of *teaching language skills*, not *testing* them. By modelling, we mean demonstrating the use of language in context, while sensitising students to phonological, syllabic, lexical, morphological and syntactic patterns, thus teaching students *how to listen*. Without skills in these areas students cannot process sound to make meaning, the ultimate aim of listening.

This implies that an important aspect of modelling relates to the *listening micro-skills* students need in order to become effective listeners. We believe these skills can be taught and the precise processes underlying them explained and practised. In other words, we need to break down the listening process and rebuild it bit by bit, to help students become more confident and skilled listeners. We call this process *Listening-As-Modelling* (LAM for short). In Chapter 2 we look at the principles of LAM in more detail, before going on in subsequent chapters to provide a wide range of activities which demonstrate the approach and help students become more confident and effective listeners.

5. A skill theory perspective

The LAM approach is partly rooted in the *skill theory* model of classroom second language acquisition, the key premise of which is that any language skill, including listening, can be acquired in much the same way as any other set of human skills (e.g. playing football or driving a car).

Within a skill theory the goal of listening instruction is the *automatisation* of the micro-skills our brain needs to perform in real time, in order to extract meaning from any utterance we hear. In Chapters 3 to 5 a range of tasks and techniques are discussed that aim at speeding up the micro-skills of aural processing, lexical retrieval and pattern recognition.

> **INFOBOX 1 Skill theory**
>
> This general approach comes from cognitive psychology-based accounts of classroom L2 acquisition (Anderson,1994; Johnson, 1996,; DeKeyser, 1998). Skill theory is one way of looking at how languages can be learned in classrooms, particularly during the early stages of teaching, less so in naturalistic environments.
>
> Essentially, skill theorists say that every complex task humans learn is made up of layers of sub-tasks. For instance, the driver of a car has to pay attention to the road and take important decisions about where to turn, how fast to go and when to brake. While taking these decisions, the driver is carrying out all sorts of lower-order tasks such as changing gear, depressing the brakes, operating the indicators, etc. These lower-order tasks are carried out subconsciously, without requiring the brain to pay much, if any, conscious attention to them. In order to be able to focus on the most important aspect of any complex activity, the brain has evolved to automatise the less complex tasks.
>
> This is because, based on models of working memory (e.g. Baddeley, 1999), the brain has very limited cognitive space to devote to a task at a given time. For instance, research suggests that we can only remember and repeat a string of about five items or unrelated words. If the words make up a meaningful sentence, the span rises to around 15 (because grammatical and semantic knowledge from long-term memory help out (Baddeley, 2010)).
>
> Automatising complex tasks takes time, requires lots of scaffolding in the early stages and a focus on building fluency. Correction is thought to play an important role in the process.
>
> Skill theorists (e.g. De Keyser, 1998) suggest that communicative language teaching which incorporates explicit grammar teaching and skill automatisation is an effective classroom methodology.

6. From incomprehensible to comprehensible input

It is generally true in learning that practice makes perfect. It is pretty obvious, therefore, that to get better at listening you need to do lots of it. But we know how quickly students get confused and switch off if they hear language they cannnot understand. Effective LAM is, therefore, not simply about the volume of input students receive, but also about its quality. Input is best when it is interesting and helps students notice whatever sound, vocabulary or structural pattern is being taught. This means choosing listening which is easily accessible both in terms of meaning and speed of delivery; in other words, *Comprehensible Input* (CI).

The use of CI is central to the LAM approach and informs the design and delivery of every exercise used to build students' listening proficiency in the early years of second language learning.

> **INFOBOX 2 Comprehensible input (CI)**
>
> This is spoken or written language that can be understood by learners despite their not understanding every single word or structure. It is sometimes described as at, or fractionally above, the students' current level of comprehension. The concept is most commonly associated with Stephen Krashen, (e.g. Krashen, 1982). According to his theory of language acquisition, all that students need to acquire a second language is meaningful messages. Krashen believes that the role of effective language teachers is to provide input and help make it comprehensible in a low anxiety situation. All second language acquisition scholars accept the fundamental role of CI in language learning, while generally believing that CI alone is not enough.

7. Integrating skills

Since most of the listening we do in real life is interpersonal, it makes sense to make the classroom a place where two-way listening occurs much of the time. The 'listening lesson' is much more than playing an audio recording and doing comprehension or decoding exercises.

In addition, it is impossible to divorce listening from the other skills of speaking, reading and writing. Firstly, to decode and get meaning from a stream of speech you need to know enough vocabulary to discern where the boundaries between words and phrases lie. These words and word-units can be taught through listening, but they are also embedded by doing other non-listening activities. Secondly, to decode properly you need to be able to *parse* the utterance, i.e. recognise syntactic and morphological patterns. These patterns can be learned by doing all kinds of non-listening exercises including oral grammar drills, written exercises and translation.

So, while listening is the focus of this book, it also considers some other aspects of language teaching which can help with the process of listening. As we shall see, listening skills development can be incorporated seamlessly into nearly every lesson, becoming an integral and natural part of the process of language learning.

8. And finally…

This book is aimed fairly and squarely at practising teachers, and assumes that the reader does not have a background in applied linguistics or second language learning theory. Technical terms and jargon are used as little as possible, but to be concise, the first language is referred to as L1 and the second language (the language being taught) as L2. A number of 'infoboxes' containing background information on applied linguistics are also included for those who have little prior knowledge about the field. Other abbreviations are explained along the way and they can also be found in the Glossary of Terms.

In general, where words are italicised, these refer to English or second language equivalents. Italics are also used when referring in the main text to the names of specific activities. You will find that the large majority of the 160 or so activities take little preparation and are easy to use with students of wide-ranging proficiency.

As anyone who has ever listened to a foreign language for an extended period knows, listening is far from a passive skill.
(Michael Lewis)

1

HOW DO WE LISTEN?

Introduction

Before focusing on practical activities and lesson sequences for the classroom, a principled basis for the activities needs to be established. Listening comprehension is a very complex process which involves an array of skills. Neuroscience suggests that what distinguishes expert L2 listeners from beginners is not just the accuracy but also the speed and ease (i.e. the *fluency*) with which they execute these skills. Therefore, the skills need to be identified in order to design an effective programme of listening and so that each listening micro-skill can be developed with focused activities.

1. A multi-level process

Researchers (e.g. Brown, 2000; Field, 2008; Rost, 2015), usually describe speech perception as a *multi-level process* involving a number of skills which allow a listener to go from recognising a speech signal, to comprehending its meaning. This process in natural language use occurs in the space of about 500 milliseconds. It is quite a feat!

The skills involved have been classified by researchers into two types: *top-down* and *bottom-up* processing skills. The use of linguistic cues when listening is referred to as bottom-up processing whereas the use of contextual clues and world knowledge is referred to as top-down processing.

Over the course of the last five decades, scholars have disagreed about which of the two skill sets is the more vital for L2 comprehension and to a certain extent the debate continues. But it is generally agreed that both are important, with top-down processing facilitating and supporting bottom-up processing. While both skill sets are at work in any listening activity, at lower levels of listening proficiency students rely mostly on bottom-up processing, and focus on words in particular. This occupies much of their working memory and can result in failing to combine the words into larger meaningful units (Field, 2004; Lynch, 1998; Rubin, 1994). For these students it is extremely important to develop linguistic knowledge (phonological, lexical and syntactic) for them to go beyond simple word recognition. We believe that bottom-up processing skills should be given a great deal of emphasis in the early years of classroom learning. Let us now look at these issues in more detail.

> **INFOBOX 3 What is working memory?**
>
> Commonly labelled short-term memory, working memory is a system for temporarily storing and managing the information needed to carry out complex thinking tasks such as learning, reasoning, and comprehension. According to an established model designed by psychologist Alan Baddeley, when we receive information it is processed by a number of systems. A *Central Executive* runs the whole system, allocating data to three subsystems: (1) the *Phonological Loop* (an 'inner ear' for sounds); (2) the *Visuospatial Sketchpad* (an 'inner eye' for visual and spatial information) and (3) the *Episodic Buffer*, which integrates data from (1) and (2). The *Central Executive* also deals with tasks such as mental arithmetic, problem-solving, sharing out time when multi-tasking and choosing what to focus on. It is also involved in daydreaming and activating long term memory when performing a task. Each component of working memory has a limited capacity, with information lingering only about 15 seconds unless it is rehearsed. It is particularly important for teachers to be aware of working memory when designing activities; if you overload it, information cannot be learned. In addition, storage is fragile and divided attention often results in forgetting.

1.1   Top-down processing skills

These help to make use of background knowledge and the context of the listening event. Knowledge of situations, contexts, conversation types and the person you are talking with, can help you understand what you hear. In other words, listening makes use of non-linguistic as well as linguistic knowledge. For example, if you hear an announcement over the loudspeaker at an airport, you already know the type of information you are likely to hear (gate numbers, delays, passenger calls). If you are having a conversation with a friend about their holiday you will probably know where they went, the type of things they talk about and where they have been before.

Background knowledge relates to what are called *schemas*. These are the mental structures we use to organise and simplify our knowledge of the world - patterns of thought or behaviour which organise types of information and the relationships between them. For every situation we come across, we use schemas based on our previous experience, together with any cultural bias acquired from the society we have grown up in. An example of schemas are stereotypes: the way we make judgments in advance about people we meet. Our brains use schemas to help us interpret everything and, together with immediate contextual and linguistic information, they help us interpret speech with greater ease and accuracy.

In our L1, top-down processing is extremely useful in situations where the language being processed is unclear. Think about having a conversation in a crowded and noisy restaurant or on a bad phone connection. Whenever you cannot understand a word, you resort to the context, including the linguistic content of the conversation so far, your interlocutor's facial expressions and body language, their intonation as well as other linguistic cues to do with that word. The latter may include a single phoneme or syllable you have identified, or a lexical item that preceded or followed the word, e.g. the definite article *the* will suggest the next word must be a noun. The structure of the sentence may also help you identify the mystery word. In other words, top-down processing skills have a facilitative, supportive and *compensatory* function, making up for any lack of linguistic knowledge.

For L2 students top-down skills are particularly valuable since they compensate for failures in decoding and comprehension due to lack of vocabulary, slower processing or insecure grammatical knowledge. Research has found that the lower the proficiency level of students, the greater their reliance on top-down processing. The overuse of top-down strategies by these students is not necessarily a good thing, however, as it often results in ineffective guesswork.

For the last few decades the teaching of listening has been 'top-heavy' in being concerned mostly with the teaching of top-down processing strategies. To this day, the modelling of strategies such as activating background knowledge and using contextual cues to predict and understand texts is a staple of listening lessons (see Chapter 11). Bottom-up processing skills, on the other hand, have been neglected in many classrooms (see below).

Table 1.1, adapted from Field (2008), provides a classification of top-down processing skills. While we believe that bottom-up processing skills should be the main focus of an L2 listening programme, teaching top-down skills is also useful, and is considered in more detail in Chapter 11. But as research points out, to be effective top-down teaching has to be explicit and frequent because:

1. With the processing capacity of working memory being so limited, any skill has to be routinised so that it can be executed quickly, creating as light a cognitive load as possible.

2. Every single skill has the potential to aid comprehension if it is carried out alongside

others, at the right time and in the right context. This requires explicit training not only in the effective use of each strategy but also how to handle them in combination. Research suggests that although lower-attaining students often make use of such strategies, they do so ineffectively. It is not just about the strategy itself but, more importantly, when, where and how it is used.

The effective teaching of top-down processing skills, or *strategy-based instruction* as it is generally called in the literature (Macaro, 2003), takes time. Our view is that it should have a secondary, supportive role in the listening curriculum during the formative years of L2 learning, and the greater focus should be on bottom-up processing. Also of note is that it is harder to design practice tasks for top-down than bottom-up processing skills. Chapter 11 considers specific, evidence-based strategies aimed at developing top-down processing.

Table 1.1 Top-down processing skills (adapted from Field, 2008)

Process	Examples of sub-skills
Context: using knowledge sources	• Drawing on world knowledge, topic knowledge, cultural knowledge
Deriving meaning	• Storing the literal meaning of an utterance • Accepting an approximate meaning • Checking understanding
Adding to the meaning	• Making inferences • Dealing with pronouns • Dealing with ambiguity
Selecting information	• Selecting what is relevant or important • Recognising redundant information
Integrating information	• Carrying forward what has been said so far • Connecting ideas • Self-monitoring for consistent interpretation of the message
Recognising the overall argument structure	• Noticing connecting words used by the speaker (e.g. *on the other hand*)

1.2 Bottom-up processing skills

These are about decoding: making meaning from all the bits and pieces of the language, i.e. individual sounds, syllables, morphemes, words, chunks, clauses and longer utterances, as well as the intonation patterns (stress and pitch) associated with the stream of sound. While top-down skills cannot be ignored, our view is that the main aim of the 'listening lesson' should be to help students develop their bottom-up skills.

Let us look at how bottom-up processing works, using a model put forward by Field (2008), and summarised in **Table 1.2**. This is then broken down in more detail.

Table 1.2 A bottom-up processing model (Field, 2008)

Process level	Processes involved
Phoneme	• Identifying consonants and vowels • Adjusting to speakers' voices
Syllable	• Recognising syllable structure • Matching weak syllables and function words
Word	• Working out where words begin and end in connected speech (segmenting) • Matching sequences of sounds to words • Identifying words which are not in their standard forms • Dealing with unknown words
Syntax	• Recognising where clauses and phrases end • Anticipating syntactic patterns • Checking hypotheses
Intonation group	• Making use of sentence stress • Recognising chunks of language • Using intonation to support syntax • Reviewing the decoding process

Note that the main micro-skills involved at each level of processing (shown in **Table 1.2**), take place more or less at the same time, not in a given sequence. If we trust that all these processes are required to be a competent L1 and L2 listener, it makes sense to design activities which practise each of them intensively and frequently as an important part of a long term approach. If students can learn to perform these processes as automatically as possible, they will gain in confidence and proficiency.

1.3   Phonemic and syllabic processing

As we listen, we receive a series of acoustic sensations which need to be successfully matched to the sounds (phonemes) of the L2 in order for effective comprehension to even begin. These phonemes are grouped into syllables and the syllables into words. Languages vary in terms of how many vowels and consonants can be included in a syllable, as well as the ratio of consonants to vowels. For instance, Field (2008) notes that most languages have a CV (consonant - vowel) and CVC structure. Spanish and Italian rely heavily on open CV syllables, while English allows very complex phonemic combinations (e.g. CCCVCCC, e.g. in the word strengths /strɛŋθs/).

Field points out that a growing body of research suggests that syllable processing contributes more to the decoding phase of listening comprehension than single phoneme processing, i.e. we process aural input by dividing it into syllables, not phonemes, since it is a faster and more efficient way to decode.

In L1 processing, our implicit (subconscious) knowledge of which syllables usually precede or follow others, and how syllables affect each other phonologically, is a major aid to comprehension. It helps us make statistically-based predictions about what we are hearing as soon as we hear the first syllable. These predictions are also based on the context, both the situation and what has been discussed so far. This is why the LAM model emphasises using syllables to help students improve their skills.

1.4 Segmenting

In order to be able to identify vocabulary in the input, we have to identify word boundaries. If you cannnot determine the beginning and ending of words (a skill known as *segmenting*) the speech signal comes across as a fast, unintelligible flow. That is why we often complain, on hearing a language we are not very familiar with, that it sounds faster than our own. (Incidentally it has been calculated that Spanish and Japanese produce syllables at a slightly faster rate than other languages, though supply no more information in doing so.) The frustration caused by the feeling that another language is too fast for us is something we need to be constantly aware of with our students. Imagine feeling day in day out that what you hear in the language classroom is just barely meaningful noise! Segmenting is, therefore, a crucial decoding skill and one we can specifically help students to develop. A student who has received extensive training in phoneme and syllable processing, as shown in 1.4, will find segmenting easier than a student who has not.

1.5 Lexical processing

Just as one syllable helps us predict what the following syllable might be, so words help us predict what lexical items are likely to follow. This helps us process speech in different ways. For instance, words often cluster to form familiar, frequently encountered chunks of language. So, on hearing the word *tea* we can predict it may be followed by one of the following: *cup*, *time*, *pot*, *bag*, *leaves*, *break*, *ceremony*, etc.

When a word or formulaic chunk activates in the brain a number of predictions of what words are likely to be heard next it is called in the literature *semantic priming*. It is a widely documented psychological phenomenon and something we can help students exploit through dedicated activities.

1.6 Syntactic processing (parsing)

Words prepare us for what comes next in another important way: by helping us predict what part of speech or even what type of clause will follow. For instance, on hearing the French definite article *la*, we expect a feminine noun or noun phrase to follow. On hearing *Je suis allée au supermarché pour...* the preposition *pour* cues us to the presence of an infinitive - most likely *acheter*, along with a complement to that verb (e.g. *des provisions pour le weekend*).

Since syntactic processing, known as *parsing*, is a vital aspect of aural processing, it makes sense to focus on activities which help develop skill in using it. This implies a focus on those small function words like articles, prepositions, connectives etc, which are useful in understanding the grammar of the sentence. Any work we do on syntax, e.g. verb forms, tenses, adjective agreement and adverb formation, will improve students' listening skills.

Words identified at the lexical stage of processing provide listeners with important cues to grammatical word class (parts of speech). This is an important part of the parsing process; knowing if a word is a noun, adjective or a verb aids comprehension by indicating how words relate to each other in an utterance.

Besides the identification of word classes, parsing is also about recognising patterns, e.g. tense, agreement and pluralisation, sentence patterns (e.g. subject-verb-object) and elliptical (shortened) forms, as well as intonation (pitch and stress). Field (2008) notes how, in English, intonation provides very important information about the grammatical structure of a sentence. The same is true of other languages.

It has also been hypothesised that recognising the communicative function of an utterance helps with parsing by providing us with important clues, both in terms of syntactic and grammatical structure (Brown, 2000). For example, identifying a request for directions activates a number of expectations about the grammatical and syntactic properties of any utterance to come, in this case the expectation that you will hear imperatives: *Turn…, go straight on, take…*

1.7 Supra-segmental features (intonation)

Tone of voice and stress yield significant clues to meaning, including emotional content. Training students to recognise intonation patterns associated with questions, or phrase and sentence ends, can help them break down the message, providing information about syntax and discourse-construction.

1.8 Meaning-making and discourse-building

During the first 200 milliseconds of processing an utterance, working memory deals exclusively with the decoding of the physical and structural aspects (i.e. the form) of the the input before starting to make some meaning from the signal (Egorova et al, 2013). This is important in terms of our brain's management of its very limited cognitive processing resources. By dealing with form first, the brain frees up cognitive space so that it can tackle the extraction of meaning from all the linguistic information obtained at the other levels of processing.

In the working-out-meaning stage, listeners also draw on a range of contextual information independent from the actual language used. This, as previously noted, requires those top-down skills, such as knowledge of the world, co-text and prediction of what may follow. Top-down skills enrich the meaning and help the listener decide what is relevant or important. So, working out meaning cannot rely solely on decoding.

Field (2008) explains that meaning-building from the bare message operates at three levels. A listener turns what they hear into a *proposition*, an abstract representation of a single idea, which is a literal interpretation of the words uttered. This occurs at the end of each clause or unit of intonation. The idea is stored in working memory, even if the listener cannnot recall the exact words used. The listener simultaneously adds meaning by referring to their knowledge of the world, the topic and the speaker to grasp the relevance of the message to the immediate situation. This results in a *meaning representation*, an enriched version of the proposition, if you like.

Finally, in the discourse-building stage the meaning representation temporarily stored in the brain is added to the listener's memory of everything they have heard so far, as well as what they hypothesise about what will be said next. As the listener hears more input, they use the information gathered so far to build a more thorough understanding of the whole discourse (connected series of utterances). So, a student listening to a textbook audio track processes one utterance at a time, on each occasion storing in their working memory its meaning representation, using this to deepen and expand their comprehension of the text as a whole. As students listen, the mental representation of the text held in working memory expands, posing a cognitive challenge which increases as information becomes richer and more complex.

1.9 Retaining chunks of language in working memory

The processes described above mean that the ability to retain chunks of language in working memory is vital (Brown, 2000). As Nation and Newton (2009) point out, this ability is thought to be a significant indicator of language learning aptitude. Given the very limited capacity of working memory, it is important, especially at the early stages of teaching, to provide students with extensive practice in this skill.

Bear in mind that working memory span can vary from one individual to another and that this ability may be hampered by a number of factors which increase the cognitive load of the material to recall, e.g. how difficult the language is to pronounce. So in a typical class, you may have higher proficiency students who are able to retain large chunks of text and others who have trouble retaining a two or three-word phrase.

2. The challenges posed by listening
2.1 Cognitive challenges

Fleeting input

The biggest cognitive challenge posed by listening comprehension concerns the fleeting nature of aural input: incoming speech signals linger in the brain for no longer than two seconds. To make things more difficult for the listener, any new speech signal erases the previous one. This means we have to process really quickly! For the L1 listener, this is usually not an issue unless the input is particularly complex (in informational or linguistic terms) or there are significant interferences from the surrounding environment. For L2 listeners it is a different story.

The processes involved in L1 listening occur automatically, by-passing working memory or merely occupying some subsidiary awareness. In L2 listening, on the other hand, especially at beginner-to- intermediate level, the same processes are usually carried out consciously, drawing on the limited cognitive space available to working memory, and on limited L2 knowledge. The chances of cognitive overload and failure to process efficiently at any stage are high. Beginners find listening hard, probably harder than we think.

Limited memory resources

To further complicate the picture, consider again the brain's very modest processing resources. Our memory capacity is extremely limited: we have seen that an average human can usually process around four or five items of information at any one time. If each unit of information corresponds to a word (e.g. *dog, nice, have*), this limits the brain's capacity to four or five words; if, however, each item is a longer phrase or chunk of language (e.g. *there's a nice dog* or *I have a nice dog*) then the capacity can be considerably expanded. That is why the brain tends to learn words which are frequently uttered together in chunks. In light of such limited capacity, even though the novice-to-intermediate listener may be aware of useful top-down processing strategies, they are likely to have little cognitive space available in working memory to use them.

Assimilation

A further obstacle to comprehension is that words sound different in isolation than in connected speech. In natural speech a phenomenon known as *assimilation* occurs. This is when the influence of one sound on a neighbouring one makes the two become similar or the same. This significantly alters the pronunciation of words, rendering the decoding process very challenging for the non-native speaker. Take the Spanish word *barco* (*boat*) with its indefinite article – *un barco*. In normal speech the /n/ of *un* becomes /m/ because you say /umbarko/. Phonologically speaking, you use a bilabial /m/ instead of an alveolar /n/ because it is easier to say alongside the bilabial /b/. This happens all the time in normal speech. In Chapters 3 and 11 we suggest ways to help students prepare for the difficulty of recognising different phonological forms of words.

Processing form and meaning

Another important limitation of working memory is its inability to simultaneously process form and meaning, especially when the cognitive load is high. This means that if we ask students to focus on meaning when answering comprehension questions, they learn little about sound, vocabulary, grammar and syntax, i.e. the aspects of the language we would like to model for them. Focusing on meaning simply tests comprehension but does not teach students how to listen. In this book the focus is shifted away from comprehension and towards modelling how listening occurs.

Comprehensibility

We also need to keep in mind something else about the limited processing capacity of working memory: the fact that for a typical L2 listener any input which contains fewer than 95-98% comprehensible words poses serious obstacles to understanding and, consequently, to learning (Nation and Newton, 2009). This implies that providing students with input below that comprehension threshold is likely to encourage the overuse of top-down processing strategies.

Noticing

Finally, it is worth pointing out that much learning starts with a phenomenon called *noticing*, which was originally formulated by Schmidt (1990). Schmidt hypothesised that for a learner to begin the complex process of acquisition, they first have to *notice* a new item before understanding its usage. Only then, and after much explicit and/or implicit learning, can they acquire it. (Not all scholars accept this is always true, by the way.) However, while salient (most noticeable) linguistic features in the input, e.g. key content words such as nouns or verbs, may be noticed quite easily, other less salient features such as word endings and function words are likely to be missed. This is owing to a number of factors, ranging from the items' *perceptual salience* (**how easy it is to hear or perceive a given form**) to their *semantic weight* (how key they are to meaning-building), and to their *regularity* and *frequency* (how often they occur in the input). The low saliency of some linguistic features is compounded by the high cognitive load which lower-proficiency students experience when listening. This means that these features are more likely to go unnoticed in listening than in reading.

2.2   The affective challenges

Anxiety and self-efficacy

Research suggests (e.g. Graham, 2017) listening is the skill that causes language students the highest levels of anxiety. This is mainly because most students perceive listening tasks as tests, and it is easy to see why: many tasks are about assessing comprehension and obtaining a score based on how many questions you answer correctly. This anxiety has a serious effect on another important feeling: *self-efficacy*.

Self-efficacy is about the expectancy of success, i.e. the extent to which you believe you are going to succeed at a task (Bandura, 1997), and is believed to be a powerful predictor of progress in language learning. We agree with Graham (2007), who argues that teachers should put a lot of effort into the development of student self-efficacy from the very early stages. If students feel confident about listening tasks and experience a sense of mastery, they will become better listeners in the future.

This means planning for success at listening in at least four ways:

1. Carefully design input and tasks so that they are matched to the aptitude or attainment of students. This means the language should be highly comprehensible (see Chapters 3, 4 and 5 in particular).

2. Prepare students appropriately for a task, e.g. by activating, through pre-listening activities, the linguistic and non-linguistic knowledge that will help them carry out the task successfully (see Chapter 8).

3. Speak or play language at a speed suitable for the students' level of proficiency. Recall that the goal is to model, not test listening skill (see Chapter 6).

4. Train students in cognitive and metacognitive strategies (see Chapter 11).

Another source of anxiety is that, very often, students cannot see the person who is speaking. This is quite unnatural for humans, and students feel more at ease when the person they are listening to interacts with them, ideally in the flesh. This suggests perhaps that relying almost exclusively on playing audio tracks can be counterproductive, especially at the early stages of learning. If you are the main source of listening input, you can pitch the speed of delivery appropriately, emphasise words and sounds you want students to notice, model language more clearly and effectively and, more importantly, use clues and gesture, reassure and even amuse students with facial expressions and body language. By the way, research indicates how useful gesture can be in supporting comprehension, e.g. Huang, Kim and Christianson (2018). See Chapter 6 for more about making language comprehensible.

Concluding remarks

Scholars offer slightly differing models of the listening process, but few would argue with the broad outline presented in this chapter. It is with this summary in mind that the next few chapters describe curriculum design, instructional sequences, individual lessons and lesson ideas. Specific exercises are matched with each of the processes described. There are no silver bullets in language teaching, but we aim to show that if you adopt this focused, process-based approach, you are more likely to develop effective listeners.

Hopefully this chapter has shown that listening is by no means a passive skill. As L2 listeners make meaning of what they hear, and attempt to build a mental representation of text, their brains are very much active, drawing on and integrating a multitude of data picked up from processing a vast array of linguistic and non-linguistic cues at very high speed. We need to bear this in mind and in some cases devote much more classroom time to listening practice, while being acutely aware of the challenges listening poses.

Questions to consider

What do your students tell you about their experience of listening?

What can you do to reduce the possible anxiety associated with it?

How much attention do you give to intonation in class?

What type of metacognitive strategies do you already get students to use?

Too often, we confuse the assessment of listening comprehension with instruction in listening.
(Beth Sheppard, University of Oregon)

THE PRINCIPLES OF LISTENING-AS-MODELLING (LAM)

Introduction

Having explained in detail how listening works and the challenges it presents, this chapter describes the rationale and main pedagogical principles behind an approach which we call *Listening-as-Modelling*. For the sake of convenience this is referred to as LAM from now on. Traditionally, as already pointed out, the teaching of listening has not really centred enough on skills instruction, e.g. Nguyen (2018). As Field (2015) explains, language teachers traditionally adopt a comprehension approach, where, typically, students listen to spoken passages and do comprehension exercises of various types (e.g. 'wh-questions' or true-false tasks). For many students this can be a sink or swim experience. High-attainers often cope well enough, but students who are less proficient, resilient or focused soon switch off. LAM, on the other hand, can be defined as follows:

> ***Listening-as-Modelling gradually builds student expertise and self-efficacy through a process of explicitly taught exercises which target the specific skills required to be an effective listener.***

What is LAM?

To expand upon the definition above, LAM is about modelling language and skills through listening input. It is a process consisting of four strands:

- **Explicit modelling**. Aural input is carefully designed and used to model speaking and assist L2 acquisition. This means simplifying and 'flooding' language with numerous occurrences of the words, lexical and grammatical patterns we teach, in the same way as a caregiver adjusts their language to the needs of young children. Activities require thorough and extensive processing to promote recycling and noticing of language forms.
- **Implicit modelling.** Input and activities are designed and used to encourage implicit (unconscious) learning of language patterns and vocabulary. The premise here is that highly patterned comprehensible input, flooded with the target L2 items, can bring about incidental learning through carefully planned intensive and extensive exposure and tasks. These tasks contain 95-98% comprehensible input and make students thoroughly process the language they hear.
- **Explicit training in micro-skills**. Students are trained to develop the micro-skills thought vital for effective listening (see Chapter 1). These include recognising phonemes and syllables, words, morphemes and grammatical patterns.
- **Explicit training in cognitive and metacognitive strategies**. Students are taught to use cognitive and metacognitive strategies to make use of existing knowledge, compensate for any lack of knowledge and develop independence.

The kind of listening practice envisaged here does not exclude traditional comprehension tasks. These are useful when working on meaning and discourse-building skills. In addition, lessons can include a mixture of LAM and comprehension-style exercises. In sum, in an ideal world, a listening lesson would activate every level of processing (see **Table 1.1** in Chapter 1):

1. phonemic and syllabic processing;
2. lexical retrieval;
3. parsing (grammatical and syntactic processing) ;
4. meaning-building;
5. discourse-building.

Key principles

1. Listening first

As noted earlier, humans are natural listeners. Various calculations have been made about the time we spend listening when compared with speaking, reading and writing. These include 45% (Wilt,

1950), 48% (Brieter, 1971) and 55% (Werner, 1975). We need to include large amounts of one-way and two-way (interpersonal) listening in lessons for at least two reasons: (1) to take advantage of students' natural acquisition abilities and (2) to prepare them for communication in the world beyond school.

2. Micro-skill teaching

As noted in Chapter 1, the brain has to process aural input extremely quickly. In a tiny amount of time, a listener has to cope with a mass of information from the five levels of processing referred to above. This means that listening ability depends on how quickly and accurately the brain can process at each level. Therefore, to improve the brain's processing abilities, the skills required for each level of processing need to be taught. Compare this with a football coach training his or her team in the separate skills required to be great players. So, especially in the earlier stages, LAM lays greater emphasis on bottom-up skills than top-down skills.

3. Alertness to sound

Students benefit from being sensitised to sounds from the very start through everyday routines and activities which send the message that sounds matter and are central to language learning. Having fun with sounds and teaching decoding skills can form a significant part of lessons (see Chapter 3).

4. Intentional contextualisation

Listening activities should be incorporated in schemes of work or curriculum plans, relating coherently to speaking, reading and writing tasks. When using listening exercises from a text book, it is all too easy to neglect linking them to other listening and non-listening tasks. Chambers (1996) notes that this is a common occurrence in L2 classrooms.

In the approach we propose, all four skills are integrated within each teaching sequence through a framework described in detail in Chapter 8. Suffice it to say for now that listening plays a central role in nearly every classroom activity, whether it be listening + reading, listening + speaking or listening + writing. This close relationship between listening and the other skills is also apparent when we discuss interpersonal listening and task-based listening in Chapters 6 and 7.

5. Comprehensible input

Listening input needs to be highly comprehensible to be useful for acquisition. With the average student any L2 input which is less than 95-98% comprehensible, i.e. understandable without help, is very unlikely to be conducive to acquisition. With high-attaining students this figure may fall to around 90%. Any input where a higher proportion of L2 cannot be understood is less than ideal since too much meaning has to be guessed. Where this is the case, students may also feel a task is unfair, which both increases their anxiety and lowers their motivation. So this means that within the LAM approach the usual goal is to provide students with input which is 95 to 98 % comprehensible.

This has implications if you are thinking of using authentic or adapted authentic sources for listening (and reading for that matter). Authentic sources can be interesting and useful, but if they require too much deciphering they may be unsuitable for efficient acquisition. The alternative is to use teacher-written texts which are sufficiently comprehensible. You might want to analyse a particular resource you use to see whether it is comprehensible enough.

Another factor which affects comprehension is the pace of delivery. Since speed of processing is such an important factor in comprehension, it is usually unwise to use material spoken at native speaker or near-native speaker pace. If the language comes too fast, once again students are quickly discouraged and may not notice crucial aspects of the input. In Chapter 6 we look at strategies you can use to make spoken language as understandable as possible. With beginners, it is sensible to speak at a moderate speed or use sensibly paced audio recordings. As students gain proficiency, so the rate of delivery can increase. This does not mean neglecting faster speech entirely. In Chapter 11 we suggest ways in which you can help students prepare for the day when they hear native speakers. How often do we hear students say "they speak much faster than we do in class"?

6. Input-flooding

Skilled caregivers provide children with large amounts of language which is simplified, repetitive, patterned and matched to their children's level of proficiency. Applied linguists call this *input-flooding* or *enriched input*. The LAM approach makes great use of flooded input. We argue that it is a good idea to include in input as many instances as possible of the phonemes, syllables, words, chunks and grammatical structures you want students to learn. To an extent this is common sense; if you want students to acquire a given item, they need to hear it over and over again across a wide range of linguistic contexts for them to be noticed, repeatedly recognised and eventually internalised (i.e. retained in memory) for future spontaneous use. You could liken this to the way young children pick up language by hearing rhyme, stories and songs.

With this in mind, a major advantage of using teacher-written texts and teacher speech over authentic, recorded texts is that you can build in multiple instances of the language you want students to acquire. To give an example, if you wanted to practise negatives, how many authentic recordings would contain multiple uses of the negative? An alternative is to write or adapt texts to contain multiple examples of negatives. Of course, some recorded texts also offer useful patterned language; songs sometimes fit the bill well (see Chapter 9).

7. Controlled input and output

We have argued for input being tightly controlled for it to be comprehensible and patterned. But we also believe that students need plenty of opportunities to transform input into output. This means sequences of activities where the same language items and patterns are modelled and practised in other tasks, including speaking and writing. In addition, this new language can be interleaved with previously learned items.

In the longer term this results in students recycling similar language many times so that they are more likely to acquire it. In secondary language classrooms, where time is strictly limited, this is especially important. For example, imagine how many times each pattern is encountered and used by your students if you (1) present and practise listening and reading a dozen new vocabulary phrases and two new syntactic patterns through a number of tasks that model those items explicitly and abundantly, then (2) practise them orally and in writing in every single subsequent task.

Note in passing the contrast with some versions of traditional Communicative Language Teaching. In the LAM approach students need to go through a number of highly controlled activities before progressing to unstructured, 'free' oral and written tasks. In this sense it has something in common with the traditional PPP approach to language teaching (Presentation-Practice-Production) with controlled activities preceding free production. The main difference, however, is the much greater amount of time the class will spend hearing modelled listening input. Whole lessons or more can be spent on LAM and RAM (Reading-as-Modelling) before free production is attempted. When time is limited it can be tempting to go from presentation straight to production without enough time for students to process large amounts of comprehensible input.

INFOBOX 4 What is PPP?

This is a common pedagogical approach in language clasrooms. The first stage is the Presentation of an aspect of language in a context students are familiar with, much the same way that a swimming teacher would demonstrate a stroke outside the pool to beginners.

The second stage is Practice, where students carry out an activity that gives them opportunities to practise the new aspect of language and become familiar with it whilst receiving appropriate assistance from the teacher. (The swimming teacher allowing children to rehearse the stroke in the pool while being close enough to give any support required.)

The final stage is Production where the students use the language in context, in an activity set up by the teacher but who now gives minimal assistance, like the swimming teacher allowing the children to swim on their own.

8. Focusing on meaning and form

Research has shown that, while listening, we cannot focus on both meaning and form of the language at the same time. We listen either for meaning or for form (Spada, Lightbown and White, 2005). In general, students may appear to be more interested in meaning than form, which is one reason why we often choose to focus on comprehension questions: Who? Why? When? However, this focus on meaning comes at the expense of noticing and learning aspects of sound, vocabulary, grammar and syntax. Intensive input-output work (Swan, 2011), with a balanced focus on both meaning and form, sums up the best way to work with listening texts within the LAM model.

9. Thorough processing

Published listening tasks and exams feature exercises of the type true/false/not-mentioned, tick the correct sentences, match the start and the end of the sentence, and so on. They then omit to get into the text in much more detail. These exercises encourage what we might call *partial processing,* since they allow students to listen out for key words, make guesses or use other clues to work out meaning, some within the text, some from general context. While these exercises have their purpose, e.g. for assessment of comprehension, when used in class to the exclusion of other more intensive tasks, they fail to develop more *thorough processing* of the text. If whole sections or sentences are not exploited during a teaching sequence then learning is likely to be less thorough and listening skills underdeveloped.

Students who intensively process a text:

- become aware of how language items behave in a range of contexts – phonological, lexical and grammatical; how words and phrases sound in context; what other words they go with and how they behave in various grammatical forms (e.g. the fact that the word *play* has associations with the words *playing, plays, played* and *playful*);
- notice new items, beginning the process of their acquisition (Schmidt, 1990);
- gain a more detailed general knowledge of the world;
- achieve a sense of mastery, success and self-efficacy.

10. Extensive Processing

Whereas thorough processing requires detailed focus by the listener on a single aspect of a text (e.g. sound or lexis), *extensive processing* means exploiting a text or texts through a series of fast-paced, engaging tasks which focus students on as many levels of processing as possible: phonemes, syllables, lexis, grammar, syntax, meaning-building and discourse construction. In other words, better to work intensively on shorter texts or sets of texts, than on a longer one only superficially. 'Do more with less', sums it up.

> **INFOBOX 5 From Comprehensible input (CI) to Input processing (IP)**
>
> After Krashen had placed the spotlight on the importance of hearing and reading comprehensible input, researchers (e.g. VanPatten, 1993) became more interested in how *input* becomes *intake*, i.e. language which learners can process for acquisition purposes. They wanted to explain more precisely how input might be processed by learners and whether teachers could manipulate the input to make it more noticeable or 'processable'. For example, do techniques such as input-flooding or 'input enhancement' (e.g. highlighting parts of a text to focus students on a particular form) accelerate the process of acquisition? When teaching past tense, for instance, if you omit a time marker phrase such as *last weekend*, does this focus students' attention more closely on the verb form itself? In other words, if a student hears *last weekend*, they might ignore the verb form and therefore acquire it more slowly. Many of the exercises proposed in this book promote noticing and use input-flooding.

11. Using L1 for scaffolding

Judicious use of L1, or any language common to the class, can help maximise comprehension and support learning. Common ways this can be done within a LAM framework are:

- When modelling new language through listening, use L1 translation as needed alongside other clues to meaning, e.g. realia, gestures or pictures. Translation can reduce the cognitive load on students and help them notice similarities and differences between L1 and L2 forms. Some research suggests that learning is enhanced by *bilingual dual-coding* (e.g. Soh, 2010); this does not necessarily mean constant *sandwiching*, i.e. following something you say in L2 with its L1 translation.
- Give metalinguistic explanations and feedback to students in L1.
- Use L1 in specific activities, such as gapped parallel texts and translation.
- Let students use *translanguaging*, i.e. with their peer students work out problems together in both L1 and L2 to make sense of the L2.

Mounting research evidence points to the value of using L1 in the contexts above, so there is no need to think that L2 should be used at all times. See Chapter 6 for further detail.

12. Interpersonal listening

As we shall see in Chapter 6, interpersonal listening, i.e. listening during conversation, is the bread and butter of everyday communication. In the LAM approach a considerable emphasis is placed on interpersonal listening through highly structured and more open-ended teacher-led and peer-to-peer communicative tasks. Everyday conversations with students build quick reactions and facility with L2 input.

13. Metacognition

As a reminder, metacognition here refers to how students think about and monitor the listening process. The LAM approach aims to develop students' self-monitoring skills, namely their ability to:

- identify their general strengths and weaknesses in specific areas of general listening competence, e.g. ability to concentrate at length, skill at recognising words in the sound stream, watching the speaker;
- monitor and evaluate their performance in the above areas and in specific tasks, e.g. skill at transcribing words and phrases, ability to hear inflections;
- develop independent strategies to tackle any identified weaknesses, e.g. practising specific tasks such as transcription;
- make a long-term effort to work on identified weaknesses, e.g. keeping a listening diary, keeping a tally of how specific issues (e.g. anxiety levels; problems with a specific task-type) evolve over time;
- work independently, planning their practice to take advantage of their own learning preferences, e.g. using video or audio, choosing favourite subject matter.

Ideally, for metacognitive training to be most effective it should be a planned programme consisting of a number of phases.

1. A modelling phase where a strategy is demonstrated. The 'thinking aloud' method works well in this respect.
2. A scaffolding phase where the strategy is practised with reminders from the teacher.
3. An autonomous phase where reminders are withdrawn.
4. An evaluation phase during which the success of the strategy is assessed.

However, given the limited time available to teachers, any metacognitive training is best done in small doses to encourage a degree of self-monitoring. Here are three simple examples:

- Model the value of searching for cognates during listening by displaying a passage and analysing how many words resemble L1.
- Help students spot intonation patterns by showing a text, reading aloud and using choral repetition to demonstrate how pitch and stress affect meaning.
- Demonstrate how certain key words and phrases give strong clues to meaning, e.g. *but, however, on the other hand*.

> **INFOBOX 6 What is metacognition?**
>
> Metacognition refers to 'thinking about thinking', 'thinking about learning' and 'self-regulation' in general. For instance, a person engages in metacognition if they notice they are finding it harder to learn A than B, or that they should double-check C before accepting it as fact. So, it involves monitoring how you are learning and thinking about what you can do to improve it. In the context of listening, an example of a metacognitive strategy would be to think consciously about using cognates (words which sound like their L1 equivalents) to make sense of a message. We go into more detail about this in Chapter 11.

14. Fair assessment

Inherent to LAM is the notion that, in assessment of listening, the process should be fair to all students. This means that students should be tested on what they have been taught and what they can possibly know. A common criticism levelled at some exams and published material is that the audio extracts contain too much unknown language which has to be guessed or inferred. Too often students emerge from listening tests feeling dispirited. Although it is understandable that exam boards require a good range of scores for statistical purposes, we would argue that assessment material should contain more comprehensible input to reflect effective classroom practice. There is a case to be made for assessment formats being adjusted to reflect the type of work done in successful classrooms. See Chapter 10 for more on the topic of assessment.

Concluding remarks

The *product approach* to listening refers to the teaching of listening comprehension with an emphasis on the product, i.e. the correct answer to comprehension questions. On the other hand, the *process approach* refers to the mental processes, skills, and strategies that underpin skilled listening. LAM is a process approach; it is about teaching listening, not testing listening. This chapter has laid out some general principles which underpin this approach, the key ones being:

- listening first;
- bottom-up processing skills as the main focus;
- the preference for texts featuring highly patterned input and input-flooding to provide as much exposure as possible to the target L2 structures and lexical items;

- 95-98 % comprehensible input to lighten the students' cognitive load as they grapple with aural texts which help enhance self-efficacy ("I can do it because I am familiar with most of the linguistic content");
- the use of thorough processing to promote noticing and recycling;
- the use of extensive processing to ensure students process the text at as many levels as possible;
- the integration of listening with the skills of speaking, reading and writing through planned sequences of controlled and less structured tasks;
- the use of fair and appropriate assessment techniques better matched to classroom practice.

Questions to consider

How comprehensible are your text book listening resources?

When you use a listening text, do you think of it in terms of *teaching* or *testing*?

What does it mean to intensively exploit a listening text?

What are the issues around choosing authentic listening sources?

3

The basic pleasure in the phonetic elements of a language and in the style of their patterns, and then in a higher dimension, pleasure in the association of these word-forms with meanings, is of fundamental importance.

(J.R.R. Tolkien)

TEACHING SOUNDS: FUN WITH PHONOLOGY

Introduction

As we have seen, if students are to process connected speech fluently, they need to acquire the bottom-up processing skills needed for decoding the speech signal. An important part of this process involves *matching*, i.e. making a connection between clusters of acoustic clues and the listener's knowledge of units (phonemes, words and grammatical patterns) (Field, 2008). An expert listener does this largely automatically, without thinking, but how do we help students work towards this level in their L2?

In this chapter we look at how learning to perceive and produce sounds, and how to link sound to spelling, make students 'alert to sound', thereby contributing to their overall ability to listen. Our focus here is therefore on phonemes and combinations of phonemes, those sounds which are often unique to the phonological system of each language. We shall look at some relevant research evidence, discuss the role of what Field (2008) calls *micro-listening tasks*, describe a range of classroom activities and consider the specific difficulties posed by French, German and Spanish as examples.

Since without awareness of the L2 phonological system students find it hard to recognise vocabulary, syntax and meaning effectively, we suggest teachers devote significant time to working on sounds and sound-spelling correspondences (phonics). By the end of the first year of teaching students should be able to master the vast majority of the L2 phonemes and phoneme combinations. French and English are examples of languages where this is more of a challenge owing to the mismatch between sound and spelling.

But phonics training on its own is not really enough for the development of sound-decoding fluency. Greater benefit comes from a regular focus on phonological awareness within a framework of engaging ear-training, reading aloud, choral reading, repeating aloud, singing, critical listening and interactional speaking games and tasks. These recycle target sounds, interleaving new sounds with previously learned ones. Extensive receptive and productive practice of this sort can help bring about decoding fluency.

Developing students' metacognition in this area of their learning will also bear fruit. Student listeners can become (1) *aware* of sounds together with the role decoding and pronunciation play in language acquisition; (2) *intentional* in their learning of the L2 sound system; (3) *alert* to the properties and qualities of L2 sounds and (4) proactive *self-monitors* (evaluators of their own performance). This work on metacognition can start from the very beginning through daily activities, e.g. during classroom entry and exit routines, lesson starters and fillers.

In the rest of this chapter we attempt to answer a number of questions. How do we:
- get students to enjoy sounds which sound strange to them?
- get them to pronounce well?
- create sound awareness and a clear grasp of sound-spelling relationships?
- get them to discriminate between L2 sounds and apparently similar sounds in their L1?
- develop good pronunciation?
- create awareness of sound and a clear grasp of sound-spelling relationships?

1. The role of explicit instruction

In her study of 359 novice students of French (from Year 7 in two English comprehensive schools), Erler (2014) found that after one year of teaching, with two contact hours a week, her informants' knowledge of spelling-sound rules was poor. Both schools obtained the same mean score in a test of rhyming words, i.e. 2.75 correct choices out of 14. She concluded:

The results seem to indicate that, with a few exceptions, pupils had little idea after one year of learning French about spelling-sound rules for principal vowel sounds in the language and for the general rule of silent final consonants. These are key rules for being able to decode from print to sound, and are essential for reading comprehension (p. 5).

In addition, only 7.6% of the students reported they felt happy when reading French aloud in the lesson; the vast majority felt negatively about decoding and spelling written French. Another finding was that 75 % of the students thought it was useful to know pronunciation and 63% stated they were aware of subvocalising sounds (sounding them out in their heads) when silently reading in French. Whether we are aware of it or not, the brain automatically converts letters into sounds as we read, even when we are not reading aloud.

These findings are a cause for concern because, as much L1 and L2 research indicates (e.g. Stanovich, 1980; Bradley and Bryant, 1983; Sprenger-Charolles and Casalis, 1995; Gathercole and Baddeley, 2001), decoding skills are crucial to comprehension of written texts. Other research indicates that a child's early phonological awareness is a strong predictor of their fluency in later years (Stanovich, 1986). Muter and Diethelm (2001) found that students of French as a foreign language who were able to tell where syllables in a word begin and end were more proficient readers than those who did not.

A clear conclusion to be drawn from the above study is that an increased focus on phonological awareness and phonics should increase students' skills, confidence and motivation.

2. Creating the right climate

Creating a climate of alertness to sound begins with the business of modelling and raising students' awareness of L2 phonemes and how they differ from similar L1 phonemes in sound and articulation. As our framework for phonological instruction shows (**Figure 3.1**), modelling and awareness-raising need to be followed by extensive receptive practice.

Figure 3.1 A framework for phonological instruction

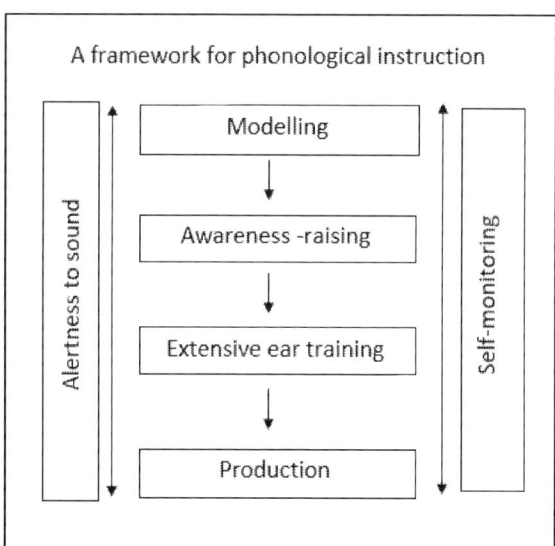

Extensive receptive processing of L2 phonemes should take place before production. Why? Firstly, less confident students may find receptive practice less challenging and threatening than speaking aloud. Secondly, it takes lots of receptive practice through recycling, spaced practice and interleaving before skills becomes internalised. De Jong (2005) notes that if students have to produce too soon they fall back on incorrect or incomplete knowledge, or on knowledge of sounds in their L1. What is more, if production is faulty it can hinder acquisition of correct knowledge. In short, it is a good idea to preempt phonological errors by doing lots of receptive practice first.

3. Ear-training

Ear-training work prior to production can be done through a series of activities carried out first at single word level and later through larger chunks of text, from sentences to paragraphs. Speed of delivery can be gradually increased to match students' progress. Higher-attaining students will need less targeted practice, so you would be wise to match your teaching to what you hear coming back. At what point are students ready to move beyond specific training to using language in less structured productive activities? When can they move on to reading aloud, choral reading, repeating aloud, pronunciation games, e.g. tongue-twisters, and communicative oral tasks?

Figure 3.1 shows that sound-related metacognition, alertness to sound and self-monitoring, are part of the whole process. Keeping a focus on sound, showing students in every lesson that it matters a lot to you helps develop students' purposefulness, encouraging them to monitor and evaluate their performance. In this way they are likely to become confident and keen to improve further. So prioritise sound from day one!

4. Pronunciation

From the outset it is important to demand accurate pronunciation. If students try to sound authentic, they will become more discerning listeners in turn. If your students develop good habits in their first year, these will continue into the future. They do not need to sound exactly like native speakers, but they do need to make a serious effort and be clearly understood. Fortunately, most students enjoy playing with new sounds if you create the right conditions.

Research suggests that having a good *phonological memory* assists with word retention in general. As we shall see in Chapter 4, part of *knowing* a word is being aware of how it sounds and knowing words is the most important thing of all for listening comprehension.

Before we look at some more research evidence and suggest useful classroom activities, here are some of our favourite general pieces of advice:

Steve's favourites

- Consider showing students a side-on diagram of the vocal tract with the main articulators and how they work to create specific sounds (see **Figure 3.2**). Give them some basic phonetics terminology to get them interested in the science of sounds and, more importantly, to share a common language (e.g. the terms *plosive, voicing, fricative, bilabial, uvula, dental, alveolar* and *palatal*). Students may find this of general interest. Explain how the articulators (mouth, lips, tongue, etc.) produce different sounds; make funny noises; demonstrate accents.

- Be acutely aware of the sounds which will cause L1 interference in the language you teach. For instance, when dealing with English native speakers: all French vowels, *r* sounds in all languages, German fricatives (*ch*), *v* and *w* sounds, and diphthongs, Spanish bilabial, sibilant (*s*) and fricative (*j*) sounds. Focus on them and have fun making them.

- Link gestures to sounds and spellings, e.g. raising your arms or fingers for certain accents or diacritics (see the exercises below). Have students do the same. Younger students enjoy this type of physical response. Some teachers do this with song, e.g. from YouTube videos.

- Model correct stress and intonation, explaining how it works in the L2 and draw slanting lines above written sentences to illustrate it. Give exaggerated examples of pitch and stress in L1 to show how it alters meaning and emotional effect. Try saying the word *really* in English to the class with various intonations to demonstrate boredom, surprise, interest and shock. Get students to copy you.

- Talk about different L1 accents, and contrast native language and L2 sounds. Have a discussion about why we react to accents in the way we do. This type of sociolinguistic conversation raises students' interest in and awareness of sound.

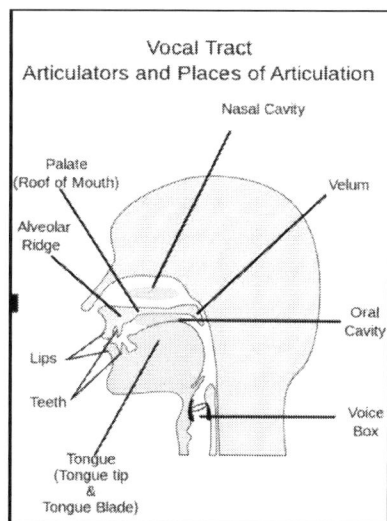

Figure 3.2 The vocal tract

Gianfranco's favourites

- Have 'sound(s) of the week' on display and referred to in lessons.
- Use classroom entry and exit tickets, e.g. questions on sounds of the week as the students arrive and leave, such as *How do you say this? What's wrong with my pronunciation of this word? Which one of these two words have I just read out?* (pointing to two *minimal pairs*, i.e. two very similar words, having pronounced one of them).
- Refer students to a 'phonological hooks' board – a sign displaying, say, French numbers one to ten. In French, when a student mispronounces *brun* as *brune* or *peur* as *pur*, point to the number which rhymes with the mispronounced word and ask students to correct themselves.
- Give frequent reminders and nudges when errors are made, e.g. a facial gesture or mouth shape.
- Give whole-class feedback when you hear common errors during oral activities, rather than interrupting individual students as they interact.
- Do quick response tasks, e.g. students react to a sound by putting their hands up, clapping or standing up.
- Use phrases or songs to practise specific sounds, e.g. French nasal vowels can be practised with the phrase *un bon vin blanc* or the song *Sur le pont d'Avignon*; in German accurate pronunciation of *au* can be practised with the phrase *Auf der Lauer auf der Mauer*; in Spanish the Peruvian children's song *La mar estaba serena* can be used to practise a range of vowel sounds.
- Get students to pronounce the target sound(s) in as many contexts as possible; the wider the range of contexts the greater the chances of transfer.
- Whenever your students listen to a text, ensure one or more tasks focus them on phonological aspects.

INFOBOX 7 Phonetics, phonology and phonics

Phonetics concerns the physical aspect of sounds, their production and perception. Articulatory phonetics is the study of speech sound production by the articulatory and vocal tract. Acoustic phoentics concerns the auditory qualities of sounds. Phonetic transcriptions using the IPA (International Phonetic Alphabet) are written using square brackets [ ].

Phonology is about the sounds (phonemes) and sound patterns of a particular language. Phonemes are sounds that can make a difference in meaning between two words, e.g. the /ɪ/ and /i:/ sounds in *ship* and *sheep* are two of 44 phonemes in English. Phonology is also concerned with 'supra-segmental' features such as intonation.

Phonics is concerned with the relationship between phonemes and spelling.

5. The role of phonics teaching

There has been much debate about the value of teaching synthetic phonics (i.e. a structured course of sound-spelling instruction) in L1 teaching during early schooling. Some argue that while phonics teaching may help with recognising and pronouncing isolated words, including invented words (also known in the literature as *pseudo-words*, *nonsense words* or *non-words*), it does little for reading comprehension (e.g. Krashen, 2001, who cites a range of studies) and Huo and Wang (2017) who looked at 15 studies on what they called phonological-based instruction in EFL lessons for primary school children. They found that phonemic awareness and reading of non-words improved, but word recognition and reading comprehension did not. Torgerson *et al* (2006), in a major meta-study on L1 phonics teaching, concluded that phonics teaching improves reading accuracy, if not comprehension, and recommended that teachers include it "…in a judicious balance with other elements" (p.49). From this it appears that while phonics teaching has benefits, it does not clearly improve L1 reading comprehension. Can it improve listening performance? Research is unfortunately thin on the ground.

There is good evidence, however, that sounding out whole words makes them more memorable. What psychologists call the *production effect* suggests that we remember items better when we say them aloud. Forrin and MacLeod (2018) carried out a study to compare how well college students recalled words depending on whether they read them silently, heard someone say them or read them aloud themselves. The words they read aloud themselves were more easily recalled two weeks later. The researchers concluded that when the students spoke the words this provided more engagement with the word, helping to make the words memorable. As they put it: "…oral production is beneficial because it entails two distinctive components: a motor (speech) act and a unique, self-referential auditory input" (from the Abstract).

Other researchers, such as Baddeley, Gathercole and Papagno (1998) have argued that when a student learns a new word it needs to be repeated aloud in order for sounds to be assigned to the word, a process which helps the word find its way into long-term memory. Woo and Price (2015) have suggested that if students are not given the chance to say a word or phrase several times they may assign the wrong sounds to the word before it is transferred to long-term memory. Service (1992) found that *phonological short-term memory* (reflected in the ability to repeat words accurately, i.e. being a good mimic) correlates with future L2 learning performance.

Finally, an influential review of language teaching pedagogy in England by The Teaching Schools Council (Bauckham, 2016), which involved observations of lessons and interviews with teachers, strongly recommended a planned approach to the teaching of phonics.

With this type of evidence in mind, together with our own long experience as teachers, a number of general points can be made:

- L2 phonology differs from L1 and students often apply their existing knowledge of L1 phonics to L2. This leads to poor pronunciation and a greater likelihood that words will not be recognised in speech. It is therefore important to model correct pronunciation and sound-spelling links, and have students *shadow* it, i.e. say or whisper it out loud after you.
- Although sound-spelling links will become established through general work in the four skills, students will benefit from being taught explicitly which sounds and syllables correspond to which spellings, notably where these spellings are in contrast to the L1 orthography. This may be of particular benefit to lower-attaining students.
- Language-specific issues may need special treatment, e.g. 'silent letters' and elision in French or the role of accented characters in French, German and Spanish.
- Although perception tasks such as distinguishing between minimal pairs (e.g. in French *des chats* versus *déjà*) are useful, saying sounds and words aloud adds an extra element in reinforcing memory. If we train students in accurate repetition this will help with their general proficiency.
- Rather than prepare a time-consuming structured phonics programme which has the potential to be tedious for students, we recommend you intersperse your other communicative work with short bouts of phonics practice. But keep in mind the areas which will cause most difficulty for your students. Whether teachers deal with phonics in a systematic or more incidental manner may depend on their preference or practical issues such as time available.
- Pronunciation of segments longer than individual phonemes is likely to be more engaging for students. Adding meaning to a task makes it more enjoyable as well as productive.
- Unusually able language learners with excellent mimicry skills may require little phonics training at all.

6. The importance of lexical segmentation

In Chapter 1 we saw that *lexical segmentation* is about spotting the boundaries between words in speech. Clearly, knowing words is vital for comprehension, but picking them out of the stream of sound is not easy for students. There are usually no 'white spaces' between words in speech. Research has shown that knowing the acceptable sounds which can appear together and at the starts and ends of words helps people decode speech. This is known in the literature as *phonotactics*. To give an example, in English /br/ and /pr/ can occur at the start of a word, but not at the end, whereas /ts/ can occur at the end of a word, but not at the start. These restrictions are specific to each language, so for example in French /bʀ/ and /pʀ/ can, phonologically speaking, appear at both the start and ends of words, e.g. ***branche*** and *ar**br**e* (the *e* is silent*)*. Does this cause problems for students when the phonotactic restrictions between the L1 and L2 are different and can we do anything about this to make listening easier for students?

Weber and Cutler (2006) and Al-jasser (2008) both found that learners usefully transfer their L1 knowledge of phonotactics to the L2. When the rules for L1 and L2 are the same, words are more quickly detected. Al-jasser (2008) also found that learners who received specific training in L2 phonotactics were even better at word spotting. He concluded, somewhat tentatively, it has to be said, that teaching phonotactics was useful in improving word detection in speech.

The practical tasks we list below should help students become aware not only of sound-spelling correspondences, but what sounds they can expect to hear at word boundaries. In the longer run students will build up their skills with lexical segmentation through large amounts of comprehensible input.

7. A repertoire of activities

In this section we offer a list of specific activities you can carry out to develop students' alertness to sound and decoding abilities. Most of these require little or no preparation on your part. Some suit one language more than another, depending on the challenges posed by the language.

7.1 Receptive activities

Phonics bingo

1. Create bingo cards featuring individual letters or letter combinations. Hand out identical cards to all students or make, say, four different ones.
2. Either read out individual sounds or single syllable words containing sounds on the cards.
3. When a student thinks they have won they read out the sounds identified. The whole class can repeat for further practice.

Minimal pairs

Minimal pairs are pairs of words or phrases where a change in one single phoneme alters the meaning. A classic example, noted earlier, is the difference in English between *ship* and *sheep*, a common problem for non-English-speaking learners whose language does not share the distinction between these two vowel phonemes.

1. Display two words which are near homophones, i.e. very similar in pronunciation.
2. Read one of them out, pronouncing it very clearly.
3. Students have to spot which word of the two you uttered.

Table 3.1 lists some examples you could use:

Table 3.1 Minimal pairs

French		German		Spanish	
blanc	*blond*	*dich*	*dick*	*casa*	*caza*
du vin	*du vent*	*schon*	*schön*	*sopa*	*soba*
déjà	*des chats*	*zeit*	*seit*	*pollo*	*poyo*
feux	*faux*	*beten*	*Betten*	*cama*	*clama*
l'écran	*les grands*	*Beine*	*Biene*	*está aquí*	*está allí*
moules	*mules*	*Mutter*	*Mütter*	*la Casa Blanca*	*la cosa blanca*

Spot the foreign sound

1. Display a set of words or a phrase containing sounds that do not exist in the student's L1, e.g. *u* in the French word *bu* for English learners of French. In this case the phrase might be *J'ai voulu manger du poulet* (*I wanted to eat chicken*).
2. Read out the words carefully.
3. Students dot, circle or underline the letters in the words which correspond to the target sound. The correct answer would be *J'ai voulu manger du poulet*.

Spot the silent endings

1. Display a set of words, phrases or short sentences containing final unpronounced consonants on the whiteboard, e.g. the French sentence *Je suis français (I am French)*.
2. Read them aloud at moderate pace, ensuring you pause between words with less proficient students.
3. Students dot, circle or underline the letters at the end of words which are not sounded.

Spot the silent letters

Give students a list of sentences like the one below then read them aloud. The task is to highlight the letters not pronounced by the teacher since they are silent. This is appropriate for French.

> Example: *Je parle avec mes amis au restaurant près du grand port.*
> (*I'm talking with my friends at the restaurant near the big harbour.*)

Contrast response

This is adapted from Field (2008). Tell students to put up their left hand when they hear one sound, their right hand when they hear another. As an example, in German, to help students distinguish between the sounds spelled *u* and *ü,* students would raise their left hand when they hear *u*, their right hand when they hear *ü*.

        Examples: *über – Mutter – für – zu – oben – unten – Wort – Hund*

Multiple options

1. Display a set of three words or short phrases which ideally share some phonological features.
2. Read one of them.
3. Students must spot the one you have read.

Listen and rearrange

1. Give students a series of four or five words or phrases.
2. Read the words in a different order to the one given and students must rearrange them, e.g.

Student's sequence (Spanish):   *buenos días, adiós, por favor, hasta luego, buenas tardes*
Teacher's sequence: *por favor, hasta luego, buenas tardes, buenos días, adios*
Tip: this works well with absolute beginners.

Writing unknown words

As an exercise for intermediate students to see how well students have established sound-spelling links simply read aloud some words which the students have not yet encountered. This could be blended with other work, e.g. pick out new words students will be meeting in a spoken or written text in that lesson. You can scaffold this task by supplying three different spellings, each containing a minor error.

Rhyming pairs

1. Give students a list of five words all with different endings, chosen based on their difficulty or simply because they contain sounds they may need to pronounce during the rest of the lesson.
2. Read out six or seven words (the extra one or two are distractors), five of the words rhyming with the five words provided initially (see French example below).
3. Students identify which words rhyme with which.

Student's words: *moi – ville – famille – travailleur – brillant*
Teacher's words: *bois – mille – peur – soleil – ailleurs – dur – jouet – cédille – mer – souriant*
(NB students cannot see the Teacher's words)

Broken words

Remove a syllable from the end or beginning of a set of polysyllabic words.

1. Display the gapped words along with the syllable(s) you removed from them, arranged in random order on the board.
2. Read out the words in their complete form.
3. Students must reconstruct the gapped words, selecting the correct option.

Tip: to make it more challenging and interesting, add in a couple of distractors which could be near-homophones of the options you gave.

Spot the wrong sound

1. Pronounce a sentence or short text making sure that you make a typical L1 transfer phonetic error. For instance, in the German sentence below, you would pronounce the *ch* incorrectly, e.g. as an English *sh* or *k*.
2. Students need to identify the pronunciation mistake. These are easy to make up on the spot.
   e.g. (German) *Ich wohne in Deutschland* (where the *ch* is incorrectly pronounced 'sh' or 'k').

Gapped letters

1. Choose or produce a text flooded with three target sounds, a new one and two that you want to reinforce. Create gaps in the words that contain the target sound(s).
2. Read the text in its complete form at moderate pace, slightly emphasising the target sounds.
3. Students fill the gaps.

Tip: to add a grammatical focus to the activity, gap nouns, verbs or adjectival endings.

Catch the first or last letter

This is a variation of *Gapped letters*, except that you gap just the first and/or last letter of each word in order to focus the students on word boundaries.

Tip: to increase the challenge, gap silent endings. Make sure, however, that if you do this you provide plenty of practice with silent endings beforehand, e.g. by doing *Spot the silent ending* or *Broken words*.

Spot the correct transcription

1. Give students a gapped version of a sentence and with three near-homophones (words that sound very similar).
2. Read out the sentence at near natural speed.

3. Students choose the correct option, e.g. (French)
   Teacher: *J'y vais avec lui (I'm going with him)*.
   Students see on the board : *J'y vais avec _____*.
   Options to choose from : *Louis – lui – l'huile*.

Syllable anagrams

1. Display the anagrams of a set of words or phrases you have practised.
2. Read out each word or phrase two or three times.
3. Students much match the word or phrase they hear with each of the anagrams provided, rewriting the word correctly.

Break the flow

First display short sentences which follow a pattern the students are familiar with, but containing familiar and unfamiliar items. For instance, your students may have learnt *I am* + adjective, or *My* + noun + *is* + adjective, so you may use sentences such as *We are* + unfamiliar adjective or *My* + unfamiliar nouns + *are* + adjective, etc. Remove the spaces between the words.

1. Read out each sentence at natural speed first.
2. Students draw lines in between the words to indicate the boundaries between words.
3. Read out each sentence a second time, this time pausing briefly in between each word.
4. Students change or confirm the word boundaries they initially identified.

Break the flow with intruder

This is the same as *Break the flow* except that you add an extra letter, syllable or word in the sentences without gaps between the words.

Syllable building blocks

1. Display a number of high frequency syllables on the board. You can work with four or five syllables at a time.
2. Say polysyllabic words which contains different combinations of two or more of the chosen syllables.
3. Students write out the words on mini-whiteboards using the syllables on display as cues.

Tip: to make it more fun with younger students, and if you have a sufficient number of building blocks, you can write the target syllables on them, ensuring that each of them is on blocks of different colours, e.g. *ca* on blue blocks, *foi* on green blocks, etc. As they listen, students assemble the relevant blocks correctly.

Faulty Echo

For raising students' awareness of commonly made decoding errors.

1. Display a list of words or short phrases which, when pronounced, produce the sounds you want to focus on. These could include new sounds you want to draw attention to or known sounds that you want to reinforce.
2. Read one of them aloud correctly at moderate pace and as clearly as possible.
3. Read the same item aloud a second time, pronouncing the sound wrongly. Make sure that the wrong pronunciation reproduces errors commonly made by students, e.g. faulty 'r' sounds in French, Spanish and German, or common vowel sounds.
4. Students spot which sound you mispronounced and give suggestions about what is wrong and why.

Spot the error

This activity is a great follow-up to *Faulty echo* and is best done after students have had enough practice with the sound you are teaching.

1. Display a list of words or short phrases.
2. Read one of them aloud, making a pronunciation mistake.
3. Students identify the error, possibly reminding the rest of the class of the phonological rule.

Track the sound

This can be used at a later stage in a teaching sequence on decoding skills, as students have to process a larger amount of input.

1. Read out a highly comprehensible text flooded with a specific sound.
2. As you read, students track as many instances as possible of the sound as they can. Ask them to note down the words they hear which contain the sound. The precise spelling of the words need not matter.

In order to make this activity more fun and to bring a bit of L2 culture into the classroom, use songs or nursery rhymes, for example.

Tip: you can make this even more fun by playing it as 'musical chairs'. In this version read out a text flooded with the target sound or syllable. Each time students hear a specific sound or syllable they sit down.

Spot the intruder

This can be used for various purposes, including developing word identification, metalinguistic awareness and parsing skills (using the grammar in the sentence to make meaning). If you want to give this task a decoding focus, the intruders should include several instances of the sounds you are targeting. You can kill two birds with one stone, of course, by choosing to add in the text (as the 'intruders') words which students typically overuse.

1. Edit a text by inserting extra words. Ideally, these would be words that are plausible or commonly misused.
2. Read out the original text, omitting the extra words.
3. Students underline every word in the text you do not read.

Tip: this activity also works very well using songs and nursery rhymes.

Spot the missing word

Words are omitted from, rather than added to, the text. You could view this as a partial dictation. To add a metalinguistic focus, the words removed could be ones students typically leave out.

1. Remove words containing the target sounds from a text.
2. Read out the text.
3. Students note down the missing words.

Write it as you hear it

1. Display a few sentences and give the students a copy of them on paper.
2. Read them out at moderate pace, pronouncing them as clearly as possible.
3. As they listen, students write under the correct version they have, their own home-made phonetic transcription of what they heard.
4. Students pair up with two other students and agree on a phonetic transcription.
5. Discuss as a class the various ways the most challenging sounds were transcribed.

7.2 Productive activities

Read and repeat

Flashcards or PowerPoint pictures are particularly useful for this, with a focus on individual phonemes which may cause difficulty. It is a good idea to show a picture alongside the word (to hold attention and aid memory) and to highlight key letter combinations in a different colour. **Figure 3.3** shows three examples of slides for practising nasalised vowels while showing common spellings in French. Some teachers deal with the phonic difficulties of reading aloud and pronouncing French by marking silent endings in some way, e.g. *enfant*. These are then reproduced in written texts until decoding is mastered.

Figure 3.3 Phonics with pictures (French) (Image: Pixabay)

un p**in**gou**in**   un mout**on**   des **en**f**ants**

The back-chaining technique (starting with the final syllable and working backwards) can be used for choral repetition of individual sounds and sound sequences. With beginners you can show a set of similar pictures and play *Mind reading* (see below), where students have to guess and say out loud the word or words you are thinking of. You can add an extra level of fun by having them guess if you will say, sing or whisper the word, or ask them to say it as if they are in love or frightened. Alternatively, choose categories of students to repeat: girls/boys, separate rows, those who prefer vanilla or chocolate ice cream, and so on. As you pronounce words and sounds to the class you can demonstrate mouth shapes for students to copy, which is quite fun in itself. You can also amuse the class by reversing syllables, e.g. saying in French *on-mout*, rather than *mou-ton (sheep)*. This will also give students a feel for word structure and stress (in French there is often a slight stress on the final syllable). These types of activity can also reinforce the effect of accented characters on pronunciation or stress if the L2 uses them.

Note that in some quarters choral repetition is frowned upon, associated as it is with the audio-lingual teaching approach to which it was central. In our view it is an enjoyable and useful part of a lesson during which students gain confidence in listening and speaking without being in the limelight.

Letters on the board

1. Display some letters or letter combinations on the board.
2. Read out words or phrases one at a time which are made up of only those letters.
3. Students must transcribe the vocabulary. You can use common words which the students do not yet know so they have to work on their sound to letter knowledge, not just their memory of known words.

Battleship phonics

In this version of the well-known game, Battleships, the vertical column can consist of word starts and the horizontal row word ends. The words could be genuine or invented. Students play the game in the normal way, identifying ships (boxes) by saying complete words which combine the starts and ending. You can prepare the grids to include target sound and letter combinations which are known to be a challenge.

Repeating long or interesting words

This works particularly well with German, but can be used with any language. Choose an interesting word with several syllables and practise saying it using back-chaining. You could use shorter words if they just sound pleasing to the ear. You will have your own favourites. Teachers have told us that students can have fun pronouncing the following words:
French - *cacahuète, brouillard, pneu, pamplemousse, poubelle, pantoufle* and *écureuil*;
Spanish - *sacapuntas, maquillaje, hablabla, ejercicio, desafortunadamente* or *mariposa*;
German - *Auspuffgase, Küchentücher, Schornsteinfeger, Schlittschuhlaufen, Fussgaengerzone* or *Strassenbahnhaltestelle*.
Words which sound rude to English native speaker ears can be worth doing with the right class.

Mind-reading (teacher-led)

This is a zero preparation game which can be played as a warm-up for the games listed below it.

1. Write a set of phrases or short sentences on the board. Choose those containing challenging sounds you wish to focus on.
2. Write one secretly on a mini-whiteboard which you do not show to the students.
3. Students guess the hidden phrase or sentence by reading out any one of the sentences on the board. Reveal the correct answer you wrote on your mini-whiteboard. You can reward correct answers.

Mind-reading (student-led)

This is a variation on the above. Students secretly write three phrases or sentences from a set of ten or more on display. They then take turns at guessing what the other has written by reading phrases or sentences aloud. The player who gets more guesses right in a given time is the winner.

Sentence stealer

1. Students are shown on the board a list of twelve L2 model sentences they have been practising. Each sentence has a number from 1 to 12.
2. Give each student four blank cards and tell them to secretly write on each card any one of those sentences, or simply the number for it.
3. The game consists of 'stealing' as many cards as possible from other members of the class in five minutes, i.e. student X approaches student Y and reads out from the board any four sentences; if a sentence that X reads is on one of Y's cards, X can 'steal' that card. To make it more fun students can play rock, paper, scissors (repeating the three words aloud in L2) to win the right to guess.

48 · BREAKING THE SOUND BARRIER

4. The student with the most cards at the end of the game wins. Note: students cannot interact with the same person more than once.

This game may best be played after modelling the target patterns through a sentence builder frame. **Figure 3.4,** below illustrates an example from a lesson with novice L2 French students. Silent letters in the word endings are underlined to remind students.

Figure 3.4 Sentence stealer game (French) (Image: Pixabay)

Voleur de phrases

1. Je ne fai<u>s</u> jamai<u>s</u> la lessive.
2. Je travaille souven<u>t</u> dans le jar<u>din</u>.
3. Je ne fai<u>s</u> jamai<u>s</u> la cuisine.
4. Je fai<u>s</u> souven<u>t</u> les course<u>s</u>.
5. Je fai<u>s</u> la vaisselle tou<u>s</u> les jour<u>s</u>.
6. Je ne fai<u>s</u> rien pour aide<u>r</u>.
7. Je sor<u>s</u> le<u>s</u> poubelles de temps en temp<u>s</u>.
8. Je ne fai<u>s</u> jamai<u>s</u> mon li<u>t</u>.
9. Je passe quelquefoi<u>s</u> l'aspirateur.
10. Je promène le chie<u>n</u> tou<u>s</u> les soir<u>s</u>.

Find your match

1. Display a number of sentences. The list might include a range of responses to the question *How are you?* such as *I'm good, thank you.*
2. Students write secretly on their mini-whiteboards one sentence (or more) from the ones on display.
3. Students go around the classroom asking a question, e.g. *How are you?* Their task is to find another student with the same sentence on their mini-whiteboard.

You can run several rounds of this game in ten minutes as students usually find their match quickly.

'Find someone who' with cards

1. Give students cards containing one or more details in L2. For instance, on the topic of food, one card might read *My name is Mark, I like chicken because it's tasty and healthy*. Students are also given a grid with a series of questions such as, on the topic of food, *Find someone who likes chicken, Find someone who loves meat*, etc.
2. For each question, they need to find a person with the matching card and write their name in the grid, asking L2 questions such as *What food do you like?*
3. The student who completes the most items on the grid in the time given is the winner.

A reason to prefer *Find someone who with cards* to the traditional *Find someone who* is because (1) it turns it into a read-aloud activity and (2) it allows you to control the students' output, eliciting exactly the patterns you want them to practise.

Sentence chaos

1. Display a set of 10 sentences on the board.
2. Put students in groups of three: two players and a reader/referee.
3. The referee decides on a set order (different from the arrangement on the board) and reads out the sentences twice, at the beginning of the game. The 10 sentences are visible at all times.
4. Players then repeat the sentences in the same order. Players have five lives. Every time a player makes a mistake the other player has a go until they run out of lives. The player who stays alive, or has managed to reproduce the longest accurate sequence of sentences, wins.

Spot the differences

1. Students A and B are each given texts which are nearly identical except for a number of differences.
2. Student A reads their text to B, then vice versa.
3. Student A or B (whoever reads the text to the other) has to spot and note down the differences.

The 'Algo' game

1. Sit the students in pairs, back to back.
2. Give student A sheet 1 and student B sheet 2. Each sheet has a different version of the same list of sentences; the sentences gapped on student A's sheet are complete on students' B sheet and vice versa.
3. Students take turns reading one gapped sentence each. As they read their sentence they say *something* (*algo* in Spanish – or an equivalent word in other languages) to signal the presence of a gap (note: each gap corresponds to a key target chunk). When student B hears student A say *something* they have to read the whole sentence twice, including the missing chunk, while their opponent writes it down and vice versa.
4. At the end of the game the students compare the two sheets to see who was more accurate.

Sentence hunt

This game is meant for younger students. It is played like 'hotter and colder'.

1. Display ten or more short sentences containing the target pattern, grammar structure or chunk.
2. Use thirty or more post-it notes. On ten post-its write the ten sentences (one sentence per post-it). On the remaining post-its write 'distractor' sentences which are different from the target sentences, but similar in structure.
3. Stick the post-its around the classroom in as many places as possible.
4. Select and send a 'searcher' out of the classroom.
5. Take a post-it containing one of the target sentences and place it near other distractor post-its. Make sure the class knows exactly where it is.
6. Referring back to the list of displayed sentences, point to the post-it you have just hidden. Tell the class to repeat it louder and louder as the searcher gets closer to the target post-it, and quieter and quieter as they move away. Get them to practise and orchestrate the volume with your hands.
7. Call the searcher back into the classroom, instruct them to find the post-it with the sentence the class is repeating aloud and play the game until the post-it is found. Then do as many rounds as you like. You might fit about one search per minute.

Tongue-twisters

These are a tried and tested way of having fun with sounds, words and longer utterances. One way to practise them is to use back-chaining (described earlier). This helps students pronounce difficult sounds, words, chunks or sentences, e.g (in English):

> Teacher: *shop*
> Students: *shop*
> Teacher: *shine shop*
> Students: *shine shop*
> Teacher: *shoe shine shop*
> Students: *shoe shine shop*
> Teacher: *I saw Susie sitting in a shoe shine shop.*
> Students: *I saw Susie sitting in a shoe shine shop.*

Tongue-twisters are easy to find for the language you teach and ideally should include the particular sounds and sound sequences you wish to target. Back-chaining can be used at any time to add fun to a question-answer or repetition sequence in class.

Tongue-twister race

1. Model the pronunciation of a tongue twister containing the target sounds.
2. Do a couple of the tasks listed above to raise students' awareness of possible pitfalls, reinforcing the target sounds. For example, play *Faulty echo* or *Spot the error*.
3. Students compete with each other in groups of four or five. Ask them to award to one person in the group three prizes: one for speed, one for accuracy, one for most improved (from the beginning to the end of the activity).

Tip: Select or create the tongue twisters based on the developmental stage of the students and ensure that they are not overloaded with difficult sounds

Critical listening

This activity is designed to enhance students' alertness to sounds, developing metacognition and a degree of autonomy. Although it may seem elaborate, it requires no preparation and produces useful conversations about sound. Here is how you can structure it:

1. Read aloud a text on a familiar topic flooded with specific sounds you want the class to hear.
2. Give students the text and 10 minutes to prepare reading aloud with a focus on pronunciation. They identify problems and attempt to solve them with the help of peers. Students note down the main issues identified and the solutions they have worked out.
3. Play a recording of yourself reading the text. Students listen to it for a few minutes before recording themselves.
4. Students now record themselves reading the text.
5. They listen back to themselves and to a partner, identifying areas for improvement.
6. Students jot down their findings, targets and reflections.

Tip: In order to encourage metacognition and self-reflection you could ask students to answer some or all the following questions:

a. What strategies did you use to prepare for reading aloud?
b. What strategies did you use when reading?
c. What sounds were hardest or easiest for you or your partner?
d. What did you pay attention to when reading?
e. What did you try to do when listening to your friends in pairs?
f. What helped you the most when reading?
g. What do you think you need to work on in the future?

Inductive listening

1. Give students the lyrics of an L2 song featuring lots of examples of target sounds and ask them to read it.
2. Ask them to underline as many occurrences as they can find in the text of specific combinations of letters (e.g. *che* and *ci*, *ce* in French).
3. Students then listen to the song a few times and work out individually or in pairs how those letter clusters are pronounced in L2.
4. Students share their findings.

Note: the above is more suitable for intermediate level students. We examine how to exploit songs in much more detail in Chapter 9.

Track the pitch

This activity makes students aware that stress and pitch can mark the ends of meaningful word groups or whole sentences. This assists with segmentation of the message.

1. Read aloud short paragraphs as students follow a transcript. Use rise and fall of pitch to indicate the ends of word groups and sentences.
2. Students mark with upward or downward-facing arrows what they hear your voice doing.
3. Show them your version with arrows on the board, modelling it once more.
4. They read the same paragraph aloud in pairs, evaluating each other's performance.

7.3 Alphabet fun

Most teachers teach the alphabet early on to beginners since spelling out words is a useful real-life skill, but it also serves to practise the new phonemes of the language. Here are a few fun activities teachers have told us they do with the alphabet:

- Sing the alphabet to familiar tune, e.g. a US army marching song, Camptown Races, Twinkle Twinkle Little Star or the theme to Eastenders (a series familiar to UK students). Repeat any letters as necessary to go with the tune.
- Who can guess the word first as I spell it out to you? Use the names of students in the class or, for example, the names of L2 country cities.
- Sing along with YouTube alphabet songs. You could play three such songs to the class, asking them to pick out their favourite to use repeatedly. In doing this, they begin to pick up the sounds implicitly.
- Make up or find an optician's sight testing chart containing letters of different sizes. Use this for repetition practice.

- Display letters in rows with each row sharing the same phoneme, e.g. in French *b*, *c*, *d*, *g*, (all sharing the *é* sound.
- Have students make up an alphabet rap or sing along with one on YouTube.
- Have students finger-write in the air on a partner's back as you read aloud letters.
- Design a 'join the dots' picture, but use letters rather than dots. Read out the right sequence of letters for students to draw the picture.
- Tell students to 'have a conversation' in pairs just using letters, gestures and intonation. Provide them with characters to use, e.g. a giant's voice or a mouse voice. Tell them to introduce emotions such as sadness, anger or mirth.
- *Beat the Teacher*: display the alphabet on the board, point at a letter and say it; if you pronounce it correctly the students repeat chorally, if you are wrong they remain silent.
- Draw a grid, e.g. 10 x 10. Write letters as coordinates (across and down), draw a shape or figure on your grid using a number of boxes and say the coordinates. Students have to shade in their empty version of the same grid. Make clear whether you are using the vertical or horizontal axis first. Whoever guesses first what the figure is wins, or students can just complete the whole figure.

7.4 Songs and singing along

Listening and singing along to a song, as some research indicates (e.g. Carlsson, 2015), does not on its own improve pronunciation. If you want to use song to improve pronunciation and alertness to sound, supplement it with exercises aimed at noticing, awareness-raising, targeted practice and corrective feedback. For more detail see Chapter 9.

Spot the mistakes and correct

Provide a set of lyrics with errors. Students have to spot the errors and replace them with the correct version. You could target particular sounds, or just keep the focus on meaning, using alternative words or chunks.

Spot and cross out the intruder

As with *Spot the intruder*, add extra words to the lyrics.

Spot the different accent

Some singers will sing with an accent which may be different from the one students most often hear in class, for example Canadian French or a South American variety of Spanish.

1. Give students a transcription of the song.

2. Students underline parts of the song where they become particularly aware of sounds which are new to them.
3. Elicit from students which words they found unusual and have a discussion about different accents they might encounter.

Note: this is a good example of using an authentic source to help students prepare for the reality of hearing the L2 in forms they do not usually encounter in the classroom.

7.5 Dictation tasks

Syllabling

Select words containing the syllable you wish to practise.

1. Dictate the words syllable by syllable. Students transcribe.
2. Dictate syllable by syllable again. Students check and make any changes.
3. Students pair up with others and compare transcriptions.

Partial dictation

Write a gapped text where the gapping depends on the focus of the task: is it decoding and transcription practice? Is it morphology? Is it syntax? All of them? If your focus is decoding skills, flood the text with as many occurrences as possible of the target phonemes and insert your gaps to correspond with these.

Delayed dictation

This is a zero-preparation activity which develops important processing micro-skills: holding chunks of language in working memory, along with decoding and transcription skills. Younger students really enjoy this one!

1. Say a sentence that students are familiar with, or containing at least 95% comprehensible input, and tell them to 'hold it inside their heads'.
2. As they do this, make funny noises or utter random L2 words to distract them for a few seconds.
3. Finally ask them to write the sentence on their mini-whiteboards and show you their answers.

Tip: follow this up with *Aural sentence puzzles* (Chapter 5) where you recycle the sentences used in delayed dictation but say them in jumbled-up order. Students have to rearrange them. Some teachers have reported that they prefer to avoid using distracting words or noises and so just remain silent.

Mad dictation

This a dictation in which you alternate between slow, moderate and fast pace. The activity is similar to dictogloss, described in Chapter 6.

Select a text containing familiar sentence patterns or highly comprehensible input.

1. Tell students to listen to the text as you read it at near-natural speed and to note down key words.
2. Tell them to pair up with another student and compare the key words they noted. Tell them they are going to work with that person for the rest of the task.
3. Read the text a second time, reading some bits slowly, some fast and some at moderate pace. The purpose of these changes of speed is to deliberately get students to miss some of the words.
4. Students work again with their partner to reconstruct the text.
5. Read the text a final time, still varying the speed of delivery.
6. Give the students another chance to work with their partner.
7. They get 30 seconds to go around the tables and compare notes with other pairs.

Tip: some of the students might panic the first time you do this activity. It is helpful to let them know in advance precisely how the activity works.

Running dictation

Create or select a text with highly comprehensible input.

1. Put the students in groups of four and name them 1, 2, 3 and 4.
2. Put up on the classroom walls, as far from where students are seated as possible, a sheet with the text for each group.
3. Students 1 and 2 take turns walking briskly to their designated sheet, memorising a sentence or more from the sheet, returning and repeating it to students 3 and 4 who transcribe what they hear. It is then the turn of students 3 and 4, etc. until the text has been written down.
4. Give students five minutes to proof-read the text.
5. Allow a minute to check anything they have doubts about by running to the designated sheet and relaying the information back to the rest of the group (students 1 / 2 first, then 3 / 4).

Tip: you may prefer to just play this game in pairs.

Scaffolded dictation

Students often find traditional teacher-led dictation difficult, but you can be scaffold the activity in various ways:

1. Supply the first letter of each word. This simple variation adds a further puzzle-solving element students may appreciate.
2. Supply all consonants, but no vowels, or vice versa. This resembles activities described above.
3. Provide a gapped version omitting chosen grammatical points such as articles, verbs or prepositions. This helps develop students' parsing skills when listening subsequently.
4. Provide a translation; give students a translation in L1 of the text you read. This allows them to focus on form (phonics) less than meaning, lightening the load on memory.

Paired gapped dictation

1. Students work with a partner. Student A has a complete text, student B a version with gaps.
2. Student A reads to student B, a phrase at a time. Student B can ask for repetitions.
3. After a given time stop the activity and get the pairs to correct the dictation.

Tip: you can add an extra element of fun by telling students to work back to back.

Group dictation

1. Students work in groups of four or five. Choose a more proficient student in each group to be the reader. Give that person a copy of a short comprehensible text, possibly with plenty of particular sound-spelling correspondences you wish to practise.
2. The reader carries out the dictation as a teacher would, reading a phrase at a time twice. The other students write their transcription.
3. After a given time display the correct transcription for all students to correct. The reader in each group can support the others, then another person can become the reader.

Tip: for some groups supply students with a gapped version to complete, rather than have them transcribe from scratch.

Grading dictation

1. Dictate a number of personalised sentences of the type *I get up at 6 o'clock*.
2. Students transcribe the sentence, adding an adverb of frequency to evaluate the statement, e.g. *never, occasionally, sometimes, often* and *always*.
3. Display the sentences and ask students how they graded the statements.

False facts dictation

1. Dictate some sentences, each one containing a false fact. The sentences could relate to general knowledge or something recently studied in class.
2. Students transcribe and try to underline where they think the error is.
3. Display the sentences and ask students what the factual problem was in each case.

The two tasks above are adapted from Wilson (2008).

Concluding remarks

As Field (2008) points out, decoding is a process during which students make tentative matches between sounds they hear and their existing knowledge of the L2 phonology, matches which may be revised. This is because the input varies – speakers have different accents, for example. In this chapter we have argued that doing targeted practice on the phonological system of the L2 can help students make the matches necessary to decode meaning. For us, this is one important aspect of helping students become confident listeners in the long run.

To recap, we have also emphasised that the exercises suggested may best be embedded within other more communicative practice. For instance, if you are doing communicative practice based on a written text, you could pick out particular problem areas for some brief focused practice. From the students' perspective it may make more sense to do decoding practice in the context of meaning-centred work. Field (2008) points out that, while we should not overstate the value of ear training, it has an extremely useful part to play in a process approach to listening.

Questions to consider

What balance of ear training and other types of work would be right for your class?

How can you make reading aloud a positive and engaging experience?

What issues are involved in managing pair and group work?

What are the pros and cons of doing teacher-led dictation versus paired dictation?

Should phonics training be planned or done on a more ad hoc basis?

How important is it for students to pronounce like a native speaker?

4

Vocabulary is a matter of word-building as well as word-using.
                    (David Crystal)

TEACHING LEXICAL RETRIEVAL THROUGH LISTENING

Introduction: the importance of vocabulary

Knowing vocabulary is a key predictor of overall language proficiency (e.g. Alderson, 2007) and much research suggests it plays a crucial role in the comprehension of aural input (Vafaee, 2016). Word recognition is vital for effective bottom-up processing (Vandergrift, 2004), while knowledge of word meanings plays an important role in the meaning-building stage of aural comprehension (Rost, 1990). Unsurprisingly students often report that lack of vocabulary is the main reason for their difficulty in understanding and using the language (Kelly, 1991; Hasan, 2000; Nation, 2012).

Research on vocabulary acquisition through listening is limited, but there is evidence (e.g. Elley, 1989, and Brett et al, 1996) that significant gains in vocabulary via listening are possible even with limited exposure to new words. Both studies suggest that learners studying in their L1 are able, through listening, to acquire target vocabulary with minimal repetition even when teachers do not stop to explain the meanings of words.

Research also indicates (e.g. Chambers, 1996) that teachers do not explicitly train students in the skill of acquiring vocabulary through listening. Vocabulary is often presented orally, usually in conjunction with visuals such as PowerPoint images, but then largely practised through reading and writing. This means that, because we tend to recall words in the form we encountered them (this is known as *Transfer Appropriate Processing*), they may not be easily retrieved while listening. In other words, if we read a word we are more likely to be able to retrieve it from memory when we read it, than when we hear it. This is particularly the case for languages such as French and English where spelling-phoneme correspondence is low.

This chapter focuses, therefore, on the explicit teaching of L2 vocabulary through listening. A repertoire of teaching strategies are provided which enhance *aural lexical retrieval*, a process which begins with the identification of word boundaries and culminates in the derivation of word meaning. To fully understand this stage in L2 aural comprehension and our approach to the teaching of lexical retrieval skills, it is useful to understand:

- what it means to *know* vocabulary;
- how vocabulary is *learned*;
- the most effective ways to achieve vocabulary retention;
- why it is important to learn vocabulary through listening.

Research into the detail of vocabulary acquisition is considered, and its relation to developing listening skills. After this preamble, a range of classroom activities supported by the research are described.

1. What does it mean to *know* vocabulary ?

1.1 The multi-dimensionality of vocabulary knowledge

It is tempting to believe students have learned a new set of words if they can recall their meaning in a listening or reading test requiring word recognition or using L1 translation (at worst as discrete items, at best contextualised in sentences or short paragraphs). However, there is much more to knowing a lexical item than knowing its meaning or translation.

Nation (2013) established a very useful framework (in **Table 4.1** below) summarising what 'knowing' a word actually means. This includes the word's *form* (e.g. spoken, written, word parts), its *meaning*, e.g. what it refers to, its associations, collocations (what it goes next to) and grammatical functions, and its *use*, e.g. what words you can use with it and when you can use it.

Nation's framework provides a valuable blueprint for vocabulary teaching across all four language skills, suggesting that a listening programme ought to include focusing on form, meaning and use. So specific aural vocabulary learning tasks can be designed to address each of these dimensions of lexical knowledge.

Table 4.1 Nation's (2013) three dimensions of knowing a word

Form	• spelling • pronunciation • morphological knowledge (knowledge about affixation)
Meaning	• knowledge of word-meaning • knowledge of the role of context in defining meaning • knowledge of synonyms and antonyms
Use	• knowledge of correct usage • knowledge of collocations (i.e. knowledge of how L2 words combine together in natural L2 usage) • knowledge of when to use and not use a word

Aural vocabulary practice of this sort is best done through as wide a range of semantic and linguistic contexts as possible for at least two reasons. Firstly, because, as we have mentioned, words influence each other phonologically in connected speech (assimilation). Secondly, if knowing a word means knowing about its usage, it is unwise to keep practising it in the same grammatical or situational context. In essence, let students hear words in different chunks, sentences and texts as well as different activities. Moreover, it is best if practice is extensive and logically sequenced.

1.2 Breadth, depth and fluency of vocabulary knowledge

Researchers have also described vocabulary knowledge as having three dimensions: *breadth*, *depth* and *fluency* (Daller, Milton, & Treffers-Daller, 2007; Nation, 2001; Read, 2000; Qian, 1999; Wesche & Paribakht, 1996).

Breadth

Breadth refers to the size of a person's lexicon, i.e. the number of the words for which a person knows the meaning (Nation, 2012; Staehr, 2009; Qian, 2002). Depth refers to how well a learner knows a word across all the three dimensions identified by Nation (see **Table 4.1).**

Breadth has been considered the most basic aspect of vocabulary knowledge, and learners with larger vocabulary sizes are more proficient language users (Meara, 1996). Definitions of breadth are complicated by the fact that we talk both about words, e.g. *bake,* and word families: *baking, bakery, baker*, but to give an idea of the number of words needed at intermediate level (e.g. in the GCSE exam in England, Wales and Northern Ireland), around 2000 words would be typical (either for receptive or productive knowledge).

Depth

While breadth implies having a superficial knowledge of meaning, depth of knowledge seems to play the main role in determining success in complex linguistic and cognitive tasks such as listening comprehension (Vafaee, 2016). As Qian & Schedl (2004) put it, in meaningful and communicative L2 contexts, "depth of vocabulary knowledge occupies a primary and central place in the multidimensional domain of vocabulary knowledge" (p 30).

Breadth and depth can interact, e.g. the more words you know, the more examples of word parts like prefixes and suffixes you will know, so breadth develops depth (Qian, 2002). Breadth usually develops before depth, meaning that beginner and intermediate students have more difficulty putting sentences together (Vafaee, 2016). As Qian (2002) notes, vocabulary knowledge develops cumulatively. Hence, words acquired at earlier stages are more likely to have more depth than recently learned ones.

Fluency

Fluency of vocabulary knowledge has been defined as how fast and effortlessly learners can recognise, process, or access the form and meaning of a word for language use (Vafaee, 2016). It is therefore important when processing aural input in 'real operating conditions', i.e. rapidly, under time pressure. Breadth and depth of vocabulary are insufficient unless students can apply it quickly, effortlessly and accurately across a wide range of communicative situations and texts. Fluency takes a lot of time, meaningful exposure and practice to achieve.

We agree with Nation's (2007) belief that fluency benefits from specific training where students, once they have learned a word explicitly, do repeated practice in its retrieval in increasingly complex contexts in order for it to be internalised. This can mean increasing over time the rate at which input is delivered and providing gradually longer texts.

One dimension of fluency is a students's ability to hold chunks in working memory as they process input. The larger the chunks our working memory can process at any one time, the more fluent processing is likely to be. Some researchers believe that working memory capacity is genetically determined and cannot be altered by teaching (e.g. Field, 2009); others (e.g. Nation and Newton, 2009) believe it can. Some recent studies suggest working memory can be improved with training, but it is uncertain by how much and what sort of training works best. We suggest that (1) teachers provide extensive practice in this skill and (2) they train students in chunking aural input in manageable multi-word units, as this lightens the load on working memory. Activities that can help enhance this skill are suggested later in the chapter.

An important point to make concerning fluency is that it is *modality-specific* (Nation, 2007). You should not assume that simply because students are fluent in the oral production of vocabulary they will be equally fluent in recognising it when listening. You sometimes come across students who can utter long, complex sentences quickly and accurately, but who struggle to understand simple questions.

Overall, it is worth spending as much time as possible on depth and fluency during listening tasks, not focusing exclusively on breadth.

1.3 Receptive versus productive knowledge

Another distinction made in the literature on vocabulary is one between *receptive* and *productive* knowledge. As you might expect, the former develops first. One study (Nemati, 2010) found that receptive knowledge may be five times greater than productive. Students therefore typically recognise words but cannot recall and use them. Interestingly, according to researchers (e.g, DeKeyser, 1997), comprehension and production rely on different knowledge systems and processing mechanisms. This means that both receptive and productive vocabulary skills need practising.

In general, it is wise to do lots of receptive work through listening and reading, before moving on to production. This produces more accurate and fluent production (N. Ellis, 2002). As mentioned above, de Jong (2005) suggests that only after correct knowledge of an item has been sufficiently established receptively should production take place. The latter can reinforce memory and establish any processes specific to production. In sum, do plenty of listening before getting students to speak or write.

2. Vocabulary versus lexis

Another distinction is sometimes made between *vocabulary*, often thought of as single items, and *lexis*, which includes not only words but also word combinations or chunks that we store in our mental lexicon as a result of frequent exposure and usage. Some writers assume that the word vocabulary includes both words and chunks. One school of thought argues that language consists mostly of chunks which, when combined, produce continuous coherent speech (Lewis, 1997). In this view, only a minority of spoken sentences are entirely novel creations.

It has been claimed that in everyday speech up to 80% of what we say is in the form of lexical chunks stored in memory (Altenberg, 1998). Lewis (1997) proposed a taxonomy of lexical items (**Table 4.2**), which identifies six types of lexical chunks: *polywords, collocations, institutionalised utterance, sentence frames, sentence heads* and *text frames*. The table is a reminder of just how many 'set phrases' we use in speech.

Table 4.2 Taxonomy of lexical chunks, adapted from Lewis (1997)

Words	e.g. *book, pen*
Polywords	e.g. *by the way, upside down*
Collocations	e.g. *to make tea, to do business, community service*
Institutionalised utterances	e.g. *I'll get it; We'll see; That'll do; If I were you...; Would you like a cup of coffee?*
Sentence frames	e.g. *That is not as .... as you think; The most important thing about ...... is ......; I didn't go to the....because I was ....*
Sentence heads	e.g. *The fact/suggestion/problem/danger was...; What I like/don't like is...; The best/worst is....*
Text frames	e.g. *In this paper we shall explore...Firstly....; Secondly...; Thirdly...*

Viewing language as a system made up of lexical building blocks which students assemble and manipulate to form utterances in the pursuit of a communicative function has advantages. Communicative functions include: asking for directions; reporting an event in the past; comparing and contrasting two people; writing an introduction to an essay, etc. One advantage is that language learning becomes less about learning abstract rules and more about communication. Building up sequences of *functional chunks* and sentence patterns through repeated exposure allows students to carry out purposeful communication. This is likely to be more enjoyable, allowing students to gain confidence and immediate mastery.

A second advantage concerns processing efficiency and the development of fluency. Research has shown that making use of formulaic expressions and memorising lengthy chunks of text (and making substitutions within them) is far more efficient than learning to assemble new linguistic strings from individual words (Nation, 2013; Ellis, 2015). This is owing to the limited processing capacity of working memory. Processing language in meaningful chunks speeds up working memory processing rate as each L2 item we assemble while producing utterances includes multi-words rather than single ones. Put another way, four items processable by working memory could be either *I - play - games* or: *I spent – three hours - playing video games – with my friends*. Wilkins (1972) claims that learning a language through lexical and grammatical chunks, instead of discrete words or word elements, can often cover in half the time what is expected from a whole year of teaching.

Many teachers and their students have experienced first-hand the benefits of 'chunking'. You can decide whether this is something you would like to explore further. Chapter 8 looks into the approach in more detail, suggesting ways in which it could be implemented with beginner-to-intermediate students, and showing how LAM incorporates chunking within teaching sequences.

Whether you favour a chunk-based approach or not, it is helpful to include in your listening input high-frequency multi-word phrases, and to encourage students to employ the chunking of vocabulary to help with receptive and productive performance. Having a repertoire of useful chunks can be a life-saver in exams, particularly for less proficient students who find it hard to learn through a traditional 'words with grammar' approach.

3. Content versus function words

All words can be classified as either *content* or *function* words. Content words carry meaning; they usually name items, concepts, qualities, states or actions. They consist mostly of nouns, adjectives and lexical verbs, i.e. all verbs except auxiliary verbs. In contrast, function words have very little lexical meaning and primarily indicate grammatical relationships between content words. They include: prepositions, pronouns, conjunctions, articles, particles, auxiliary verbs and some adverbs. They form important elements in the structure of sentences; in a sense they are the glue that holds sentences together.

Function words usually constitute only a tiny percentage of the total number of words in a language. For instance, in English 99.9 % of words are content words. Yet function words occur very frequently in spoken and written discourse, making up over 50% of any English text (Pennebaker, 2013).

Despite their high frequency in speech, function words are less noticeable than content words. This is particularly the case for L2 listeners, who are much more successful at identifying content words (Field, 2008). Why? Since function words do not carry meaning, and owing to working memory limitations, listeners focus on content words and ignore function words in order to comprehend in the most efficient way. In addition, function words tend to be shorter and less noticeable than content words. In English, content words always have at least one stressed syllable, whereas function words are often completely unstressed in the stream of speech.

This chapter focuses on content words, since function words are more relevant to syntactic knowledge and processing, which are considered in Chapter 5. Evidently, though, the two sets of words are interdependent as function words bind content words together

4. How do we learn vocabulary?

There are said to be two types of vocabulary learning: *intentional* (explicit or conscious) and *incidental* (implicit or unconscious).

Intentional learning

Deliberate attempts to learn new words can be through direct instruction such as call and response flashcard work, matching tasks, gap-fill, or through personal learning from lists. There is research to suggest that intentional learning is more efficient (e.g. Webb, 2007) than incidental. Laufer and Rozovski-Roitblat (2011) found that intentional exercises (practising words out of context, synonym and antonym work, selecting the right meaning from options, writing the words in sentences) led to better short and long-term recall than incidental approaches. Bilingual word lists and flashcards have been found to be useful. Using meaning-focused output (e.g. writing new words in sentences) is also supported by research.

Incidental learning

This means picking up words where vocabulary acquisition is not the main goal and learning happens with little or no conscious effort. Lots of learning occurs this way during lessons when listening and reading is going on, although uptake can be slower and more uneven. This is because the number of exposures needed to learn implicitly is high.

Exploit both dimensions

Research, not to mention common sense, suggests that the best approach is to combine intentional with incidental learning, where the latter reinforces the former. As Carroll (1966) wrote: "the more numerous kinds of associations that are made to an item, the better are learning and retention" (p.105). For the students focused on in this book, intentional teaching of vocabulary is likely to be productive and indeed was strongly recommended in a major review of language teaching methodology in England (Bauckham, 2016).

5. Why is it important to learn vocabulary through listening?

Since knowing vocabulary partly means knowing what words sound like, it makes sense to introduce and practise words and chunks aurally, as well as by other means. A key component in remembering vocabulary is the *phonological loop,* the working-memory device which deals with sound or phonological information entering the brain.

As **Figure 4.1** shows, the phonological loop is one of the three sub-systems used by working memory to deal with any incoming data which requires conscious processing. It is thought to play a key role in the acquisition of both L1 and L2 vocabulary by rehearsing new, unfamiliar words while they are being added to our mental lexicon, i.e. the long-term 'word dictionary' in our brain (Baddeley, Gathercole & Papagno, 1998). This function is very important, since acquiring a large vocabulary when young is a significant determinant of a child's eventual intellectual and educational progress (Treffers-Daller & Milton, 2013).

Figure 4.1 A model of working memory (Baddeley, 2003)

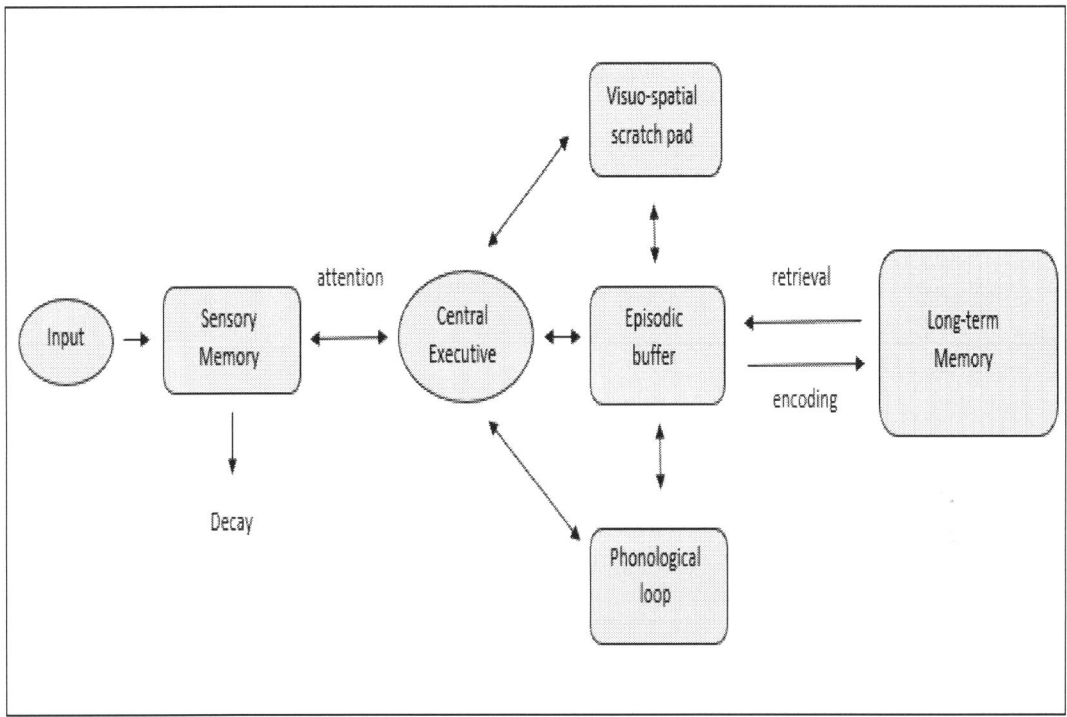

The phonological loop consists of two parts (see **Figure 4.2**): (1) a short-term *phonological store* with auditory memory traces that decay, and (2) the *articulatory loop*, which can revive the faded traces. Aural input is thought to enter the phonological store, while written input can be transformed into a phonological version by 'saying words in your head' (subvocalisation). The phonological store acts as an 'inner ear', remembering speech sounds in chronological order, while the articulatory loop acts as an 'inner voice' which repeats the sounds or words on a loop for two seconds to prevent them from decaying, e.g. when we repeat a number to ourselves aloud or silently in order not to forget it.

There are also important individual differences which depend on how good one's *phonological rehearsal ability* is. Biedron and Szeczepaniak (2012) found that accomplished multilinguals have superior memory abilities with respect to the phonological loop and the central executive component of working memory, which suggests there is a correlation between being a multilingual, having a strong working memory and having a high IQ.

As a teacher, you may be able to identify students with poorer phonological memory early on, e.g. if they find it hard to mimic what you say, or hold phrases in memory. These students need more attention and support. Some of the activities below, such as *Mind reading, Delayed repetition* and *Delayed dictation* are very useful in this respect.

Figure 4.2 The phonological loop structure (Baddeley et al, 2000)

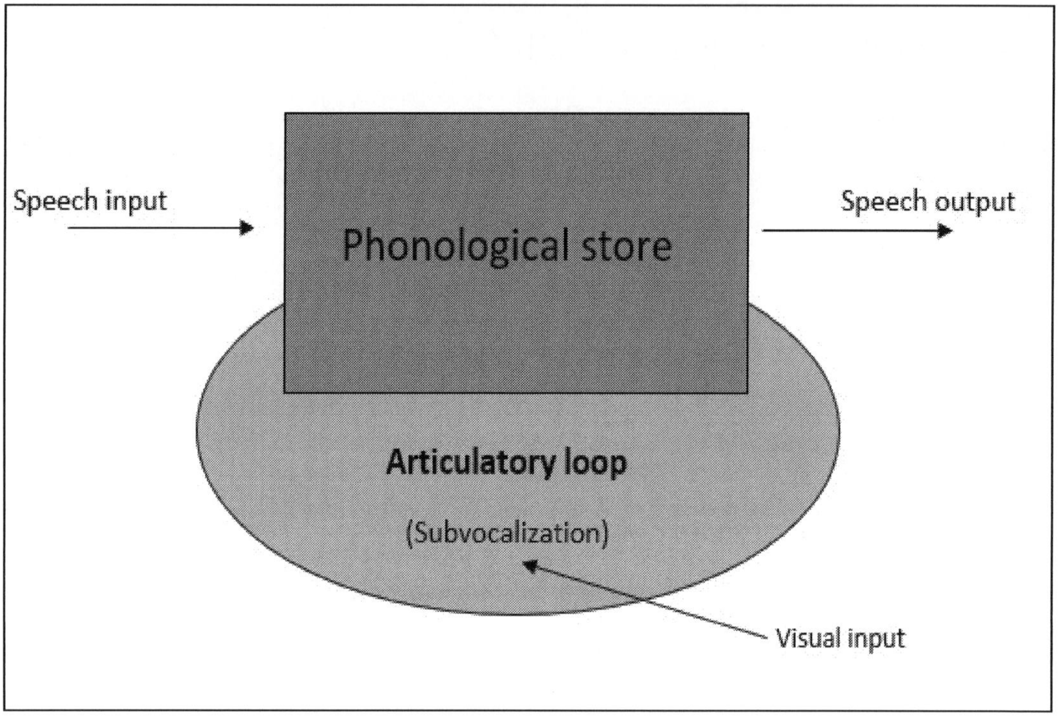

Speech input → **Phonological store** → Speech output

Articulatory loop (Subvocalization) ← Visual input

The number of words the phonological loop can handle simultaneously depends mainly on how naturally strong a student's phonological memory is. It can also be a function of how fluently they can process sounds, i.e. the slower they are at decoding or pronouncing words, the fewer words they produce. This suggests that unless students get practice in fast vocabulary decoding and pronunciation through listening and speaking tasks, it will not be efficiently retrieved. Lots of deliberate aural/oral practice through LAM tasks, repeating and reading aloud, choral reading and speaking will help. Lower-proficiency students may be the greatest beneficiaries of this strategy.

INFOBOX 8 The mental lexicon

This is our 'mental dictionary' – the store of words, word families and chunks, together with their meanings. It has been claimed, e.g. by Milton et al (2010) that this knowledge is primarily stored in phonological form. In other words, when we think of a word we think mainly of how it sounds. Try it! If we focus on teaching words aurally, as well as by other means, they will be better retained and be more retrievable when listening.

6. Principles for teaching vocabulary through listening

6.1 Select words carefully

Choose the vocabulary you plan to teach based on:
- *Learnability* (how easy or challenging it is in terms of length, pronunciation, spelling, meaning, grammar, word order in a sentence etc. See **Table 4.3**);
- *Frequency* (give priority to lexical items with high *surrender value*, i.e. how often they will be heard or used);
- *Relevance* (choose words relevant to students' interests, background and culture or sub-culture, not to mention the syllabus);
- *Semantic relatedness* (the more strongly interrelated the words are semantically, the stronger the chances of retention).
- *Word class* (ensure there is a good balance of nouns and verbs (the latter are sometimes neglected).

Some research suggests that teaching words from the same semantic field, e.g. countries, vegetables or furniture, may result in slightly poorer retention since words from that field may interfere with each other, causing confusion. If your text book contains an over-abundance of topic-specific vocabulary, you may want to be selective about which words to prioritise. This is one potential danger of 'teaching by topic'.

Table 4.3 Learnability: how hard are words to learn? (adapted from Nation, 2007)

Meaning	Form and meaning Concept and referents Associations	*Is the word a loan word in the L1?* *Is there an L1 word with roughly the same meaning?* *Does the word fit into the same sets as an L1 word of similar meaning?*
Form	Spoken form Written form Word parts	*Can the learners repeat the word accurately if they hear it?* *Can the learners write the word correctly if they hear it?* *Can the learners identify known affixes in the word?*
Use	Grammatical functions Collocation Constraints on use	*Does the word fit into predictable grammar patterns?* *Does the word have the same collocations in the L1?* *Does the word have the same restrictions on its use as its L1 equivalent(s)?*

6.2 Work across all six dimensions of lexical knowledge

Consider all the dimensions of vocabulary knowledge referred to already:
- *form* (sound, spelling and morphology);
- *meaning*;
- *use* (collocations and stylistic appropriateness);
- *breadth* (vocabulary size);
- *depth* (how well a lexical item is known);
- *fluency* (how spontaneous is retrieval and use of lexis).

Bear in mind that without fluency the other dimensions of knowledge have less value in the listening comprehension process, as a high rate of retrieval speed is required.

6.3   Teach words in context

Model and consolidate words in context; words are rarely used in isolation.

6.4   Teach chunks and encourage chunking

Include formulaic language and multi-words in the core vocabulary you plan to teach. Teaching words in chunks, as we have seen, is better for developing fluency. Get your students into the habit of chunking words in meaningful, useful and manageable multi-word units.

6.5   Ensure repeated retrieval in the short and long term

Students need to encounter vocabulary repeatedly in order to acquire it. We suggest four key strategies to make sure this happens:

- **Input-flooding**: ensuring multiple occurrences of the same items in the input students process in a given lesson. This can make input sound artificial, but is worth doing.
- **Thorough processing tasks**: activities designed to force students to process the input in detail, rather than simply skimming and scanning.
- **Highly patterned input**: providing aural texts which are very similar in structure but may differ in detail, like the narrow listening tasks in **Table 4.4**.
- **Recycling**: ensuring that students process vocabulary both receptively and productively as many times as possible in the course of a lesson.

Table 4.4 Sample narrow listening texts, i.e. near-identical texts which contain exactly the same syntactic and discourse structure but differ in small details, mostly content words.

My name is Jane. I am 13 years old. I live in Kajang, a village near Kuala Lumpur. I have a brother who is older than me. He is 20. He is very arrogant, selfish and nasty. I don't get along with him at all!	*My name is Mike. I am 18 years old. I live in Penang, a beautiful town very far from Kuala Lumpur. I have a brother who is much older than me. He is 27. He is very intelligent, hard-working and kind. I get along with him well!*
My name is Mark. I am 15 years old. I live in Batu Pahat, a town far from Kuala Lumpur, near Johor Bahru. I have a sister who is younger than me. She is 12. She is very friendly and affectionate, but at times she is a bit annoying. I get along with her, though.	*My name is Suzie. I am 16 years old. I live in Ipoh, a town quite far from Kuala Lumpur. I have a brother who is younger than me and one who is older. My brother is only 9, but my sister is 17. My brother is very nice and generous, but my sister is weird and not very nice. I don't get along with her at all!*

6.6 Do not forget forgetting rates!

Bearing in mind how quickly we forget words (see **Table 4.5** below), practice should continue extensively in a spaced fashion for as long as it takes until we are satisfied the vocabulary has been acquired. Of course some words and phrases can be recalled after a single encounter if that encounter is particularly memorable, e.g. associated with a teacher's anecdote or striking picture.

Table 4.5 Human forgetting rates (Ebbinghaus, 1885)

Time elapsed since learning	(% of information retained)
Immediately	100
20 minutes	58
1 hour	44
9 hours	36
1 day	33
2 days	28
6 days	25
31 days	21

INFOBOX 9 Human forgetting rates

Hermann Ebbinghaus (1885) studied the issue of memory loss over time. He found that when you first learn something, the information disappears at an exponential rate, i.e. you lose most of it in the first couple of days, after which the rate of loss tapers off. He found that by spacing out learning over a period of time you improve long-term retention of information.

Ebbinghaus also found that information is easier to recall when it is built upon things you already know. This is known as interleaving. Every time you reinforce memory training, the rate of memory decline reduces. What is more, by simply testing a person's memory of something, that memory becomes stronger.

6.7 Interleaving

As mentioned in the infobox above, the brain learns best when spaced practice occurs together with interleaving, i.e. when we mix in new knowledge with past knowledge. It is unwise, therefore, to use *blocking,* where one set of vocabulary is taught at a time, i.e. following the pattern AAA - BBB - CCC. It is more effective to practise mixing different sets of vocabulary together, following the pattern ABC – ABC - ABC, where the current vocabulary is combined with past.

6.8 Provide comprehensible input

We have previously made the point that new vocabulary is best learned in a highly comprehensible linguistic context which is at least 95 to 98 % comprehensible. If a text unusually falls below this threshold provide a vocabulary list (gloss) to help make the text comprehensible.

6.9 Draw on L1 to establish meaning

Although L2 use should be the classroom default, there is no need to avoid using the L1 translation of an unfamiliar word or chunk if it is the most efficient way to establish meaning. Although Zhang and Graham (2019) have noted that there is little research into the value of when and how to use L1 when teaching vocabulary studies, including their own, suggest an advantage for L1 use. They found that there was "some, but only short-term, advantage to be gained through code-switched explanations" (Zhang and Graham, 2019, p.22).

6.10 Use dual coding

Research supports the use of pictures to assist with vocabulary recall, e.g. Carpenter and Olson (2012).

INFOBOX 10 Dual Coding Theory

Developed by Allan Paivio in the 1960s, Dual-Coding Theory is a theory of cognition which states that humans process and represent verbal and non-verbal information in separate but related systems. For example, the brain uses a different kind of representation for the word *bus* than it does for the image of a bus. A verbal cue can trigger a thought of something non-verbal and vice versa; the image of a square can bring to mind the word *square*, while *square* can prompt you to visualise a square. Paivio argued that all cognition involves associations between verbal and non-verbal systems. Some psychologists believe dual-coding theory explains intelligence and memory. Critics argue that the brain processes information using only one kind of representation. For language teachers, it is easy to take from this that visual representations (pictures) reinforce word recognition and recall.

6.11 Exploit the production effect

Repeating words aloud is a more effective way to memorise new vocabulary than listening to others or oneself on a recording (Forrin and McLeod, 2015).

6.12 Promote depth of processing

Research shows that the deeper and more elaborate the level of semantic analysis of new vocabulary is, the stronger the chances are of ensuring retention. Tasks which engage the brain in building associations between words, contrasting and comparing them, inferring their meaning, or which elicit any other mental operation requiring higher order thinking, are more likely to result in stronger retention.

6.13 Exploit the distinctiveness principle

Anything that stands out is more likely to be noticed and remembered. There are plenty of ways to make vocabulary stand out, ranging from the way you say words, to the context you say them in. An amusing picture, anecdote or classroom incident all help.

6.14 Avoid cognitive overload

Bearing in mind the limited number of words human working memory can accommodate and that words which are hard to pronounce are heavy on capacity, ensure you prevent cognitive overload by not asking students to process aural input or perform tasks beyond their processing ability.

INFOBOX 11 Cognitive Load Theory

In general terms, Cognitive Load Theory, developed by John Sweller in 1998, is built on the premise that since the brain can only do so many things at once, we should be careful about what we ask it to do. Working memory is limited, so learning experiences should be designed to reduce working memory 'load' in order to allow schemas (patterns, structures, concepts) to form. Too much load leads to poor understanding, confusion, or the inability to store new information in long term memory. In a word, do not give students too much difficult material to process at once.

7. Modelling vocabulary use

Sentence builders like the one in **Table 4.6** can be used to introduce new vocabulary in context, alongside already known items. New vocabulary in this style of sentence builder is translated in brackets so that students receive 100% comprehensible input throughout the modelling process. The translations can be removed as students gain familiarity with the vocabulary.

With a class sharing a common L1 the following procedure is suggested:

1. Explain what sentence pattern or patterns you intend to model, what communicative function they serve and what semantic and/or situational context the vocabulary relates to. For example, "Today you're going to learn how to describe the rooms in your house and say how much you like or dislike them and why. The sentence pattern we're going to practise is: *I* + verb expressing like/dislike + room of the house + causal marker (e.g. because or as) + *it is* + adjective."
2. If you feel it would help, raise students' awareness of the grammar underlying the target sentence pattern. Make the grammar explanation concise.
3. Make up L2 sentences using the various combinations the sentence builder allows, reading them aloud at a moderate pace while students write down the L1 meaning on mini-whiteboards.

Modelling vocabulary this way ensures that new lexical items are presented and practised in context through dual coding, i.e. listening and reading at the same time. Sentence builders have a number of advantages:

- They enable you to present words and lexical patterns in context.
- They allow you to model chunks and patterns through listening and reading.
- They help prevent agreement and word order mistakes in languages like French, German, Spanish, Italian, etc. because words are presented in chunks, masculine/feminine nouns with masculine/ feminine adjectives;
- They make it easy to recycle old material and to plant the seed of new linguistic items you plan to teach in the future (implicit learning). Just put such items in a column of the sentence builder with the translation and they will be acquired through exposure.
- You can use them as a scaffold for playing enjoyable and non-threatening interactive oral games (e.g. *Sentence puzzles, Guess what comes next, Faulty echo, Delayed dictation*, etc.).

How modelling fits in a typical LAM teaching sequence will be discussed in detail in Chapter 8.

Table 4.6 Example of an Italian sentence builder modelling *play/do* + noun + *because* + copula *(is)* + adjective in the context of leisure.

GIOCARE (to play) Gioco (I play)	a scacchi (chess) a pallacanestro (basketball) a carte (cards) ai videogiochi (videogames) a pallone (football) a tennis (tennis) a pallavolo (volleyball) con il computer (on the computer)	perchè (because it is) però è (but it is)	noioso (boring) faticoso (tiring) appassionante (exciting) divertente (fun) duro (tough) emozionante (thrilling) malsano (unhealthy) pericoloso (dangerous) sano (healthy) una perdita di tempo (a waste of time)
FARE (to do) Faccio (I do)	equitazione (horse riding) jogging nuoto (swimming) pesi (weights) pugilato (boxing) scalata libera (rock climbing) sport (sport) una passeggiata (I go for a walk) vela (sailing)		

8. Deep processing tasks

These engage students in semantic processing. They include sorting vocabulary into semantic categories, ordering it (e.g. in decreasing order of size), finding opposites and synonyms, matching words to their definition, working out their meaning from context, playing odd one out and creating mnemonics to make them easier to recall (e.g. in German DOGWUF to recall the prepositions which take the accusative case, or in French MRS VANDERTRAMP to recall the verbs which use *être* as ther auxiliary in the perfect tense).

Below are examples of activities which generate deep processing. For the sake of clarity, we have grouped them according to a number of categories: *associations, inferencing, information transfer, listen and do, error identification, vocabulary recognition, note-taking, spot the difference, substitution, reordering, prediction* and *recall*. In reality not every task fits neatly under a given heading.

8.1 Associations

Odd one out

Read aloud four sentences. Students pick the odd one out. We suggest sentences rather than single words so that vocabulary is heard in context, e.g.

     1. *Yesterday I went to the beach.*
     2. *Yesterday I sunbathed.*
     3. *Yesterday I went snowboarding.*
     4. *Yesterday I went swimming.*

Find the near synonym

1. Write a numbered list of five words or short sentences on the board.
2. Say in random order, six words or sentences (with one item a distractor) which are near-synonyms of the items on the board.
3. Students match each item on the board to the number of its near-synonym and write it down.

Associations

1. Write up a numbered list of five words or short sentences.
2. Say in random order six words or sentences which are strongly associated in meaning with the items on the board. For instance, if one of the items is *I see a building* you could say *It's an office block* or *It's very tall* or *It has twelve floors*.
3. Students match your utterances to the items displayed and write down the answer.

Gapped sentences

1. Write a few gapped sentences on the board and tell students you are going to say in random order a number of words or phrases needed to complete the sentences.
2. Say the words or phrases and ask students to match them to the correct sentence.

Categories

1. Tell the class you are going to read out words or short sentences which refer to four categories, e.g. *At the beach, At the gym, At school, At the shop*). Students tell you what category they belong to.
2. Read out a short sentence, e.g. *Yesterday I worked out* or *Yesterday I bought a gift for my dad*.
3. Students note down their answers on mini-whiteboards and hold them up to you.

TEACHING LEXICAL RETRIEVAL   77

Put in the right order

This requires sequencing L2 vocabulary in increasing or decreasing order of size, length, duration, speed, etc. Any measurable information can work, e.g. after a series of lessons on Italian geography ask students to listen to the following Italian statements as you display a map of Italy on the classroom screen/board. Students place the statements in rising order of distance.

1. *La settimana scorsa ho viaggiato da Genova a Bari* (*Last week I travelled from Genoa to Bari*)
2. *Due settimane fa ho viaggiato da Torino a Milano* (*Two weeks ago I travelled from Turin to Milan*)
3. *Venerdì scorso ho viaggiato da Firenze a Pisa* (*Last Friday I travelled from Florence to Pisa*)
4. *Ieri ho viaggiato da Roma a Palermo* (*Yesterday I travelled from Rome to Palermo*)

Climb the wall

1. Hand out a sheet depicting a grid resembling a brick wall, as in the picture in **Figure 4.3**. Each brick in the wall contains a word from your current topic or a previously practised one (for retrieval).
2. Read out simple definitions of words on the wall, e.g. *You go to the swimming pool for this; You play with ten friends and a ball; It's a combat sport*. Students must shade in the brick, starting at the bottom. As each definition follows they gradually work their way up the wall, moving left, right or upwards. There will usually be three or four options in play. You can play this repeatedly with the same grid, ensuring repetition of the definitions.
3. Students raise a hand when they think they have reached the top. Pairs could work on this together.

Figure 4.3 *Climb the wall*

football	gymnastics	golf	swimming	basketball
judo	table tennis	swimming	rugby	hockey	golf
gymnastics	tennis	football	basketball	ice-skating
golf	swimming	ice-skating	table tennis	tennis	judo
table tennis	basketball	football	swimming	hockey

78 BREAKING THE SOUND BARRIER

8.2 Inferencing

Match

1. Write a numbered list of twelve words (including two distractors) on the board and read out the definition of ten of them in random order.
2. Students match the definitions they hear with each of the items on the board, by writing down the numbers, until only the two distractors are left unmatched.

Work out the word

1. Give the class the definition of a familiar word, e.g. having learned fruits and vegetables, say: *It's a fruit. It's long and yellow.*
2. Students write the answer on their mini-whiteboard: *It's a banana.*

Definition chains

This game consists of describing an item by providing a series of L2 clues, starting with a very broad one, then gradually narrowing them down until the answer is pretty obvious. Every time you provide a clue students guess the item. Example:

> Clue 1: *it's a vehicle.*
> Students' guesses: *bike, motorbike, car, moped.*
> Clue 2 : *it has four wheels.*
> Students' guesses: *bus, quad bike, van, jeep.*
> Clue 3: *it's big.*
> Students' guesses: *motor home (RV), coach.*
> Cue 4 : *it carries goods, not people.*
> Students' guess: *truck.*

Tip: if you do more than one chain try and stick to the same pattern as in the examples below.

First time:

It's thin.
It's black. It has many teeth.
It's made of plastic.
You can find it near a mirror.
It costs a euro.
Everybody uses it.
It's used for combing your hair.

What is it?

Second time:

It's thin.
It's silver. It has a sharp point.
It's made of steel.
You can find it in the house.
It costs ten cents.
You need good eyes to use it.
It's used for sewing things.

What is it?

Same or different?

1. Give students a card with a list of items, e.g. in the example in **Table 4.7** a list of eight rooms in a house. You have a card with eight definitions of rooms in the house, only a few of which match the items on the students' cards. For instance, the definitions in number 1, 2, 4 and 7 on the teacher's card refer to the corresponding items on the students' card, but 3, 5, 6 and 8 do not.
2. Read out out each definition on their card, e.g. *Number one: You make food in there* and then ask *Same or different?*
3. Students write *same* or *different* on their mini-whiteboard and if they get it right they score a point.

Table 4.7 *Same or different* cards

Student's card	Teacher's card
1. A kitchen	1. You cook meals in there
2. A living-room	2. There is a big sofa in there
3. A garden	3. My parents keep their car there
4. A play room	4. We play games in there
5. A bedroom	5. I mow the lawn there
6. A dining-room	6. I shower there
7. A garage	7. My sister keeps her motorbike in there
8. A bathroom	8. My parents sleep there

Detectives

1. Write on the board a number of unfamiliar words (no more than one for every couple of sentences to be heard) and tell students they are going to listen to a text containing those words. The task is to infer the L1 meaning of those words from context.
2. Play or read the text twice as students listen individually.
3. Students pair up with one or two others and compare notes.
4. They listen to the text a third time and finalise their answers.
5. Show them the transcript. Working in pairs, students confirm or revise their answers.

Mystery words

This game, which loosely resembles the classic *20 questions*, elicits lots of deep processing as it involves inferencing, processing and associating old and new material as well as requiring students to ask questions.

1. Tell the class you are going to introduce new words on the current topic in order to expand their repertoire of vocabulary. Their task is, working in groups, to infer the meaning of these words. They can ask you as many questions as they want. The group guessing the most mystery word meanings first will be the winner.
2. Ask the groups to brainstorm as many questions as possible which may help them work out the meaning of the mystery words. (If you have played the game before they may have a bank of questions already in their books.) The questions may be open or closed and even metalinguistic in nature (*is it an adjective?*). Encourage them to ask you if the mystery words can be used in combination with words they already know, e.g. if the word is *camion* (French for *truck*) they may ask you *On peut conduire un camion?* (*Can you drive a truck?*).
3. Students now share their questions with the class and you note them down on the board, making corrections if necessary.
4. Write a word you have been practising recently and ask your students (in pairs) to ask questions to find out what it is. You can give them a clue as to what broad theme or category it belongs to or the word class (e.g. *it is an adjective*). Tell them each pair has two lives only and they lose a life each time they guess wrongly.
5. Students ask you questions, guessing the word based on your answers whenever they feel ready. After giving your answer orally, you could write it on the board before being asked the next question for them to keep track of the cues.

8.3 Information transfer

Brain teasers

These tasks involve students in some sort of problem solving and they respond in speaking or writing. The task in **Figure 4.4** is based an example from Nation and Newton (2009).

1. Give the class a relatively simple problem to solve (e.g. show them the cross-shaped diagram in **Figure 4.4** and ask one of the questions beneath, e.g. *A boy is facing the city, what's on his right?*
2. Students write their answers on their mini-whiteboards in full, e.g. *The sea is on his right* or *On his right there's the sea* and show you their answers.

This can be done as a pair-work activity. You could have a series of cards with similar diagrams gradually becoming more complicated and challenging.

Figure 4.4 A listening brain teaser for near-beginners

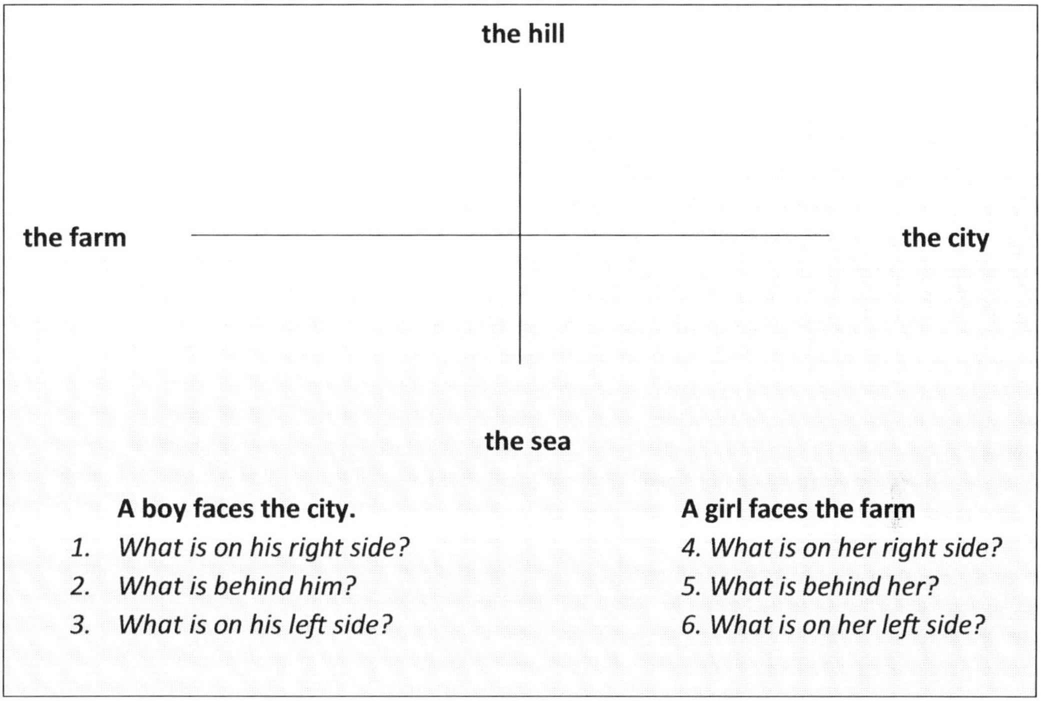

```
                    the hill
                      |
                      |
   the farm ──────────┼────────── the city
                      |
                      |
                    the sea
```

    A boy faces the city.   **A girl faces the farm**
1. *What is on his right side?*   4. *What is on her right side?*
2. *What is behind him?*   5. *What is behind her?*
3. *What is on his left side?*   6. *What is on her left side?*

8.4 Listen and do activities

These are activities where students follow instructions given to them orally, transforming the input into actions. They are an integral part of the approach known as Total Physical Response (Asher, 1969). There are all sorts of variations on *listen and do* activities, ranging from giving directions to a group of students as you take them around your school (e.g. *go straight on, turn right, cross the corridor*, etc.), to instructing them on how to make a traditional dish of the target language country in a cooking lesson (e.g. *take the tomato, now take a knife and slice the tomato*, etc). They have something in common with the type of task-based activities we describe in Chapter 7. Below are three examples.

Listen and colour in

1. Hand out a black and white image or line drawing of a room (e.g. **Figure 4.5**) containing a good range of furniture and other items. (Tip: you can remove colour from pictures using Format in Word.)
2. Describe the room, including prepositions and the colours of items, while students colour in the picture. Build in lots of repetition as you read your description.
3. If possible, display a complete version of the picture and describe it again.

Figure 4.5 Example picture for *Listen and colour in.* (Image: Pixabay)

> ## Gianfranco's favourite: Blind mimes
>
> This is a great task to practise verbs, although it also allows you to practise virtually any other parts of speech.
>
> 1. Prepare a highly comprehensible story to tell your students, in which you recycle your target vocabulary. This could be something very mundane, such as what you did yesterday, or something more creative and elaborate, depending on the class.
>
> 2. Mime the story as you relate it at moderate pace. Students mime along with you. You may display the story on the board. Do not be afraid to occasionally use L1 with novices.
>
> 3. Retell the story without acting it out. Students use the gestures you used the first time or their own. The text can still be displayed on the board.
>
> 4. Retell the story, but this time students keep their eyes shut and rely simply on what they hear.

> **Steve's favourite: A walk through town**
>
> This would work with a proficient intermediate class. Scaffold the task in advance by displaying some vocabulary on the board.
>
> Tell the students to stand up. Describe, in the second person, a series of actions and events which they have to act out. Something like this would be fine (specific actions are marked in bold):
>
> > *You are **walking** along the street. You **look right** and see your friend on the other side of the road. You **stop**, **smile** and **wave** to her. You continue **walking**. It starts to rain, so you take a **small umbrella out of your pocket** and **open** it. You **carry it in your right hand**. Suddenly you **look down** and see a small bag lying on the pavement (sidewalk). You **glance left and right**. You **bend down** and **pick up** the bag with **your left hand**. You tuck the umbrella handle under your arm. You **open the bag** and **look inside**. You are **amazed**! You see a wad of euro banknotes and **take it out** of the bag with your **left hand**. You **look left and right** again. You **look around** to see someone who may have dropped the bag. You start **to count** the money. Suddenly you **hear a noise** behind you. You **turn around** and see three young men looking threatening. You **hand over** the money, **turn** and **run away**.*
>
> Note: if students fail to understand any descriptions they will quickly get the meaning by observing what their peers do. At the end of the task you can display the description to reinforce the vocabulary – in this case there's a focus on bodily movement and directions.

8.5 Listen and draw activities

These are tasks where students translate what the teacher (or another student) says into symbols and/or pictures. It is useful to display some key vocabulary indicating positions, e.g. *at the top, at the bottom, on the left, on the right, in the middle, in the corner*. Here is an example:

Our sitting room

1. Hold in front of you a picture of a fully furnished room so students cannot see it. Students have one or more sheets with the template in **Figure 4.6** on their tables.
2. Describe the room while students draw each item you mention based on what they hear. The description(s) will be quite short and flooded with the same pattern. For example:
3. *This is our living-room. In the middle there is a large round table with four chairs. Both the table and the chairs are black. They are very stylish. On the right, there's a long sofa. It's brown. It's very elegant and comfortable. On the left, there's a big TV. It's grey. It's brand new,* etc.
4. After listening to the description two or three times, students are shown the transcript of the description they heard and revise their initial answers.
5. Display your version of the picture on the classroom screen.

Figure 4.6 *Listen and draw:* Our sitting room

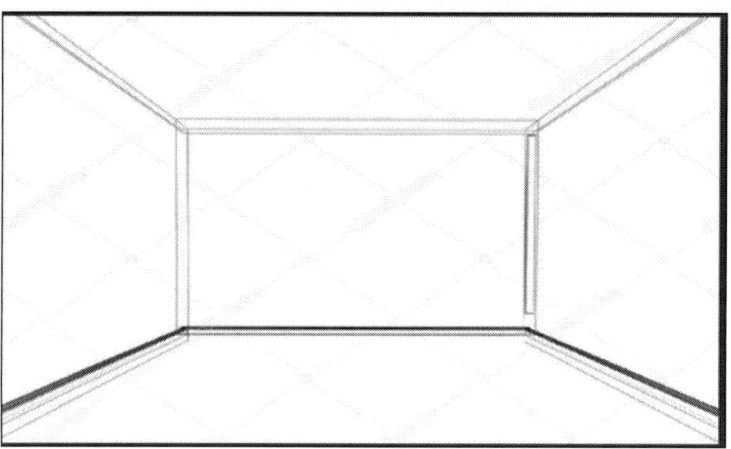

Photofit

1. Students work in pairs, taking turns, with one person providing a description of a criminal suspect and the other being a police artist drawing a representation of the person. You can either provide students with ready-made pictures or have them draw their own. Make sure they cover certain areas of vocabulary which you can display on the board: height, body shape, clothes, face shape, hairstyles, eye colour and distinctive features (the latter can be a good source of humour. e.g. a huge scar, tattoo or strange beard). It would be a good idea to model a descripiton first, before students begin.
2. Students compare original drawings and copied versions.

8.6 Error identification

Spot the nonsense

1. Tell the class they are going to listen to some sentences or a text in which you planted a few words that clearly do not fit the context as they verge on the absurd: statements like, *This morning I showered in the car* or *Last night for dinner I ate my homework.*
2. As the text is read or played to them they react by writing on their mini-whiteboards P for Possible or I Impossible.
3. Say each sentence again as students note down a/the correct alternative, e.g. the first sentence in the example below (**Figure 4.7**) could be *A few years ago I used to be fitter* or *When I was young I used to be fitter.*

Note: students often enjoy activities which contain some absurd content and it makes them listen extra carefully.

Figure 4.7 Example of a *Spot the nonsense* task

1. Tomorrow I used to be much fitter
2. Yesterday I ate the cupboard
3. Usually I surf the web
4. I enjoy football because it is fun
5. From time to time I go canoeing
6. After dinner I usually watch the shower for a couple of hours
7. For breakfast I don't eat much, only a dozen eggs
8. The worst thing about my father is his temper
9. The worst thing about my mother is that she gives me a lot of money and is very patient and generous
10. In my free time I often go rock climbing with my friends

Spot the missing detail (content words)

This task gets students to focus on words you want to be noticed. As pointed out in the next chapter, this is an effective means of focusing on the role of function words in sentences. It can also be used to raise students' awareness of common mistakes, e.g. in French the frequent omission of the auxiliary *avoir* before the past participle when forming the perfect tense ('*je joué*' instead of *j'ai joué*).

1. Tell the class they are going to listen to a text in which some words have been left out. There are no gaps to indicate where the omissions are.
2. As the text is read or played to them, they provide their answers.

Figure 4.8 Example of *Spot the missing detail* in Spanish. Some adjectives, verbs and nouns have been omitted.

Teacher's version	Students' version
A mí y a mi novia nos gusta viajar en **bici**. Hacemos **viajes** muy largos en bici. El año pasado, por ejemplo, fuimos a Italia. Fue un **viaje** muy **largo** y agotador. ¡Tuvimos que **atravesar** Francia! Pero fue muy interesante y **divertido**. Conocimos a mucha gente interesante y vimos muchos **sitios** hermosos y famosos.	A mí y a mi novia nos gusta viajar en. Hacemos muy largos en bici. El año pasado, por ejemplo, fuimos a Italia. Fue un muy y agotador. ¡Tuvimos que Francia! Pero fue muy interesante y. Conocimos a mucha gente interesante y vimos muchos hermosos y famosos.

9. Vocabulary recognition

As previously noted, recognising words and chunks in the stream of sound is a key skill. Any work on vocabulary helps develop this ability, but below are some activities which develop it specifically through the medium of listening. Remember that knowing a word in isolation and recognising it in the sound stream are not the same.

9.1 Matching tasks

These tasks involve matching up words or phrases in the aural input with their L1 translation.

Multi-choice match

Read aloud, or play two to three times, a description of a holiday you would like to take if you had the chance. Students must match the L2 input they hear to the correct option from the sets of three provided (see **Table 4.8**).

Table 4.8 *Multi-choice match* task

	1	2	3
A	I would go to the US	I would go to Germany	I would go to the Caribbean
B	I would go to the coast	I would go to the mountains	I would go to the countryside
C	I would go there by plane	I would go by car	I would go on foot
D	I would go there by boat	I would go there by coach	I would hitch hike
E	I would stay in 3 star hotel	I would stay in a cheap hotel	I would stay in a luxury hotel
F	I would eat traditional dishes	I would take photos	I would buy clothes
G	I would go rock climbing	I would sunbathe	I would play golf
H	I would go bungee jumping	I would go clubbing	I would go sight seeing
I	I would go to the beach	I would go shopping	I would visit historic places

Listening bingo

Students write the L1 translation of some words or chunks chosen by the teacher on their mini-whiteboards or on a sheet of paper, laying them out as on a bingo card. Then play bingo, but uttering short sentences containing those words or chunks. Students score points if they have the word or chunk on their card.

Quickfire translation

This is a zero preparation starter or plenary aimed at consolidating familiar vocabulary and developing fluency. It makes for an easy way to link with practice from previous lessons and is a good example of simple retrieval practice.

1. Say out loud familiar sentences, e.g. ones used in recent or earlier lessons.
2. Students translate on mini-whiteboards to a short time limit.

Listening slalom

This activity is ideal for beginners.
1. Give students a grid like the one in **Table 4.9**.
2. Play or read out a simple text. Students have a grid containing its L1 translation broken up into key words or phrases, along with some distractors. Each row in the grid contains one correct item and two or three distractors.
3. As they listen, students must select the item they hear on each row, working their way down the grid as the text unfolds.

Table 4.9 *Listening slalom*

	1	2	3	4
A	I play	I do	I go	I never play
B	weights	football	to the swimming pool	with videogames
C	rarely	every now and then	very often	every day
D	even though	but	because	because it is
E	competitive	it is tiring	it is exciting	fun
F	I often play basketball	I don't play tennis often	I never go jogging	I go rock climbing very often
G	because	even though	because it is	but
H	healthy	it is tiring	tough	thrilling
I	and dangerous	and exciting	and boring	and fun

Gapped parallel texts

1. Give the class a gapped L1 translation of a text which the students will subsequently hear (**see Table 4.10**).
2. Ask students to spend a few minutes with a partner translating as many words as they can in the L1 gapped text into the L2.
3. The text is read or played to students who complete the translation based on what they hear.

Table 4.10 *Gapped parallel texts* (Spanish example)

| Por lo general me levanto a las seis y cuarto, y me ducho rápidamente enseguida. Luego, desayuno pan tostado con mermelada y mantequilla y bebo un vaso de zumo de naranja. A eso de las siete me lavo los dientes y me pongo el uniforme. A las siete y cuarto salgo de casa y cojo el autobús a las siete y veinticinco. Por lo general llego al colegio a eso de las ocho. Las clases terminan a las tres y diez pero salgo del colegio para volver a casa sobre las cuatro. Luego me ducho, hago mis deberes y ceno. | Generally, I _____ at 6.15, and I _____ quickly immediately after. Then I have toast for breakfast with _____ and _____ and I drink a glass of _____. At around seven I _____ and _____ my uniform. At 7.15 I _____ and catch the bus at _____. Generally, I arrive at school around 8. Classes end at _____ but I _____ of school around 4. Then I shower _____ and have dinner. |

Bad translation

1. Give the class an L1 text based on highly comprehensible L2 input (see **Table 4.11**).
2. Read out the L2 text after warning students the L1 text they have is an inaccurate translation containing (X) number of semantic errors.
3. Students spot the errors. There are nine errors in the Italian example in **Table 4.11**.

Table 4.11 *Bad translation* (Italian example)

| Io sono brava. Ubbidisco sempre a mia madre, aiuto sempre mio padre e mia madre in casa, ordino sempre la mia stanza e ascolto sempre i miei professori.
Mia sorella Marina, invece, è una peste! Non ubbidisce mai a mia madre, non ordina la sua stanza, prende sempre le mie cose, arriva sempre tardi a scuola, non aiuta mai mio padre e non finisce mai i compiti. | I am naughty. I always obey my father, I help my father and my mother in the garden, I always tidy up the kitchen and always listen to my parents.
My sister Marina, instead, is lovely! She never helps my mother, doesn't tidy up her room, always takes my money, always goes to school late, doesn't listen to my father and doesn't finish the house chores. |

Running translation

This is played exactly as *Running dictation*, except that students translate the language which the runner has retrieved from the classroom wall.

No snakes, no ladders race

Students work in threes - two players and a speaker/referee. The latter has a list of L2 sentences and their translations, one for each of the squares on the race track grid (in **Figure 4.9**). Players 1 and 2 take turns throwing a dice. If, for instance, Player 1 scores a three, they move their counter to square 3 and the referee asks them to translate sentence 3 on their list. If they give the correct translation, they can throw the dice again; if not, the referee gives them the correct answer and it is Player 2's turn to play.

Figure 4.9 *No snakes, no ladders*

	1	2	3	4	5	6	7
Départ							
	14	13	12	11	10	9	8
	15	16	17	18	19	20	21
	28	27	26	25	24	23	22
Arrivée							

Oral ping-pong

Students work in pairs. They each have a card with the same L1 sentences to translate into L2, but Partner A has the translation of half the sentences (e.g. sentences 1 to 10), whereas Partner B has the translation of the other half (e.g. sentences 11 to 20). The two partners take turns challenging each other with a sentence. After one partner has attempted the translation, their opponent shows them the correct answer and points are awarded (3 for a perfect sentence, 2 for one mistake only, 1 if there are mistakes but at least the verb is correctly formed). Give students a time limit of about 10 minutes. When the time is up, the person with the higher score wins. It is best to have students of similar proficiency in each pair. The activity can be done in writing too.

Musical chairs

1. Tell the class they are going to play musical chairs, but that instead of music they are going to listen to a short narrative which contains words belonging to a specific semantic field or word class (e.g. adjectives) with which they are very familiar. Make sure the category is as narrow as possible.
2. Read out the text to them. If the category is 'animals' students sit down whenever they hear the name of an animal.

Guess how often

1. Display a series of time-frequency words on the board: *never, occasionally, sometimes, often, every day*.
2. Read to the class in L2 a series of statements about your personal life, sticking to easy, comprehensible language that students are familiar with, e.g. *I go to the cinema; I eat pizza; I visit Spain; I play tennis*, etc. Students must guess how often you do these things by choosing one of the words or phrases displayed. Answers may be written on mini-whiteboards.
3. Give the answers. Students could get points for correct guesses.

9.2   Note-taking

As many as you can

Students simply note down in L1 as many points as they can while hearing a text three times. Pairs can then compare their notes. If you wish to make the task competitive, the pair with the highest number of correct points wins.

Listening grids

Students listen to a text and fill in a grid such as *Who, What, Where, When* shown in **Table 4.12**.

Table 4.12 *Listening grids*

News item	Who	What	Where	When
1				
2				
3				
4				

9.3   Spot the differences

Spot the differences with pictures

1. Display a picture relating to your current topic or area of vocabulary, e.g a beach or street scene. Pairs must make up as many sentences as they can using the target chunks. Scaffold the task by separately diplaying a bilingual glossary of words.

2. Read out three descriptions of the picture using the same general text structure each time. Only one of the descriptions is correct while the others contain one or more inaccuracies, e.g. about the appearance of the people in the image, their clothing, what they are doing, their location, etc.
3. Students are told in advance to look out for 'X' number of inaccuracies per text. They listen and note down the inaccuracies for the faulty descriptions.

Spot the differences with translation

This is similar to the previous activity, except that students are given a written text in the L1 rather than a picture to compare with what they hear. The three or more L2 versions of the text are nearly the same, except for a few minor details.

1. Ask students to try translating the text with a partner.
2. Students listen to three or four L1 versions of the text. They identify the only one which matches 100% accurately and the differences contained in the other versions they hear (see **Table 4.13**).

Table 4.13 Three texts designed for *Spot the difference*.

Passage 1	*Last weekend I had a really good time. I went shopping with my friends, then I went to the cinema. I saw the new Marvel movie with my friend Amy. On Saturday evening I went to an Italian restaurant with my parents. I had a pizza and chocolate ice cream. It was delicious.*
Passage 2	*Last Friday I had a really good time. I went out with my best friend, then I went to the cinema. I saw the new X-men movie with my girlfriend. On Sunday evening I went to an Indian restaurant with best friends. I had a chicken curry and some beer. It was yummy.*
Passage 3	*Last Friday I had a really good time. I went shopping with my sister, then I went to the cinema. I saw the new Frozen movie with my cousin. On Sunday evening I went to a French restaurant with my girlfriend. I had a salad and a glass of wine. It was nice.*

9.4 Substitution

This example shows how specific sentence structures can be manipulated by changing some of their parts.

1. Give the class a short text where specific words or chunks have been underlined. If you plan to do a few rounds, give students several copies of the same text. For example:

Yesterday I went <u>hiking</u> with my brothers. Afterwards, since we were <u>hungry</u>, we decided to have <u>something to eat</u>. So we went to a nearby <u>Italian</u> restaurant were they make <u>great pizza</u>, etc.

2. Students listen to one or more versions of the text, identical except for the parts underlined which have been replaced by other vocabulary. So for instance, if a sentence in the students' version reads *<u>Yesterday I</u> went <u>hiking</u> with my brothers*, the version they will hear could read ***Two days ago** I went **rock-climbing** with **my brothers***.
3. Students replace the underlined vocabulary in their text with the items they hear.

As a follow-up, students could do a guided writing substitution task where they are given a similar text with underlined words or phrases to substitute with their own.

9.5 Re-ordering pictures or words

1. Display a set of pictures, each one corresponding to one of your target words or chunks.
2. Say aloud the target items (A, B, C, D, E, F) in three or four different sequences.
3. Students note down the exact order in which you sequence the items each time round. So, the first sequence may be BCDEFA, the second FBDCEA, etc.

Note: instead of pictures you could simply display L1 words and chunks (as in **Figure 4.10**). In this instance read three descriptions, one for Marc, one for Jean and one for Julien. In each case the order of activities will be different. Alternatively, you could display the word and chunks in the L2. This has the merit of reminding students of sound-spelling relationships.

Figure 4.10 Re-ordering task using L1 sentences instead of pictures

John	Marc	Jean	Julien
a. He went to the cinema	....	....	....
b. He had an icecream	....	....	....
c. He fell off his bike	....	....	....
d. He made a phonecall	....	....	....
e. He met his girlfriend	....	....	....
f. He bought a book	....	....	....
g. He drove back home	....	....	....

9.6 Prediction

Guess what comes next

Write your own written narrative of a past event or series of events. Produce a gapped transcription of the same (see the example below). Scaffold the activity by displaying a set of words from which students can choose.

> *On Saturday morning I decided to go into town with my (pause) friend. We took the bus and arrived in the city centre just opposite the (pause) supermarket. First we walked to the café. I ordered a (pause) coffee and my friend ordered a (pause) coffee too. We stayed in the café for fifteen minutes. We talked about my (pause) dog and our school work. We left the café and crossed the (pause) street. We entered the (pause) bank because I had to get some money from the cash dispenser...*

1. Slowly recount a story at or just above the class's level. Every now and again pause.
2. During this pause students should write on a mini-whiteboard their best guess at the next word then hold it up.
3. Ask a few students to say their word.
4. Reveal the actual word you wrote. Any student who guesses the right word gets a point.

Scenarios

1. Give the class a series of scenarios related to the current topic or another topic they are familiar with, for instance: *Yesterday at the supermarket* and tell them that they have to guess three things you or someone else did there.
2. In groups of two or three, they have one minute to brainstorm and write down as many full sentences as they can, e.g. *Yesterday you bought some chocolate*.
3. Tell them the three things you did. The group getting the most guesses right wins that round.
4. Provide a new scenario and repeat.

9.7 Recall

Disappearing text

This invaluable activity can form part of any lessons where text is displayed on the board. Once a text has been read and become familiar to a class, ask students to close their eyes while you remove a certain number of words. Students open their eyes and raise their hands to fill in the blanks. Then ask them to close their eyes once more as you remove more words, and so on. Students enjoy this short term memory challenge and some classes will be able to gradually recall whole paragraphs of text, listening to them multiple times as the text gradually disappears. The words you choose to erase first can be chosen for their lexical or grammatical significance, including less salient function words.

Concluding remarks

We have deliberately gone into some detail with regard to vocabulary since knowing and being able to recognise and retrieve words and phrases quickly is such an important aspect of skills for listening. Creating a vocabulary-rich classroom environment with multiple opportunities to hear, see and use words will pay dividends for listening in the long run. The next chapter looks more closely at teaching grammar through listening and in the process explains why divorcing vocabulary from grammar is not as easy as you might think.

A running thread through this book is that listening skills are rarely taught in isolation. From this chapter it should be obvious that skill in lexical retrieval and collocations, for example, can also be developed through non-listening tasks. If students get plenty of access to and interaction with comprehensible reading material they will further develop their listening skills. Targeted activities such as the many described in this chapter can be a powerful part of mixed exercises which get students interacting with patterned, comprehensible language. Experience tells us that when students receive such a diet over several years they can become very successful listeners.

Questions to consider

What is the relative value of using apps such as Quizlet or vocabulary lists for learning words?

How do you prefer to introduce vocabulary and why?

To what extent to you think vocabulary is picked up incidentally?

Do you focus equally on different parts of speech, e.g. nouns and verbs?

Language is not a collection of rules and target forms to be acquired, but rather a by-product of communicative processes.
(Nick Ellis, University of Michigan)

5

Teaching parsing, grammar and lexicogrammar

Introduction

Recognising words and chunks is clearly not enough to understand every element of a text; students need to be able to detect, consciously or otherwise, the grammatical form of utterances. Thus, having described a wide range of activities which can help develop phonological decoding and lexical retrieval skills, this chapter turns to how we might help improve students' ability to parse sentences. In other words, how do we make meaning from spoken texts through interpreting the morphological and syntactic aspects of the message.

Firstly, there is a concise description of research into the teaching of grammar and how the traditional distinction between grammar and vocabulary has been challenged by proponents of what is known as *lexicogrammar*. The role of syntactic knowledge in aural comprehension is then discussed and a rationale given for teaching grammar through listening. Finally, multiple examples are provided of activities you could use with your classes.

1. The teaching of grammar
1.1 A brief summary of the research

Can teaching grammar explicitly help students comprehend and use a language more proficiently? Does learning develop primarily through explicit teaching and conscious manipulation of structures, or merely through unconscious processes when people have extensive exposure to meaningful input (known as *implicit learning*)? This is a long-standing controversy in second language acquisition research.

> **INFOBOX 12 Two types of grammatical knowledge**
>
> Explicit learning of rules leads to *explicit knowledge*, often called *declarative knowledge*, i.e. 'being able to explain the rules'. This, in itself, is not much use when it comes to speaking and understanding in real time. *Implicit* or *procedural knowledge*, on the other hand, is usually said to occur based on extensive meaning-focused input, acquired with little or no awareness and stored implicitly (so typically you can speak the language without being able to explain the rules). Nearly all researchers believe that explicit declarative knowledge, and practice thereof, helps develop procedural knowledge. The arguments centre on how much and in what ways.

What is the relationship between these two types of knowledge, explicit and implicit, conscious and unconscious? In particular, can explicitly gained knowledge become implicit, i.e. automatic? Put another way, if we teach and practise a verb conjugation or drill a tense, can this knowledge become internalised and available for spontaneous use?

N. Ellis (2007) points out that explicit and implicit learning are functions of separate memory systems in the brain. Brain scans appear to support this, showing that explicit learning is supported by neural networks located in the prefrontal cortex, whereas implicit learning involves other areas of the brain, the perceptual and motor cortex. This would seem to confirm the relative distinctiveness of the two types of learning and knowledge. But can explicit become implicit?

There have traditionally been three views about this issue, which involve what has become known in the scholarly literature as the *interface* between explicit and implicit knowledge:

1. The *non-interface position* (e.g. Krashen, 1982) holds that explicitly, consciously learned language cannot become implicit. Grammar instruction makes little or no difference to acquisition; all you need is a lot of meaningful exposure.
2. The *strong interface position* (e.g. DeKeyser, 1998; Suzuki & DeKeyser, 2017); is that implicit knowledge can always result from automatisation of explicit knowledge, i.e. you can become proficient through explanation and skill practice.
3. The *weak interface position* is that conscious knowledge can help with gaining implicit knowledge, but does so indirectly by helping students notice language features which they can add to their implicit knowledge when they are ready (e.g. N. Ellis, 2005; R. Ellis, 2008).

Should we bother teaching grammar then? Does teaching grammar *really* make a difference? Long (1983) looked at twelve studies comparing exposure learning with explicit grammar learning and concluded that, overall, instruction made a positive difference at all levels with both children and adults. Ellis (1990), Ozkan & Kesen (2009) and Larsen-Freeman & Long (1991) also found that instruction helped with the rate and ultimate level of acquisition. Other studies have reached the same conclusion, most famously Norris & Ortega (2000) and Spada & Tomita (2010). There is a good discussion of these issues in Nava & Pedrazzoni (2018) who conclude that explicit teaching of grammar plays a useful, perhaps indirect, role in acquisition. A few scholars continue to throw doubt on the research referred to above, so it is fair to say that the case is far from closed.

> **INFOBOX 13 Pedagogical versus internalised grammar**
>
> Most of us think of grammar as a set of rules about how words are constructed (morphology) and put together (syntax). These rules are described in simplified form in school text books and result in a *pedagogical grammar*. These are the rules we usually teach in classrooms. Through learning and practice, these rules get established in our brains and we become better at speaking accurately and fluently. Applied linguists, however, tell us that what is actually in our heads has very little to do with pedagogical grammar and is not open to observation. Most researchers believe that students develop their own, internalised grammars based on the input they receive, and that these are at least somewhat immune to what we teach them. In particular, the evidence suggests that students acquire grammatical forms in their own, somewhat or very predictable order (Pienemann, 1984).

1.2. What does this mean for teachers?

Based on our experience and review of the literature we recommend the following principles:
- Use implicit and explicit learning **in synergy,** with one supporting the other. For instance, after students have worked on a text or series of texts containing multiple occurrences of a structure, you can teach it explicitly or through a guided-discovery approach.
- Be aware that conversion of explicit to implicit knowledge requires **a long period of extensive exposure and practice** across all language skills and a wide range of contexts. Nation (2007) recommends providing specific training in the recognition and production of L2 to time limits in order to develop automaticity (fluency training).
- Provide opportunities for **repeated use of L2 grammatical forms in meaningful contexts**, using both controlled and free practice. Recycle language through extensive spaced practice consistent with human forgetting rates and interleaving (see Chapter 4).
- Use explicit teaching, lots of input-flooding, extensive recycling and attention-enhancing techniques **for forms which appear only rarely in input** (e.g. in French, less common negatives such as *ni...ni*; connectives such as *à moins que*; present and imperfect subjunctive verb forms).

- Bear in mind that some grammatical features are much less noticeable ('salient') in the input to native English learners, e.g. adjective agreement. **Since low saliency negatively affects learnability, make such structures as salient as possible** if they are considered important and flood the input with them.
- Use **extensive receptive practice before moving on to production**. Ensure that target structures are consolidated through listening and reading before being used in speaking and writing.
- **Avoid cognitive overload**. For instance, model and practise new structures within very highly comprehensible input to decrease the cognitive load on students' working memory. Use L1 to teach grammar points with all but the most highly proficient classes.
- Consider whether your class is **developmentally ready** to learn certain grammatical forms. In a highly mixed-proficiency class this is problematic and is a possible argument against such classes.
- Use **formative assessment** techniques, e.g. listen for frequent errors students make in conversation or written output to guide future grammar teaching.
- **Give feedback on errors** which are **within the developmental grasp** of students. Correction which **focuses only on a few specific areas at a time** is likely to be more effective than feedback than focuses on many errors (Sheen, 2007; Ellis et al, 2008; Alroe, 2011). For instance, you may decide to focus on only three or four important problem areas every few weeks.
- Bear in mind the whole range of differences between learners, e.g. **age, ability, attitudes, cultural background and attitudes towards learning**. Use a wide range of teaching techniques to cater for such individual differences.
- Teach for **mastery rather than coverage**. Better to teach a few key grammatical structures deeply than many superficially. Less is more!

INFOBOX 14 Morphology and syntax

Morphology is the study of words and their parts. Morphemes, like prefixes, suffixes and base words, are defined as the smallest units of meaning. Morphemes can be free (single words) or bound (parts of words). Syntax refers to the arrangement of words in an utterance. The term grammar is usually taken to mean morphology and syntax combined, e.g. both knowing the conjugation of verbs and position in the sentence.

2. Lexis, grammar and... lexicogrammar
2.1 What is lexicogrammar?

Let us return to an issue raised in Chapter 4, namely the relationship between vocabulary and grammar. The discussion which follows will be relevant to how we teach listening.

> *Traditionally, there has been a clear-cut distinction between vocabulary and grammar in foreign language teaching. The prevailing attitude has been that vocabulary is about learning words, whereas grammar is about learning rules and generalisable patterns based on sentences. Vocabulary consists of a specific set of lexical items while the main function of grammar is to put words together in a rule-governed manner to construct new phrases and sentences* (Hutz, 2018, p. 3).

Although in line with traditional views, and intuitively appealing, such a division is misleading since these two domains are too closely interdependent to be considered as totally separate entities. Take the adjective *beau* (*beautiful*) in French, for instance. To be able to claim you know it, besides its pronunciation, spelling and meanings, you also need to know its masculine and feminine forms, how it is pluralised, its position in relation to the noun it accompanies and how it changes when preceding a noun beginning with a vowel. What can be drawn from this? You cannot know a word without knowing how it behaves grammatically.

The interdependence of lexis and grammar is even more obvious if we consider words not in isolation, but as interacting with other words in the chunks of language and patterns in which they most frequently occur. Look at the use of the word *good* in English; we can identify specific recurring syntactic patterns such as:

- *to be* + *good* + *at* + (verb) *–ing* (e.g. to be good at skiing, keeping appointments, making friends);
- *to be* + *good* + *at* + noun (e.g. to be good at languages/science);
- *to be in a* + *good* + noun (e.g. to be in a good state / mood / condition).

Proficient speakers use a huge number of such language patterns which students need to become aware of over time. Every word in a language is involved in a complex network of patterns and relationships. In particular, a distinction is made between lexical patterns (*collocations*) and grammatical patterns (*colligations*).

Collocations are common multi-word units such as *to have dinner, to break a record, a worthy cause, to waste time* or *spick and span*. Words are attracted to some words more than others, e.g. we talk about *express trains*, but not *express cars*. You can have a *quick look*, but not a *fast look*. Words are closely linked in the mind so that one word triggers its associated collocates (Willis 2003).

Colligations, by contrast, work at the syntactic level and refer to how words form specific grammatical patterns with other words. Words colligate (are tied together) with certain grammatical patterns. Examples of colligation patterns are:

- verb + -*ing* (*I went swimming*);
- verb + pronoun + infinitive (*I want you to go*)
- verb + infinitive (*I began to understand*) ;
- verb of perception + adjective (*it sounds fab, it looks great*);
- *with/without* + possessive + noun (*with my approval; with my family*)
- *a* + noun + *of* + noun (*a pack of wolves, a box of chocolates, a kilo of potatoes*).

This all suggests that the traditional split between grammar and vocabulary is not as clear cut as commonly thought. Some applied linguists nowadays prefer to use the term lexicogrammar, first coined by Halliday (1961), to describe the overlapping and interdependent nature of lexis and grammar. Other researchers have chosen to use terms such as 'pattern grammar' or 'construction grammar'.

2.2 Implications for teachers

When we put together what is known about working memory and the nature of lexis and grammar, it should be clear that there is great merit in going beyond single word teaching and isolated verb conjugations. This calls for a focus on words and grammar in the form of chunks and sentences. What does this mean in practice?

To take an example, the verb *to play*. Instead of focusing on the isolated verb and its various forms, we would be better off letting students hear, read and use *I played tennis* + noun phrase (e.g. *my brother*), *I played cards with* + noun phrase (e.g. *my siblings*) , *I played video games* + noun phrase (e.g. *my best friend*), and so on. These chunks of language are more meaningful, serving a greater communicative purpose than the verb *to play* used in isolation. In particular, paying more attention to chunks based on verbs (e.g. verbs + noun or prepositional phrase) will pay dividends because, with a good command of verb-based chunks, students can understand and produce a great deal of language. As Macaro (2003) notes, verbs are the most important part of a sentence. Failure to master verb collocations restricts the development of L2 proficiency.

Chapter 8 expands on the concept of lexicogrammar, provides a framework for combining lexicogrammar with listening for beginner-to-intermediate students, and offers three example teaching sequences.

3. Grammatical knowledge in listening
3.1 The parsing process

As explained in Chapter 1, when listening we process the input at different levels to access meaning. To recap, the first level of processing means identifying sounds in order to make sense of the speech signal and to segment the stream of sound. The second level, lexical retrieval, is about word recognition and meaning. The third level, of interest in this chapter, involves structural analysis of the input, known as *parsing*. According to Brown (2000), parsing is about applying syntactic knowledge, i.e. the ability to recognise a range of grammatical features:

- **L2 systems**: the rules which govern morphemes such as tense, gender, pluralisation, etc. Recognising systems provides valuable linguistic clues as to the meaning of a sentence. These systems often take the form of *inflectional affixation* (e.g. adding the suffix *s* to the verb in the third person of the present simple in English).
- **Word parts**: affixes, especially prefixes and suffixes provide us with important clues about the meaning of words, their role in the sentence, as well as the tense, gender, number of the agent or recipient of an action, etc. Other types of affixations are: *suffixoids* (e.g. *cat-like*), *simulfixes* (e.g. *mouse* to *mice*) and *circumfixes* (e.g. *en*ligh*ten*). Affixation can be inflectional and derivational (e.g. in English, *un-* in *unhappy* or *-ness* in *happiness*).
- **How lexical items relate to one another and typical word order patterns**: e.g. if we recognise a colligation such as '*a* + noun + *of* + noun', but we do not recognise the fourth item, at least we know it is going to be a noun, so we can use top-down processing and other cues to infer what it might be. Hence the importance of teaching colligations, collocations and sentence patterns in general.
- **Parts of speech**: by identifying these we have more chances of reconstructing the meaning of words and the overall sentence or phrasal pattern.
- **Function words**: words such as determiners and prepositions provide valuable clues about which part of speech is likely to come next, e.g. on hearing the French possessive adjective *ma* (*my*) a feminine noun is expected, but hearing its masculine version *mon* anticipates a masculine noun.
- **Cohesive markers (connectives)**: these provide us with clues about how words and clauses fit together. *Because* cues us to the presence of a causal cause, *in order to* of a final clause, etc. In this sense, they are key both to the meaning and discourse building processes.
- **Elliptical constructions:** a word or phrase implied by context is omitted from a sentence, usually because it is a repetition of a preceding word or phrase. The main forms of ellipsis are:
  - **noun ellipsis** (e.g. *I went jogging and my girlfriend went too.*)
  - **verb ellipsis** (e.g. *She likes action movies and her husband comedies.*)
  - **verb phrase ellipsis** (e.g. *They went for a swim, but we didn't.*)
- **Clause types:** recognising different clause types (see **Table 5.1** for English), and knowing the most high-frequency patterns which govern them, helps with discourse building.

Table 5.1 Clause types in English

Type of clause	Introduced by	Example
Adversative	but, however, on the other hand, whereas, whilst, etc.	My father is mean with money, whilst my mother is very generous.
Causal	as, as a result, because, consequently, by, due to, for lack of, for that/this, reason, for the reason that, since, that's why, etc.	As I was tired, I didn't go out.
Comparative/ Elliptical	better than, just as, less than, etc.	The house was bigger than I imagined.
Concessive	although, even though, despite, in spite of	Although he works hard, he gets low grades.
Conditional	if	<ul><li>If I drink coffee at night, I can't sleep.</li><li>If I drink coffee tonight, I won't sleep.</li><li>If I drank coffee tonight, I wouldn't sleep.</li><li>If I had drunk coffee last night, I wouldn't have slept.</li></ul>
Consecutive	so...that, in such a way that, to such an extent that, too...for	He was so nervous that he could not speak.
Exclamative	what, how, etc.	What a brilliant idea you gave me!
(Direct) Interrogative	If, why, what, when, etc.	I wonder if you know.
(Indirect) Interrogative	why, what, when, etc.	Do you know?
Final	to, in order to, so as to, etc.	I went to the beach in order to relax.
Instrumental clause	by, through, etc.	I improved my German by practising with native speakers.
Limitative clause	as far as, in this regard, as for, etc.	As far as I am concerned, the deal's off.
Modal clause	more than, less than, as...as..., higher, etc.	I study as much as I can.
Objective clause	I believe that, I know that, I think that, etc	I firmly believe (that) this is wrong.
Place clause	where, wherever, etc.	I play tennis near where I live.
Relative or restrictive clause	that, which, who, etc.	The sport (that) I like most is tennis.
Impersonal clause	impersonal phrase + that (it is important that...)	It's important that he be (is) vigilant.
Time clause	after, as soon as, then, whenever	After getting up, I go for a run. When I feel down, I watch a movie.

Syntactic knowledge, therefore, plays a key role in aural comprehension, more so at lower than higher levels of proficiency. For L2 syntactic knowledge to help with aural comprehension it needs to become 'routinised', i.e. practised so much that it becomes instantly applicable. Students can then process quickly, in real time, without compromising working memory capacity.

> **INFOBOX 15 Parsing**
>
> The term parsing is used to describing the way we analyse a spoken or written utterance in terms of its grammatical parts, e.g. identifying the parts of speech and syntactic relations between words. Unless students can parse rapidly, either unconsciously or consciously, they can only make partial sense of spoken utterances. In the LAM approach, it is assumed we can train students to do this more effectively with focused practice.

3.2 Implications for teachers

Below are some points of guidance to consider.

- Teach syntactic knowledge **through the oral/aural medium**. Simply practising grammar through reading and writing will have much less impact on listening comprehension than doing so through the aural medium.
- Teach students to recognise **high-frequency patterns**: collocations, colligations and discourse patterns. Presenting language through sentence builders is a very effective way of modelling collocations, colligations and how to use clauses. Plan for the explicit and systematic teaching of subordination through all four skills, including listening. Incorporate into your curriculum the full range of clauses in the language you teach, such as those in **Table 5.1**.
- Draw students' attention to **function words,** ensuring they are made as salient as possible. Input-flooding is an effective way of achieving this. Of all function words, cohesion markers (words and phrases such as *perhaps, although, because, in order to, for example*) need particular emphasis, especially when dealing with more complex texts.
- Develop students' ability to identify **parts of speech,** including their understanding of elliptical constructions in which parts of speech are omitted (if applicable to the language you are teaching). Using parsing grids in conjunction with dictations is one easy way of doing this (see below for an example).
- Focus on **word order** through listening from the outset. This can be done in a playful and engaging way through *Aural sentence puzzles* or other sentence reconstruction tasks (see below).
- Raise students' awareness of how L2 **affixation** works and teach them how to recognise derivational and inflectional affixation (especially prefixes and affixes).

4. Presenting grammar through listening

Just as with vocabulary, verb-based chunks are held in memory in an aural form, so it makes sense to teach them aurally too. A well-established routine for presenting grammar to students is to have them hear how that new grammar sounds. Let us suppose you want to introduce a major new tense such as the perfect (preterite) in French. This can be done by modelling the verb forms aurally in meaningful chunks with the aid of a sequence of pictures, either presented all together on a screen or one by one, typically using PowerPoint.

The first form-meaning phonological feature you want students to hear with the perfect tense are those sounds in regular verbs taking *avoir* as their auxiliary *j'ai joué, j'ai écouté, j'ai regardé*. These sounds need to stand in clear contrast to those in *je joue, j'écoute* and *je regarde* (where the 'e' is not sounded). This phonological difference is a key marker of time (past versus present) so it needs to be clearly established in memory by repetitive meaningful exposure and spoken practice.

Below is a classic oral-situational teaching sequence for practising the perfect tense, or, if you prefer, the communicative function *talking about what you did in the past*. You will see that this lesson features a good deal of LAM. We assume that students have already been exposed to examples of this tense in other listening or reading tasks, but with some classes you might use this as first step in a PPP sequence (Presentation, Practice, Production).

Steve's favourite: exploiting a set of pictures (French example)

1. Explain to the class in L1 that you are going to teach them how to talk about what they did last weekend. Give some L1 examples of past and present to make the contrast clear. Tell students that by the end of the lesson they will be able to understand and talk about a range of actions in the past. (A simple objective clearly laid out with success criteria.)
2. Show about 10 PowerPoint slides (or hand-held flashcards) depicting simple actions, e.g. watching TV, listening to music, playing sports. Say a sentence aloud for each slide, allowing students to simply listen, e.g. *J'ai joué au tennis; J'ai regardé la télé*. Do not introduce any new vocabulary at this stage so that students have a chance to focus on your key objective – what 'pastness' sounds like. Some disagree but, on balance, avoid showing the written word initially so that students are not influenced by spelling.
3. Show and read aloud the same slides with the sentence captioned. This gives more time for students to get to grips with sounds and meanings without putting pressure on them to perform. Sound spelling links are getting established and you could emphasise certain sounds, e.g. the 'é' of *joué*.
4. Do step (3) but add choral and individual repetition (with hands-up or no hands-up). This is another recycling opportunity allowing students to gain confidence and familiarity.
5. Show a single slide with all ten uncaptioned activities, point to each image and get students to respond, or give pairs of statements only one of which is correct. Students must identify the correct one.
6. Play *Mind-reading* where you think of one of the ten activities and students must guess which. With some classes you might even throw in the second person of the verb at this juncture.
7. To allow individuals to stretch themselves you can ask if anyone can list off all ten activities without stopping.
8. This could then be the time to ask students what they have noticed about how the verb works ('pop-up grammar'), before proceeding to some simple transcription work on the verb forms.

This type of sequence (images with spoken language) is very much in keeping with the so-called oral approach where the focus is on grammatical skill being developed aurally. It can be applied to plenty of areas of grammar, e.g. tenses, adjective agreements and adverbs.

Gianfranco's favourite: using sentence builders to model lexicogrammar

Table 5.2 presents a pattern through a sentence builder. Although modelling of the target structure initially occurs implicitly (see step 1 below), it is only after much receptive processing and highly structured production that the explicit learning of grammar actually takes place (see step 11 below), usually through an inductive (guided-discovery) approach. Look at the sequence below.

1. Create a sentence builder flooded with the sentence and/or morphological pattern you want to practise **(see Table 5.2)**. Use colour coding or other typographic devices to draw students' attention to specific items (e.g. superlatives). This is sometimes called *input enhancement*. Make sure any unknown vocabulary is translated in L1.
2. Using the sentence builder, read aloud L2 sentences at a slowish pace (remember, you are modelling, not testing).
3. As you say each sentence, students translate them into English on mini-whiteboards.
4. Play *Faulty echo* and *Spot the error* (Chapter 3) to draw attention to words which may be phonologically challenging and use phonological-awareness tasks such as *Spot the foreign sound* or *Spot the silent letter* to highlight or consolidate specific phonological features.
5. Play *Delayed dictation* (Chapter 3) to reinforce grapheme-phoneme correspondences.
6. Play *Aural sentence puzzles* (Chapter 5) to focus on word order.
7. Draw the students' attention to the pattern you want them to learn and any other grammar detail you think they should be aware of. This use of pop-up grammar is aimed at encouraging noticing and is not a lengthy grammar explanation with note-taking.
8. Ask students to translate sentences from L1 to L2 using the sentence builder as a scaffold.
9. Play a few interactive read-aloud games such as *Mind-reading, Sentence stealer, Find your match, Find someone who* (Chapter 3) etc, ensuring the input and output are flooded with the target patterns.
10. Provide extensive receptive practice with texts containing many occurrences of the target pattern or structure, e.g. use a set of narrow listening and narrow reading texts, exploiting them at various levels of processing: sounds, spelling, vocabulary, morphology, grammar, meaning and discourse-building.
11. Provide extensive output practice to generate oral and written production, e.g. through oral translation games, structured role-plays and short guided compositions.
12. Get students to extract any grammatical rule or pattern and note the similarities and differences between L1 and L2.
13. Do extensive controlled output practice through speaking and writing tasks which force students to use each target item model many times over.
14. Gradually move on to semi-structured exercises where scaffolds (e.g. the sentence builder or other knowledge organisers/literacy mats) are still being used if necessary.
15. Students can then do less structured and unstructured communicative tasks (Chapters 6 and 7) with scaffolds removed.

Table 5.2 Sentence builder modelling the 'Noun + relative pronoun + verb phrase + demonstrative pronoun + noun'. Words with the translation in brackets are assumed to be unknown to students.

Noun	Relative pronoun	Verb phrase	Verb + pronoun	Noun
La prof Le prof	*que* *(whom)*	*j'aime le plus* (I like the most) *je déteste* (I hate) *je n'aime pas* (I don't like) *je respecte le plus / le moins* (I respect the most/ the least)	*s'appelle*	*Madame* ……….. *Monsieur* ………..
	qui *(who)*	*a le meilleur sens de l'humour* (has the best sense of humour) *a le pire sens de l'humour* (has the worst sense of humour) *m'aide le plus* (helps me the most) *me donne le plus de devoirs* (gives me the most homework) *me donne les meilleures notes* (gives me the best grades) *me gronde toujours* (tells me off always) *ne m'aime pas* (I don't like) *travaille le plus / le moins* (works the most/least)	*est celle d'* *est celui d'* *est celle de* *est celui de*	*allemand* *anglais* *biologie* *EPS* *espagnol* *chimie* *dessin* *français* *géographie* *histoire* *maths* *religion* *sciences*
	avec qui *(with whom)*	*je m'entends le mieux* (I get along best) *je ne m'entends pas* (I don't get along)		

Having considered two general approaches to the teaching of grammar through listening, below are a set of specific classroom exercises which further develop parsing skills.

5. Parsing skills activities

For convenience a range of specific activities are listed below, as in Chapters 3 and 4. These are categorised under the headings parsing, editing, grammaticality judgement tasks, cross-language comparison tasks, collocational competence-building tasks, narrow listening and focus on affixation.

5.1 Parsing

Faulty echo (for parsing)
This can be used to draw the students' attention to specific morphological or syntactic features that they usually struggle with. For instance, in French, the teacher could say the following sentence correctly:

L'année dernière je ne suis allée nulle part.

Then repeat it incorrectly by adding in *pas*, as many students of French do:

L'année dernière je ne suis pas allée nulle part

Students note down on their mini-whiteboards what was wrong in the 'faulty echo' and why.

Aural sentence puzzles
1. Write the short-hand / symbols of a sentence pattern you have modelled and your students are familiar with. For instance (in French):
   a. Time marker + subject + verb + adverb of place (as in *Yesterday I went to the cinema*).
   b. Ask students to copy out the above on paper or on mini-whiteboards.
2. Then read out a jumbled-up version of a sentence which follows that pattern. Ensure students are very familiar with every word in the sentence
3. Students now rearrange the sentence under each heading. The correct answer is:

Time marker	Subject	Verb	Adverbial of place
Hier	*je*	*suis allé*	*au cinéma*

Note: this type of task sensitises students to word order and how it can affect meaning. This is particularly important when interpreting sentences using the passive voice, where the usual sequence of subject + verb + object is disrupted.

Partial dictation (for parsing)
Partial dictations can be used to focus students on morphology and syntax by omitting from the gapped text a key part of the target structure. For instance, imagine again teaching the perfect tense of French verbs; you could gap all the auxiliaries to draw attention to these forms.

Another example involves word endings in highly inflected languages, which could be gapped to draw the students' attention to the gender and number of nouns/adjectives or to verb tenses and/or conjugations.

Parsing grids
These can be used in combination with partial dictations, except that they focus students more explicitly on grammatical terminology. Here is a French example where students complete the boxes on listening to sentences read aloud (see **Table 5.3**). Field (2008) points out that this task can be used with high-frequency groups of words. In this case, you would stop during one such group and students guess the word that follows.

Table 5.3 A parsing grid

Subject	Relative pronoun	Verb	Proper noun	Verb	Intensifier	Adjective
Mon frère		s'appelle	Marc		très	fainéant
	qui		Louise	est		radine
Mes parents			Julien et Sandrine		assez	

Spot and rewrite the pattern

Once students are very familiar with a specific sentence pattern, they could listen to a short narrative flooded with that pattern and note down as many sentences as they can identify. Parsing grids can be used for this task too. For instance, a parsing grid for the text below, could look like the one in **Table 5.4**.

> In the morning, after getting up I usually have a shower. After showering I get dressed and go into the kitchen to have breakfast. While having breakfast I usually watch television. After having breakfast, I usually brush my teeth and around 7 am I leave my house to go to school. Before leaving my house I usually kiss my mum goodbye.

Table 5.4 *Spot and rewrite the pattern*

Adverb	Verb (gerund)	Subject	Verb (present ind.)	Object
After	getting up	I	have	a shower
After	showering	I	get dressed	n/a
After	having (breakfast)	I	brush	my teeth
Before	leaving (my house)	I	kiss	my mother

Guess what comes next (for parsing)

In Chapter 4 we showed how this task can be used with a focus on nouns. Applied to parsing skills practice, *Guess what comes next* tasks can be made to elicit predictions requiring the understanding and application of grammatical knowledge. For instance, using the example in **Table 5.4**, if you want to focus students on the structure *After/Before/While* + gerund in English, pause after each time you say *after* and *before*, ask the students to guess what comes next and display it on their mini-whiteboards. Example:

> Yesterday evening, after ………. (having lunch) we went to the beach. Before ……. (arriving at the beach), my brother wanted to have ice-cream, so we stopped at a bar on the way. After ………. (having the ice-cream), we drove to the beach. Before ……..(going for a swim), I sunbathed for an hour. Etc…

Aural gap-fill

Give the class a written text flooded with chunks and/or sentence patterns they know. After working on it in various ways (e.g. vocabulary hunt, jigsaw readings, sorting tasks) play the game as *Guess what comes* next, except that in this case students must recall – rather than guess - the words or chunks that come next. Students enjoy this type of short-term recall activity which can reinforce both parsing and lexical retrieval.

Listen and change

This task is about how a chunk of language can be used in different ways by changing a verb from one person or tense to another, or a noun from singular to plural or masculine to feminine. Here is an example aimed at consolidating how in Spanish the preterite *fui* (*I went*) changes to other persons, e.g. *fueron* (*they went*).

1. Write a set of sentences on the board. For instance: having practised the preterite of the verb *ir* (*to go*) in Spanish, write the sentence: *Ayer fui al campo con mis padres*.
2. Now say the same sentence changing the verb *fui* (*I went*) to *fueron* (*they went*). This consolidates the different persons of the verb *ir* in the preterite
3. Now utter the same sentence:
   *Ayer **fueron** al campo con **sus** padres*
4. Students rewrite the sentence they hear immediately or, if you are playing *Delayed dictation*, 5-10 seconds later.

Categories (for parsing)

This classic sorting game can be used to develop the students' parsing ability.

1. Provide some metalinguistic categories, such as parts of speech (e.g. 'verbs; 'adjectives', 'nouns') or different tenses (e.g. 'present indicative', 'perfect indicative', 'future indicative').
2. Read out phrases and ask students to assign them to the correct category.

Either… or…

This can be valuable in focusing students on grammatical dichotomies such as masculine versus feminine nouns, singular versus plural, regular versus irregular verb forms, present versus past, etc. In the example below (**Table 5.5),** for instance, the task focuses students on the differences between German verbs forming the perfect tense with the auxiliary *sein* versus those forming it with the auxiliary *haben*. As they listen to a passage, the students are required to pay selective attention to the perfect tense verb forms in the text and to sort them.

Table 5.5 Sample *Either...or* task

Gestern habe ich mit meinen Freunden Matthias und Dieter einen tollen Abend verbracht. Zuerst sind wir ins Kino in der Nachbarschaft gegangen. Wir haben einen Superheldenfilm mit Chris Hemsworth gesehen. Er war sehr gut. Dann sind wir in ein italienisches Restaurant nicht weit vom Kino gegangen. Wir haben alle Spaghetti mit Meeresfrüchten gegessen. Es hat gut geschmeckt. Wir sind bis neun Uhr im Restaurant geblieben. Dann haben wir in der Innenstadt einen Nachtklub besucht. Es war schön. Wir haben zwei nette Mädchen getroffen und haben bis zwei Uhr getanzt. Dann sind wir mit einem Taxi nach Hause gefahren. Als ich Zuhause angekommen bin, hatte ich wieder Hunger, also habe ich eine Wurst gegessen.

Perfect tense with SEIN	Perfect tense with HABEN

Delayed dictation (for parsing)
Delayed dictation can be used to model or reinforce a specific sentence pattern. This activity was described in Chapter 3 as a means to practice grapheme-phoneme correspondence and spelling.

Delayed dictation with a cue for combining sentences
1. Show the sentence to be combined with the cue in brackets. For instance:

I have a sister (who)
Her name is Marie

2. Combine the sentences, e.g. *I have a sister who is called Marie* and say it to the class
3. After 10 -20 seconds, students write the sentence out on their mini-whiteboards.

Delayed dictation with open sentence combining
1. Show the sentences to be combined. For instance:

I have a sister
My sister is called Marie
She is friendly, pleasant and helpful
I argue with her from time to time
She is too talkative

2. Combine the sentences according to whichever pattern you intend to model or reinforce:

> *My sister, who's called Marie, is very friendly, pleasant and helpful, but from time to time I argue with her because she's too talkative*

3. After 10 -20 seconds students write the sentence as you uttered it.

Find the object

1. Produce a Battleships style rectangular grid. The vertical axis contains a set of L1 sentence starters, the horizontal axis the ends of the same L1 sentences. The teacher has their own grid with cells shaded in to resemble an object, e.g. a means of transport. See **Table 5.6** for an example with a focus on past tense, with the teacher's object shaded. Remember that students do not see this object.
2. Read aloud complete sentences from the grid twice in L2. Students have to understand the sentence and shade in the cell which corresponds correctly. Repeat the process until the first student puts up their hand to recognise the object. Ideally the sentences would focus on a grammatical pattern you wish to students to notice.

Table 5.6 *Find the object.* (It is a ship, by the way.)

	then I drank a glass of coke	then I ate my dinner	then I saw a film	then I ate in a cafe	then I called a friend	then I read my book	then I played ping-pong	then I went online	then I played golf
I watched a new TV programme				▓		▓			
I played tennis				▓					
I listened to music		▓	▓	▓	▓	▓	▓	▓	
I read a magazine		▓	▓	▓	▓	▓	▓	▓	
I bought a new T-shirt		▓	▓	▓	▓	▓	▓	▓	
I took a selfie with mum		▓	▓	▓	▓	▓	▓	▓	▓
I made a coffee		▓	▓	▓	▓	▓	▓	▓	▓
I drank some water		▓	▓	▓	▓	▓	▓	▓	
I did my homework			▓	▓	▓	▓	▓		

5.2 Editing tasks

Students frequently do not pay attention to error correction (Cohen and Cavalcanti, 1990); Conti, 2004), but research clearly suggests that error correction ('negative feedback'), if carried out in certain ways, is useful (Uysal, 2010). The tasks below focus students' attention on corrective feedback through listening. They focus students' attention on form, making them aware of their own errors.

Listen and correct

Give students a text like the one in **Figure 5.1** below, containing a number of commonly made mistakes. Better to focus only on a few error types. Then read the correct version a few times as students (possibly working in pairs) cross out and correct the discrepancies between the text and your version. When the task is over and you have gone through the corrections, ask students to discuss with their partners and explain in writing what the errors were and the grammar rule they referred to. This builds metacognitive skills.

1. Tell your students they are going to listen to a text containing an 'X' number of mistakes.
2. Read or play the text twice.
3. Working individually, students have to spot the mistakes and note them down on their mini-whiteboards.
4. Students discuss their findings with a partner.
5. They listen to the text one more time.
6. They discuss their findings again and agree on a list of errors and their corrections.

You may wish to adopt a narrow focus, i.e. flooding the text with one error type only, when dealing with specific issues such as incorrect agreement, pluralisation or word order. These require extensive exposure, practice and sustained monitoring to reduce their frequency.

Figure 5.1 Listen and correct (French)

> *Je suis pas allé au cinéma avec mons copains hier soir car j'ai étais fatigué. J'ai resté chez moi et je regardé la télévision. Il a été relaxant mais un peu ennuyeux. Puis, je suis fait mes devoirs jusqu'à huit heures. Vers huit heures et quart j'ai dîne avec mons parents. Après avoir dîne, je suis douché et puis je me couche.*

Spot the missing detail (for parsing)
This task can be used to focus on features of a linguistic structure that your students tend to omit in their output, e.g. (in French or Italian) the auxiliary of verbs in the perfect tense. In the example below (**Figure 5.2**) the auxiliaries are omitted from the perfect tense forms (e.g. *ho* from the correct *ho scaricato*).

Note that no gaps are placed where words have been omitted. This is deliberate in order to enhance thorough processing, as the gaps cue the students as to where the words occur promoting selective attention and consequently, partial processing.

Figure 5.2 *Spot the missing detail* task aimed at practising use of the auxiliary in the perfect (preterite) tense in Italian

---

Venerdì scorso suonato la chitarra, poi scaricato giochi e canzoni da Internet e ascoltato musica. Stato rilassante e divertente. Poi andato al centro commerciale con i miei amici. Stato forte. Nel pomeriggio io e il mio migliore amico visto un film giallo molto appassionante, fino alle sette. Lui poi tornato a casa e io fatto i miei compiti fino tardi. Mi addormentato verso l'una e mezza.

5.3   Grammatical judgement tasks

Multiple options (for grammatical accuracy judgement)
Read out two sentences, one correct and one incorrect. Students need to decide on the correct sentence and note on their mini-whiteboard '1' for the sentence you uttered first and '2' for the second. With more proficient students, you could choose more options. Examples:
Option 1: *Hier je suis allé en ville* (correct)
Option 2 : *Hier j'ai allé en ville* (incorrect as the auxiliary should be *suis*)

Minimal pair sentences
Show students two L1 sentences which are very similar in wording, except that they exemplify different grammatical or sentence patterns. The example below (**Table 5.7**), for instance, was designed to focus students on verb formation in French across a range of tenses, including conditionals. Read aloud the L2 translation of one of the two options, e.g. for '*a*', 'Je suis allé au gymnase a six heures trente' (*I went to the gym at 6.30*); students identify which of the two L1 options it matches with.

Table 5.7 Minimal pairs - structure recognition

	Option 1	Option 2
a	*I went to the gym at 6.30*	*I am going to the gym at 6.30*
b	*I used to train every day*	*I train every day*
c	*I go to the gym every day*	*I would go to the gym every day*
d	*I would be thinner, if I followed a healthier diet*	*I would have been thinner, if I had followed a healthier diet*
e	*I would like to travel abroad at least once a year*	*I used to travel abroad at least once a year*

5.4 Focus on sentence patterns

Sentence breakdown

This focuses attention on the role played by each element of the sentence through a parsing grid in which the headings show metalanguage (e.g. subject) alongside meaning (e.g. through the question: *Who did the action?*). Design a grid so that the answers occur in a different order to the one read out. Example (French) :

Avant-hier mes parents sont allés au théâtre

Who did the action? (subject)	What did they do? (Verb)	When? (temporal adverb)	Where? (locative adverb)
mes parents	*sont allés*	*avant-hier*	*au théâtre*

Sentence frames

Write on the board a number of sentence frames such as the following. Make sure you provide one or more examples for each of them. For example:

1. Time marker + subject + perfect tense + preposition + place + preposition + means of transport
   Hier   je   suis allé   au   collège en   voiture
2. Consessive + subj + subjunctive + adverb + subject + negative + present indicative + object
   Bien que   je   travaille   dur   je   ne fais   pas   de progrès
3. Preposition + infinitive + subject + modal + infinitive + adverb
   Pour   réussir   je   dois   étudier   davantage

Read out a few sentences each containing one of those patterns. Students have to match each sentence to one of the patterns given.

5.5 Cross-language comparison tasks

Same or different? (for parsing)
This aims at raising or reinforcing students' awareness of the differences and similarities between L1 and L2.
1. Give students a set of L1 sentences containing examples of the target pattern(s), such as (French) *I didn't do anything, I didn't see anything, I said nothing*.
2. They hear and transcribe the L2 version, e.g. *Je n'ai rien fait, Je n'ai rien vu, Je n'ai rien dit*.
3. Each student now teams up with one or more others to identify the similarities and differences between the L1 and the L2 and to work out the rule(s) governing the structure.

Dodgy translation
1. Give the class the literal L2 translations of a set of L1 sentences containing the target structure. Note that, while the literal L2 translation of each item is factually correct, it is not grammatically correct. Example : the English sentence *I have done nothing* would be incorrectly translated as *J'ai fait rien* (to reflect the English word order, instead of *Je n'ai rien fait*).
2. Students listen to the correct L2 versions of those sentences. As they listen to each sentence twice, they must rewrite them correctly.
3. Working in pairs or groups, they work out the rule.

Mystery position
This focuses attention on the differences between the L1 and L2 in terms of word order; notably, how specific words behave, e.g. the position of *déjà* (*already*) and other time adverbs in French sentences. This is particularly valuable in targeting function words, which, as we have seen, are less salient.
1. Provide students with a set of written L2 sentences with a gap before and after every single word. If not using familiar language, provide the L1 translation alongside. For example:
    J'ai _____ *vu* _____ *ce* _____ *film (I have seen this movie)*
2. Read the sentences adding in the item you want to draw their attention to. Let them know which word you are going to add in (e.g. *déjà* means *already*). As they listen, students add the target item in the right gap.
3. After a number of examples (10-12 sentences?), ask your students to work out the rule(s) inductively

5.6 Collocational competence-building tasks

These are tasks which aim to develop the ability to recognise and anticipate common collocations, a key micro-skill when it comes to grammatical, as well as lexical processing.

Collocational grids

Grids can be used to model collocations, as in the activity below:
1. Give students a grid like the one in **Table 5.8**, designed to practise verb collocations, using known vocabulary, in which the first collocation partner is provided, e.g. *I play, I do, I listen to, I watch.*
2. Read out sentences which contain both the first and the second collocation partner, e.g. *I do gymnastics, I play tennis, I watch a film, I listen to a song* while students note them down in the appropriate row of the grid (e.g. *tennis, piano, football, guitar* will be written on the same row as *play*.

Table 5.8 A collocational grid used to practise the collocational patterns of French verbs used to discuss leisure

	1	2	3	4
Je joue				
Je fais				
J'écoute				
Je regarde				

They can also be used for consolidation. For instance, going back to the example in the grid, you could say the noun phrases *a TV programme, shopping, some songs, trumpet*, etc. in random order, and the students have to write them on the correct row.

Collocations ping-pong

This is very similar to the above. There are two versions. In the first, students are given a card each with a list of ten or more second collocational partners, for instance, referring back to the previous example, the noun phrases *a film, some music, lots of shopping*, etc. You then say out loud the first collocational partner (i.e. the verb phrases *I play, I watch*, etc.). Students choose from the list and write on their mini-whiteboards the noun phrase which matches each verb phrase. In the second version, students are not given cards, but need to recall the missing collocation partner. So, for instance, you say *I read* and students write on their mini-whiteboards, to a time limit, a complete sentence including the missing collocational partner, e.g. *I watch a TV programme*. To stretch the students, you can ask them to add a time marker, e.g. *I watched a film last night*.

Spot the wrong collocation

This is an effective follow-up to any of the above tasks.
1. Read out a short text which contains some faulty collocations.
2. Students must spot the wrong collocations and correct them, e.g. instead of *I watched a good song* they would correct by writing *I watched a good film*. With any listening task never underestimate how much students enjoy correcting faulty information!

5.7 Narrow listening

As already mentioned, *narrow listening* texts are an excellent source of flooded input. They usually consist of a set of short passages (typically four to six) which are similar in terms of topic and linguistic content (see **Table 5.9**). We examine their use in more detail in Chapter 8.

Table 5.9 Beginner-level Italian narrow listening texts on the topic of leisure

> **TEXT 1** - Mi chiamo **Franco**. Nel mio tempo libero di solito gioco a **scacchi**. Adoro giocare a **scacch**i perchè è **emozionante** e **divertente**. Mi piace anche molto **giocare ai videogiochi** ma è **malsano**. Non **faccio sport** perchè è **faticoso** e noioso. Ogni tanto vado **in discoteca con i miei amici** nel week-end.

> **TEXT 2** -Mi chiamo **Maria**. Nel mio tempo libero di solito gioco a **pallone**. Adoro giocare a **pallone** perchè è molto **competitivo** e divertente. Mi piace anche molto **arrampicare perchè è sano e divertente**, ma è un po' faticoso. Non **gioco al computer** perchè è noioso e **malsano**. Ogni tanto vado **al centro commerciale con i miei genitori** nel week-end.

> **TEXT 3** - Mi chiamo **Sonia**. Nel mio tempo libero di solito gioco a **pallavolo**. Adoro giocare a pallavolo perchè è molto **emozionante** e **avvincente**. Mi piace anche molto **fare equitazione** perchè è **rilassante** e **appassionante**. Non **gioco alla playstation** perchè è **una perdita di tempo**. Ogni tanto vado **in chiesa** e **al cinema con la mia ragazza** nel week-end.

In this version, the narrow listening texts are nearly identical. **Table 5.9** clearly illustrates this, the highlighted words signalling where the three narrow reading texts differ in linguistic content. The way to create narrow reading texts is to produce a text flooded with the target patterns, then copy and paste it several times changing key details each time. This ensures that, while the discourse structure and patterns of the text stay the same, they are interleaved with a range of vocabulary, thereby enabling the students to process them multiple times. This means that, while students feel they are tackling different texts, they are actually reprocessing the same *discourse frame* repeatedly. At higher levels of proficiency, the texts can vary to a greater extent, while recycling the same key patterns and lexical items.

It should be pointed out that although narrow listening texts are a means of flooding the input with the same sentence and discourse patterns, we recommend exploiting them at all levels, from phonological to syntactic, from meaning to discourse-building. How this approach, that we term *extensive processing* is applied to narrow listening in practice will be demonstrated in one of the three instructional sequences detailed in Chapter 8.

5.8 Focus on affixation

These tasks focus students on prefixes, suffixes and other forms of affixation (see above). The ultimate goal is to enhance word awareness by training the students in the recognition of word parts which may suggest the meaning, part of speech and role those words play in a sentence.

Word completion
Give students a grid similar to the one in **Table 5.10** (but with 8-10 rows), containing various parts of speech. Whilst the word root is provided in its full form, its derivatives are gapped. The students listen to the teacher and fill in the gaps.

Table 5.10 *Word completion* (French)

Nouns	Adjectives	Verbs	Adverbs
lent___ (slowness)	lent (slowly)	__ lent_ _ (to slow down)	lent_____ (slowly)
facil___ (easiness)	facile (easy)	facil____ (to facilitate)	facil_____ (easily)

Morphology chart (with or without translation)
This activity is an effective follow-up to *Word completion*. It can be carried out with or without the translation. Dictate L2 words with the same stem and students write them next to their correct L1 translation in the grid (**Table 5.11**).

Table 5.11 *Morphology chart*

Noun	Adjective	Verb	Adverb
slowness =	slow =	to slow down =	slowly =
easiness/ease =	easy =	to make easier =	easily =

Speed of retrieval

Listening fluency is, as we have seen, a function of how fast a student successfully processes input. Training students in fluency involves lots of repetition and building up of speed. Many of the activities outlined above can be used to foster speed of retrieval by increasing the rate of delivery, by requiring students to produce a response to a time limit or by adding in a time-related competitive element where the individual or group completing the task most quickly wins.

Concluding remarks

It has been said that with vocabulary alone you can understand and say something, with grammar alone you can say or understand nothing (Wilkins, 1972). Nevertheless, we have seen that a grasp of syntax and morphology is clearly needed to make full sense of utterances. In this chapter we have also tried to make clear that the distinction between vocabulary and grammar is not as clear-cut as many think.

As with earlier tasks suggested in the book, you can pick and choose those which suit you and your class, interspersing them with other types of work. It is the underlying principles of teaching listening through modelling and the focus on micro-skills which need to be kept in mind, whatever lesson you plan for listening.

The next couple of chapters, while keeping an eye on LAM, move us into slightly different areas of listening which you may or may not have explored already, those which are a more traditional part of the communicative language teaching field: interpersonal and task-based listening. Within the whole LAM framework they can be seen as the least structured of activities, founded on groundwork done through developing micro-skills.

Questions to consider

How useful is it to give students detailed explanations of grammar?

In what circumstances would you begin a lesson with the explanation of a rule?

Does 'knowing the rules' help students become more proficient language users?

How would you like to learn a language yourself?

We teach language best when we use it for what it was designed for: communication.
   (Stephen Krashen)

6

INTERPERSONAL LISTENING

Introduction

So far this book has focused on opportunities to practise the *process* of listening, e.g. phonological awareness and decoding, lexical retrieval, grammatical parsing and so on. Classroom listening lessons also frequently involve comprehension work based on audio texts. But the form of listening most common in everyday life occurs in the context of oral interaction between two or more individuals and is referred to variously as *two-way listening, listenership, interactive listening* or *interpersonal listening*. Let us not forget, therefore, that listening is above all a social activity and, as Goh (2018) has pointed out, listening activities should engage students in listening for a communicative purpose. Interpersonal listening can be a great source of tightly controlled, input-flooded speech, or can take the form of relatively open-ended dialogues.

Gu (2018) defines interpersonal listening as follows:

> *…the listener's active involvement in a communicative situation where at least one other interlocutor is involved. In two-way listening meaning is perceived, inferenced and predicted, synthesised, negotiated, and co-constructed with interlocutors. In addition to comprehension and interpretation of meaning, the cognitive process is accompanied by the rapid and appropriate exchange of listener/speaker roles so that social purposes and emotional balances are achieved* (from the abstract).

In the L2 classroom interpersonal listening takes place in the context of an oral exchange, either between the teacher and student(s) or between students in pair or group work. If L2 is your normal means of classroom communication, students are exposed in every lesson to large amounts of listening input. We are not talking here about routine formulae such as *Open your book, Look at the board, Work in pairs* and so on. These are handy phrases which are easy to teach and use, but they represent a tiny and, in a way, the least useful type of input, since they are examples of barely transferable language, and are not particularly capable of helping develop internalised grammatical or lexical skills.

This chapter examines some of the research background to interpersonal listening, then suggests a number of engaging and productive practical classroom activities which not only improve listening skills, but also encourage oral spontaneity – the holy grail for language teachers and students.

1. Theoretical and research background

Two research strands can be drawn upon with regard to interactive teacher use of L2 in the classroom to support the teaching of listening. These centre on the role of *input* and *interaction*.

1.1 The role of input

Firstly, research has shown that providing comprehensible input at or just above the students' current level promotes acquisition. Krashen (1982) advanced his *Input Hypothesis* which claims that meaningful messages are all that is required for acquisition. All scholars in the field of second language acquisition give a very high priority to input.

1.2 The role of interaction

Secondly, Swain (1993) argues that output is also required to enable students to recognise where there are gaps in their knowledge and to modify their speech. Furthermore, research indicates that language learning is enhanced when students have the opportunity to take part in dialogues in which they try to make themselves understood and to understand their interlocutor. The theory of *modified interaction* (Long, 1981) suggests that speakers modify their L2 to make it more comprehensible. Teachers do the same. Donato and McCormick (1994) and Swain (2000) take this further by referring to *collaborative interactions*. As students interact with their peers or teachers they often talk about the language, question their own language use, ask for help or correct themselves or each other (Glisan and Donato, 2017).

To state the obvious perhaps, all this suggests an important role for interpersonal communication in both language acquisition generally and listening skills in particular.

2. Teacher-led interpersonal listening

2.1 Skilled questioning

A key technique for teachers in making language comprehensible and useful for acquisition is the expert use of question and answer (QA). This is a fundamental technique used in the direct method of language teaching and, in particular, the British oral-situational approach, described in Thornbury (2016). It also shares roots with audio-lingual language learning theory in which QA interactions are just one type of repetitive drill shown to have some success in building spoken and aural skills. QA is also known as *circling* or PQA (Personalised Question and Answer) by practitioners of the TPRS (Teaching Proficiency through Reading and Storytelling) approach (Lichtman, 2018). **Table 6.1** shows the hierarchy of question types you can employ when working from the front. It often makes sense to start with the easier question forms and progress to the harder, but with practice you learn to mix them up in response to the class:

Table 6.1 Hierarchy of question types

Question type	Example	Commentary
True/false statement.	*Paul is an actor. True or false?*	Students simply process a statement rather than a question form where the sentence structure varies. Students just have to produce true or false.
Yes/no question through intonation.	*Paul's an actor?*	Students just say yes or no. There is no question form to decode. The intonation of the voice shows it is a question.
Yes/no question.	*Is Paul an actor?*	Students have to do a little more decoding here, but still only have to say yes or no.
Either/or question.	*Is Paul an actor or a journalist?*	A little more decoding is required, but students only have to choose between the two options they are given.
Multiple-choice question.	*Is Paul a journalist, an actor, a teacher or a doctor?*	Slightly harder than the above because of the added options.
Question word question.	*What does Paul do for a living?*	A harder question type since the students cannot use much in the input to help them produce their answer.
Opinion question	*What do you think of Paul?*	The most open-ended question.

Through skilled QA technique students get to hear numerous repeated examples of words, chunks, whole sentences and even individual sounds and syllables (if you build this in to the teaching sequence). This is a further example of input-flooding, maximising the chances of language being processed and acquired, e.g. VanPatten (2014).

Interestingly, when thinking of QA or peer-to-peer work we usually see it in terms of its value for speaking. In fact, with teacher-led QA sequences, students are listening most of the time. This means that, although teacher-led work can be criticised for allowing too little student speaking time, it can foster excellent listening skills. In paired work students listen around 50% of the time; in teacher-led work the figure will be over 90%.

In addition, during whole class QA exchanges, when one student is answering, it is frequently the case that other students are engaging in what is known in the literature as 'private speech', namely rehearsing their own answers in their heads (Nava and Pedrazzoni, 2018). The mini-whiteboard is an excellent tool for ensuring this is taking place. In sum, we can view QA primarily as an opportunity to provide tightly controlled and scaffolded aural input.

To demonstrate how much input students can get during a QA sequence. Look at **Table 6.2**, where we describe a QA exchange.

Table 6.2 Modelling the imperfect tense through QA

Teacher	Student(s)	Commentary
Hide the pictures depicting the past and ask: *Does Debbie live in a flat or a mansion?* *Where does she live?* *Does she drive a Mini?* *What type of car does she drive?* etc.	(Hands-up and occasional no hands-up.) She lives in a mansion. She drives a Rolls Royce.	Mix up your question types, using yes/no, either/or and open questions. Adjust this to the speed of your class. Throw occasional questions at non-volunteers ('cold calling'), get individuals to repeat correct responses.
Hide the present tense pictures in the left-hand column and display the imperfect tense (*used to*) ones on the right. Repeat the above routine.	As above.	As above. Be prepared to recast (say correctly as a means of correction) faulty verb forms and any other errors.
Reveal the two columns of pictures together again. Mix up past and present questions.	As above. Use group repetition when you think it will help internalise the verb forms or endings.	Intermediate groups can do choral repetition if they are trained into it. It keeps everyone on the ball and they can even find it amusing.
Now, leaving all the pictures displayed, tell the class you are not going to ask a question, just point at a picture. They will have to give a response.	Students give responses.	This subtle change of activity changes the mood of the lesson and allows you to repeat the same work in a slightly different way. This is a key principle to remember: same, but different.
Pair up students and ask each partner to describe the two columns of pictures to their partner. The partner may correct.	Students try to recreate your original commentary in pairs.	Another change of perspective to the lesson, building the level of challenge.
Ask an individual to summarise in full either one column or both.	Hands-up.	Get two or three students to do the task. This lets the best students stretch themselves. It is a minor example of effective 'differentiation by task'.
Reveal a written version of the commentary and read it aloud once more.	Students listen and read.	This allows students still in any doubt to see the different verb forms and spellings they may have been curious to see.

126 BREAKING THE SOUND BARRIER

2.2 Example: modelling the imperfect tense through QA technique

This is a QA sequence based on a two columns depicting pairs of pictures, as suggested in **Figure 6.1**. Imagine the left-hand column showing Debbie's life now, the right hand column showing her life in the past (what she *used to* do). This is one way of introducing or practising the imperfect (*used to*) tense, with a focus on the sounds involved in recognising the imperfect. The commentary on the right of **Table 6.2** reminds us that we can recycle lots of language to get students to listen to the key point, in this case the phonological and meaning contrasts between present and imperfect tense verbs. Note how grammar is closely mapped to sound and meaning here.

Figure 6.1 Present and imperfect contrasted

The sort of QA techniques above can be used time and time again when working with pictures or written text. The secret to success is to be rigorous with the amount of repetition you do, while varying the interaction type: hands-up, no hands-up, choral repetition, individual repetition etc. This type of practice can work at all levels, although experience suggests it is of most use with beginners and low intermediate-level students. For QA to be successful all students need to be involved. It is often observed that teachers favour some students over others, usually the keenest ones who like to put up their hands. In addition, it is wise not to let whole class QA continue for too long. Very often QA can be a modelling session before students continue in pairs. Good generic teacher skills such as moving around the classroom and maintaining good eye contact play a role. For more examples of detailed descriptions of interpersonal exchanges see Steve's book about language teaching (Smith, 2017).

2.3   Beyond QA: other interactions

But QA is just one type of teacher-student interaction which generates comprehensible listening input. Summarised below are a range of interactions you can use apart from QA. This will be followed by an example of a teaching sequence exemplifying how you might incorporate them. Below is the text they are based on:

> *I often go to the cinema with my friends. It's expensive, but my dad pays! I like action movies the most, for example the Avengers. My favourite Avenger is Iron Man because he's cool and very funny. I also like Ant-Man - the special effects are amazing when he changes size. Last weekend I went with my friend Jane to the Odeon to see the new James Bond movie. It was really good, one of the best in the series. Next week I am going to visit the theme park Harry Potter World near London. It'll be amazing! (Amelia)*

False statement
Provide false statements to be corrected, e.g.
Teacher/student: *Amelia often goes to the swimming pool.*
Student(s):   *No, she goes to the cinema.*
Note: this can involve reading aloud, adapting or even paraphrasing of L2 items.

Answer-question
Give answers to which students must supply the questions.
Teacher/student: *She prefers action movies.*
Student(s):   *What type of film does she prefer?*
Note: this activity is useful if you have previously been focusing on question use or simply wish to review it from earlier in the year.

Finish the sentence
Supply starts of sentences which students complete. You can pause at a key point in the utterance to make students aware of a particular grammatical or lexical issue. For this you need to hide the source text. This activity can be extended to the whole text.
   Teacher/student: *Her favourite Avenger...*
   Student(s):   *... is Iron Man.*
   Note: tailor your gaps to the class depending on their capabilities; choose gaps to elicit

targeted words or chunks. Some students are able to recite longer chunks of language, providing more input to the class. This type of task helps students develop their skill at dividing the sound stream into meaningful words and chunks.

Start the sentence
Provide the end of a sentence to which students suggest possible beginnings.
Teacher/student: *... to the Odeon.*
Student(s): *I went with my friend...*

Note: with some classes you could let them invent their own starts, some of which might even be absurd or amusing in some way. Again, however, the main aim is for students to hear chosen phrases reused.

Correct the pronunciation
Read sentences with a deliberate pronunciation error for students to correct. In this instance students repeat the given sentence correctly pronounced.

Correct the grammar
As above, but this time the teacher's or students' sentence contains a grammatical error. A variation would be to ask students if there is an error before correcting. Focus on your target lexis or structure.

Translate into L1
Individual students act as interpreters, translating your sentence. Again, you may focus on target items you wish to reinforce.

Repeat the last few words
Warn students that every now and again you will ask someone to repeat the previous few words you uttered. This encourages the class to maintain full attention.

You could add some of the activities described in Chapters 3, 4 and 5, maybe pointing out their purpose (e.g. focus on phonemic, lexical, parsing, meaning-building level). With all the above activities mini-whiteboards can be used to ensure you get visible feedback from the class.

3. A suggested teaching sequence for exploiting texts

1. **Pre-reading activity** of some sort. This could be linguistic, e.g. a vocabulary brainstorm from the topic area, or non-linguistic, e.g. some taster questions in L2 or even L1 to stimulate some interest in the subject matter. In general it is not a great idea to go into a text 'cold'.
2. **Read aloud the text**. This helps ensure the class reads along at the pace you read and gets to hear sound-spelling relationships. To make sure every student is reading, use a trick such as warning that you will pause randomly and select a student to say the next word. Or tell the class you will make some deliberate mistakes they have to spot. Your intonation will also help students decipher meaning.
3. Try giving an immediate off-the-cuff **translation into L1** of the text. This can work well particularly with a lower attaining group. Think of this as a sort of instant parallel translation.
4. Do **choral repetition** of part or all of the text, insisting on accurate pronunciation and full participation. This reinforces the first reading, builds some phonological memory and allows another pass at the meaning.
5. Have some individual students **read aloud short sections**. Alternatively get students to read a sentence at a time to each other in pairs. The previous teacher reading and choral reading should make personal reading aloud easier. Another technique is to have students all read aloud individually with fingers in their ears. This has the benefit of discouraging distractions between students.
6. Do a **'find the French/Spanish/German'** style whole class exercise where students, by reading the text, have to find the L2 translation of the English word or phrase you read out. This gets the class to scan the text again. You could use hands up or no hands up. To ensure full participation students can write answers on mini-whiteboards.
7. Do a **'correct the false statement'** task. Give the class false statements which they have to correct from reading the text. They could give oral answers or write them down. These false statements can be tailored to the level of the group.
8. Do a **QA sequence** using the full range of questioning types described above. On hearing a good model answer from their peers or from your own recast (corrected version), students can write these down. This builds listening and transcription skill.
9. Give a similar set of **written questions**. Students work in pairs, with one as the teacher, one as the student. They can swap roles after a few minutes of questioning. This reinforces the previous oral practice.
10. Do an **aural gap-fill task.** Students hide the text, you read aloud and pause at certain points to ask the class what the next word is (see Chapter 5). Answers could be given orally or written down. Again, this can be tailored to the class; the next word to be given might be quite memorable, obvious, or more difficult.
11. Give a **comprehension task** such as true/false/not mentioned, tick the correct sentences or match the starts and ends of sentences.

12. Hand out a **gap-fill task**, either with options available to choose from or not. You could make the focus on either grammar or meaning, depending on your aims at the time.
13. Do a **traditional dictation** or **running dictation** activity. Running translation is another option. Both of these are motivating for students and get them out of their seats for a bit.
14. As a quiet written task give sentences from the text to **translate into English**, or do **retranslation into L2**. This provides more recycling of language and helps reinforce meaning for students who may still have any issues.
15. If the text is appropriate there may be a more **creative oral or written task** which could be done with some classes. Students may be able to make up interviews, tell the story from a different point of view or summarise the key points in their own words.

4. Making input comprehensible

Chapter 1 noted how important it is for listening input to be around 95-98% comprehensible for learning to be most effective. Let us consider this now in more detail. Input comes in various forms. Kumaravadivelu (2005) makes the distinction between three types:

- *interlanguage input:* the developing language of students and their peers, including both accurate and deviant language forms;
- *simplified input:* the language used by teachers, textbook writers and other speakers when they are talking to language learners;
- *non-simplified input:* the language of competent speakers and the media.

In most classrooms it is the first two which are most commonly encountered. Non-simplified ('authentic') listening input is also used, but chosen by the teacher to be accessible. Bear in mind, however, that *input* does not necessarily become *intake*, i.e. even though the language that students hear may be *comprehensible*, it may not actually be *comprehended* (noticed and processed). As Corder (1967) pointed out, language has to be comprehended to be acquired. Anything you can do to help this happen is valuable.

Kumaravadivelu (2005) has put forward an apt acronym for the factors which affect intake:

- **I**ndividual factors: age and anxiety;
- **N**egotiation factors: interaction and interpretation;
- **T**actical factors: learning and communication strategies;
- **A**ffective factors: attitudes and motivation;
- **K**nowledge factors: language and metalanguage knowledge;
- **E**nvironmental factors: social and educational context.

Thus, a key skill for teachers when doing interpersonal listening is to make the input understandable to students at all times, (e.g. Pica, Doughty and Young, 1987). If classes are subject to lots of language they simply cannot understand they will soon switch off. Alongside the skilled use of QA, a number of specific techniques can be used to make language comprehensible and learnable when talking to students. These techniques include Long's (1981) *modified input* and *modified interaction*, whereby we simplify input and check for understanding (as a caregiver would with a young infant). They form part of an effective use of formative assessment.

- In general, pitch your language at or fractionally above the current level of the students' comprehension. Avoid using too many new words or phrases.
- Modify the input to make accessible by simplifying the syntax, e.g. by using simple sentences and avoiding subordinate clauses.
- Select vocabulary students are more likely to recognise, e.g. cognates or vocabulary they have encountered before.
- Do not speak at native speaker speed; use repetition, rephrasing and pausing.
- Allow students to ask questions or seek clarification, including by gesture. Teach them simple phrases such as *Can you repeat, please?*
- Maintain eye contact with as many students as possible, using facial expression to enhance meaning. 'Teach to the eyes.'
- Use generic teacher skills to hold attention, such as varying your physical position in the class, scanning left to right and front to back.
- Use humour to reduce anxiety and produce more engagement. Research suggests that students echo their teacher's behaviour and are more likely to use language spontaneously when relaxed (Hawkes, 2012). Put another way, students learn better when their *affective filter* is lowered (Krashen, 1982).
- As mentioned previously, make judicious use of translation into L1 when there is no efficient alternative. Do not feel obliged to use 100% L2.
- Use gesture, pictures and classroom objects. You can spot a language teacher by the number of gestures they use when making everyday conversation!
- Be predictable in your routines, including questioning style, use of choral and individual repetition; students become familiar with what is expected of them.
- Reinforce listening by using the written word, e.g. writing words and chunks on the board or providing transcripts of dialogues.
- Use formative assessment techniques such as mini-whiteboard responses to check for meaning, e.g. students may write *true* on one side of their board and *false* on the other. Or check for understanding by asking individual students to translate back what you have said.
- Avoid talking for too long; observe when a class may be losing enthusiasm for an activity. Make use of your emotional and cognitive empathy skills.

Making it comprehensible: an example classroom exchange

Here is an example of a typical classroom dialogue which allows you to model language repeatedly in an organic, communicative fashion (adapted from a lesson observed in Nava and Pedrazzini, 2018). Suppose you want to explain the new word *sporty*.

Teacher: *Are you sporty? I love sport. I'm very sporty. I play football, tennis and love to go walking (gestures). Do you like sport? Hands up (gesture) if you like sport.* (Students raise hands)
Teacher: *Lionel Messi is sporty, isn't he? Harry Kane is sporty. Who else is sporty?*
Student: *Rafael Nadal.*
Teacher: *Yes! He's sporty. Is Homer Simpson sporty?*
Students: *No!*
Teacher: *Homer loves sport!*
Students: *No! He loves donuts!*
Teacher: *Is an elephant sporty?*
Students: *No!*
Teacher: *Is a hippopotamus sporty?*
Students: *No!*
Teacher: *All together: "sporty".*

And so on. Note how students receive plenty of modelled L2 input, including multiple repetitions of the words *sport* and *sporty*, before they are expected to produce much language themselves.

5. Example activities

These tasks have been divided into those which are primarily led by the teacher from the front and those which mainly involve students working with each other.

5.1 Teacher-led tasks

Below are some specific teacher-led two-way listening activities which generate large amounts of comprehensible input and varying degrees of interaction. Each one can be scaffolded to meet the needs of the class. Activities of this type help build motivation and the teacher's relationship with the class. Wherever possible, it is sensible to have in mind a specific language pattern or communicative function before opting for a particular task. Make sure also that your class has mastered the relevant language patterns and vocabulary before beginning. These tasks represent opportunities to use largely pre-known language in a less rehearsed, more spontaneous context. It should go without saying that the class's work ethic and behaviour allow the tasks to run successfully. They depend on a positive and supportive classroom atmosphere where language can be used without too much fear of error.

The difficulty level of each task is classified using two level reference points, first using the terminology of the ACTFL in the USA, followed by a CEFR equivalent. A2 in CEFR terms is broadly equivalent to the Foundation Tier of GCSE in England and Wales, while B1 roughly equates to Higher Tier GCSE.

The Price is Right

Level: Novice High to Intermediate Mid (A1/A2). **Time** 30 minutes.
Language focus: comprehension of numbers, household item vocabulary and descriptions.
Preparation: bring in a range of small household items or prepare a 10-slide PowerPoint presentation with items displayed.

Pre-listening: it is assumed that the class knows numbers from 1-100 and a range of simple descriptive vocabulary such as *cheap, expensive, useful, stylish, modern, popular*. If necessary, review these on the board before the game, e.g. using translation or a matching task with L2 words on the left, L1 on the right. Ensure students are confident with this vocabulary before proceeding. You can introduce some new vocabulary as you go along, particularly given that the items will be clearly visible.

Task: Students guess the price of household consumer goods to win them. The class can compete as individuals, pairs, small groups, or, if you want to make it more of a spectator sport, ask students to come up to the front and be contestants with you as the host. Offer alternative prices (multi-choice) or just get the students to make a guess. (Assuming you have revised numbers and prices by now.) Have your individuals or teams read out their guesses before revealing the actual price paid. (If in doubt, make them up.) Points for the closest answers, prizes for the winners. Classes enjoy this, pay close attention and get plenty of chances to hear numbers, items of vocabulary and prices (input) and to say them (output). With a high-attaining class you could use a good student as host, perhaps obtaining some theme music, and make it even more fun.

Post-listening: as a 'warm down' activity do some simple mental math(s) with the class, reading aloud some simple additions, subtractions, multiplications or divisions for them to work out and write down as you read them.

Note: this style of task can be used with a wide range of themes such as guessing the age of famous people or the height of recognisable landmarks. Whichever task is chosen, it can be matched with a specific communicative objective or language pattern you have in mind, e.g. describing height, talking about ages or giving prices.

Describe a memorable event

Level: Intermediate-Mid to Intermediate High (A2/B1). **Time:** 30-40 minutes.
This is adapted from Richards (2015). The original lesson was planned by Diana Croucher, an English language teacher in Barcelona. It could be used with a good intermediate class.
Language focus: using the perfect (preterite) tense.
Preparation: find a photo reflecting an important event in your life, e.g. a wedding, holiday highlight, graduation or sports achievement. Prepare a list of high frequency past tense verb forms to be displayed on the board.

Pre-listening: introduce the activity and tell students they will need to use some common past tense verbs. Do a practice drill with the verb forms on the board, e.g. get students in pairs or individually to make up sentences using chosen verbs to a time limit. For some classes scaffold the task further by displaying some other language options. They can show their sentences on mini-whiteboards or you can circulate, checking if they have written appropriate responses.

Task

1. Display the photo you selected. Do some whole class QA on describing the picture. *Where is it? Who is it? What do you see? What was happening?* Scaffold this with some pre-prepared sentence options on the board.
2. Describe the event in your life, making frequent use of perfect tense verbs. You might bring in an artefact of some sort to support your story, e.g. a souvenir. The account can be short and easy for some classes, longer and more complex for others. Tell the class they must note down in L1 anything they understand. Recount the story at least twice, making sure you use your techniques for making language comprehensible; slowing down, repeating, rephrasing, using gesture, for example.
3. Ask students in either L1 or L2 (depending on the class) to share their notes with a partner, then report them back to the teacher. If the class reports back in L1, then write up notes on the board in L2 (instant translation). Make sure to reuse language you used in your account, saying it out loud repeatedly.
4. Then erase parts of your displayed language, as much or as little as suits the class (*Disappearing text*). Get students in pairs to recreate your original account in L2. They should then report it back to you, at which point you might make some light-touch recasts or corrections.
5. (Optional for higher-attaining classes) Tell students they are going to talk about an important event in their own life. Give them 10 minutes to make some L2 notes, but not to write a whole script. They then deliver their account to a partner. Select a small number of students to report back what their partner said. As a written task, possibly for homework, students can write out and/or record their account.

Your account could be something like this (perfect tense verbs which you displayed for the pre-listening task in bold):

*Last year my wife and I **had** a fantastic holiday in Canada. We **took** the plane to Toronto. We **spent** three days with our friends in an Air BnB in Toronto and **visited** the sights of the city. It was great. Then we **took** a train from Toronto all the way to Vancouver. What a trip! The journey **took** four days. We **slept** three nights on the train. we **saw** forests, lakes, prairies and stunning mountains. The food and service on the train were excellent and we **met** lots of interesting people of different nationalities.*

'My house' video

Level: Novice Mid (A1).   **Time:** 20 minutes.
Language focus: rooms in the house, basic furniture and the phrase *there is/are*.
Preparation: go around your house, or someone else's if you prefer to maintain your privacy, and produce a videoed commentary with your phone. If you have a proper microphone, the sound will be even better. The clip should last no longer than about two minutes.

Pre-listening: it is assumed you have previously worked on rooms in the house and furniture. Do some quickfire translation or QA on this topic to prepare them for the task.

Task:
1. Play the video to the class twice. If you have filmed your own house then students should be particularly interested!
2. Play the video again without sound, pausing to ask questions to the class. You can use hands-up, no hands-up or mini-whiteboards with answers written down.
3. In pairs students should now try to recreate the whole description. It is fine if they make mistakes.

Post-listening: address any points of difficulty, then students can write up the description for homework. For lower-proficiency classes you can provide a template.

Talk about your family

Level: Novice Mid (A1).   **Time**: 20-25 minutes.
Language focus: family, ages, simple descriptions.
Preparation: find some pictures of your family to be displayed, together with a glossary of simple vocabulary.

Pre-listening: do some quick QA with the class, revising family vocabulary: *Do you have any brothers and sisters? How old is your brother? Is your dad tall or short?*

Task:

1. Describe your family members while looking at the pictures displayed and with the key vocabulary displayed separately on an adjacent whiteboard. Use repetition and pausing to keep the language understandable.
2. Repeat the description as the class write down notes in L1 on paper or mini-whiteboards.
3. Elicit answers from the class, writing up partly completed sentences.
4. Students now copy and complete the gapped sentences.

Post-listening: students could write their own brief descriptions using the language you modelled on the board and they copied.

Dictogloss

This task can be traced back to Wajnryb (1990) who saw it as a way to work on grammar through listening. Since then a number of studies have provided further evidence of its effectiveness, e.g. Nable (1996) and Gallego (2014).

Level: Intermediate Mid to High (A2/B1). **Time:** 30 minutes.
Language focus: any.
Preparation: write a short text describing, for example, a recent event. Build in repetitions of a target phrase or grammatical structure.

Pre-listening: explain that you are going to read a short account and that the class, working in pairs, will have to take notes in L1 or L2 (or both), then recreate the story between them in L2. Brainstorm a few words from the text, writing them up on the board with translations where needed.

Task: as you read the text quite slowly at least three times, building in pauses, the pairs jot down their notes. Do not go so slowly that the task becomes a dictation. Then give them about 10 minutes to discuss together how they will summarise the account in L2. Then invite a couple of pairs to give their accounts as you write up language on the board.

Post-listening: as a follow-up task students can write a final version of the account.

Dictocomp

This activity is very similar to the above, but more demanding in as far as students are not allowed to write anything down. Whether this would work with your class depends on the simplicity of the source text and the proficiency of your class. On the whole, it may be better reserved for high-attaining classes as it requies very good memory and concentration.

Alibi

This is described in Smith & Conti (2016) and elsewhere, but is worth repeating since it is such an excellent source of structured listening input. In particular, you can use the game to model multiple examples of the perfect (preterite) and imperfect tenses.

Level: Intermediate Mid to High (A2/B1). **Time:** 40 minutes.
Language focus: hearing past events narrated; hearing and using perfect and imperfect tenses.
Preparation: none.

Pre-listening: Tell your class in L1 or L2 - in your best deadpan and convincing fashion - that a crime was committed the previous night at 8.00 p.m. (For example, say that an elderly lady was attacked and robbed on the town square.) Explain that the police suspect a pair of young people. Then say that they are suspected to come from your school. Add solemnly that the two suspects are thought to come from this very class. (Some will look quizzical, a few will cotton on that you are joking.) Then confess that you have made up the crime and explain that you need two volunteers to leave the room to work out an alibi between them.

Task: The pair should agree on something they did together, such as a trip to the cinema or a restaurant, and plan in every detail what they did. Warn them that they will have to come in one by one to be questioned by the rest of the class. This means that their alibi must be very detailed (what clothes they were wearing, how they got to their destination, where they sat, what they ate, who paid, who was there, what they talked about and so on).

While the pair are outside, prepare questions with the rest of the class and write them on the board. Make a point of modelling the key grammar point, the distinction between perfect and imperfect tense: *what were you wearing?/how did you get there?* etc.

After about five minutes invite one of the suspects in and have them sit at the front. Ask them to swear an oath on an L2 dictionary: *I swear to tell the truth...* (classes like that bit). The class then puts up hands to ask L2 questions, using the displayed questions on the board to help. Your job is to choose who will speak and suggest extra questions if students dry up. One student may act as a scribe to record testimony. After about 10 minutes the second suspect is invited in, swears the oath and answers questions. The first suspect may stay in the room if you are sure they will not cheat by gesturing answers to their alleged partner-in-crime. Finally, having weighed up the similarities and differences between the two stories, the class can vote to decide if the suspects are guilty or innocent.

In a large class of, say, 30 students most of the time they are listening to input which they find interesting, amusing and which is quite highly structured and repetitive in nature, giving them a chance to further internalise high frequency language, e.g. *I wore, I paid, I bought, we watched* and so on.

Post-listening: an optional written task would be for students to write up an account of the two volunteers' story. Scaffold this with some notes or a template you have prepared after the original activity.

Creative storytelling from a picture

Level: Intermediate Mid to High (A2/B1). **Time:** 30 minutes.
Language focus: various but, in the example below, using three time frames (past, present and future).
Preparation: choose a photo you intend to use.

Pre-listening: for this task it is important that the class knows that *they* will be telling the story with your help. Encourage the class to be imaginative and try out any ideas and language they have.

Task: below is an example of a picture you could use for creative storytelling (**Figure 6.2**). Display it on the class screen.

Figure 6.2 Picture for creative storytelling (image: pixabay.com)

The series of suggested starter questions below will vary a lot according to how the class responds. Accept all suggestions before agreeing with the class what the preferred answer is. Write up examples of language on the board. Remember that this task is primarily about generating comprehensible listening input.

- *Where are these two girls? What are their names? How old are they? What are they wearing?*
- *What are they doing? What time of day is it?*
- *Why are they in this field? How did they get there?*
- *Who is in the space vessel? Is it a space vessel? Where did it come from? How long was the journey?*
- *What's going to happen next?*

End the activity by summarising the class's story, clarifying any remaining difficult points of language.

Post-listening: focus on one or two grammatical patterns which have cropped up. As a written task tell the class to write up the story, or, if they are able to, write their own imaginative story based on the same picture.

What can I take on holiday?

Level: Intermediate Mid (A2). **Time**: 15 minutes.
Language focus: topic-specific vocabulary.
Preparation: none

Pre-listening: explain to the class that they are going to review holiday vocabulary by playing a game. They have to suggest items they can take on holiday, then have to work out why you allow them to take the item, or why you will not. They can choose absurd items such as *castle*, *crocodile* or *tree*. In other words, they need to fathom what your criteria are. Below are two possible criteria you may choose in advance:

1. This is the hardest and most fun. You must say *um* or *uh* (or equivalent L2 hesitation sound) before you make the statement for the item to be allowable, e.g. *Um… I'm going to Florida and I'm going to take a camera*. In order for this to work well, it is best if you use no hands-up as opposed to having students raise their hands. If the students have planned out what they are going to say, they will not often say *um*. Your students who are confident at speaking in public may get frustrated because they do not use fillers, so they will not ever be allowed to take their suggested items
2. The items must contain the same number of letters, e.g. *food, door, lion*. In this case you would need to plan your own examples ahead of the game.

Task: This assumes you use criterion (1). Give students an example of an item which can be taken, enclosed in a model L2 statement, e.g. *I'm going to Florida and I'm going to take a... um.... swimsuit*. Write up this example on the board. Then ask the class *What are you going to take on holiday?* After each suggestion spoken in the same form you respond by saying *Yes, you can take...* or *No, you can't take...* Your answer depends on whether the student includes the hesitation sound. Then give another example of your own: *I'm going to go to Florida and I'm not going to take a dinosaur* (*not* because you did not hesitate).

It can take a while for students to work out why they can and cannot take items. You will need to decide how obvious to make your hesitation noises.

Post-listening: recap via quick translation from L1 to L2 some of the items mentioned during the game.

Note: this game generates many repetitions of the language patterns *I can/I can't* and *you can/you can't*. The game can be played in other ways, e.g. to practise using the prepositions *from* and *to*. *I take the plane from... um... London to Washington, but I can't take the plane from Washington to London.*

5.2 Student-led tasks

This section looks at interpersonal listening between students. When pairs (or groups) of students are working on an interpersonal listening task, a complex process is taking place. Meaning is perceived, inferenced, predicted and worked out between speakers (Gu, 2018). As mentioned earlier, this so-called *negotiation of meaning* is thought to be a significant contributor to acquisition (e.g. Long, 1981; Allwright and Bailey, 1991).

The basic premise of most pair-work listening activities is that there is an *information gap* which creates a need to communicate. Practical considerations here include whether the class is able to do pair work productively without wasting time and whether the activities are clearly structured enough, as well as within the linguistic capability of the students, i.e. have they had enough input and practice of the language to be used. Ground rules need to be made clear and enforced, especially if students are new to regular paired activity. In general, pair work is preferable to group work principally because it is more efficient, allowing each partner more time for speaking, but also because it is harder for some students to let others do the work. When pair work is underway you can usually monitor from a distance, offering help or keeping pairs on task when needed.

Below are some suggested peer-to-peer tasks.

> **INFOBOX 16 Information gap activities**
>
> An information gap activity is one where learners are missing the information they need to complete a task and need to talk to each other to find it. For example, student A has some details about a city, while student B has others. Together they can complete the information by asking each other questions. Information gap activities are useful as they provide an opportunity for extended speaking practice, they represent real communication and they require sub-skills such as clarifying meaning and re-phrasing. Typical information gap activities include 'describe and draw', 'spot the difference', 'jigsaw reading and listening' and paired gapped dictations.

Liar, liar

Level: Novice High to Intermediate Mid (A1/A2). **Time**: 30 minutes.
Language focus: personal identity, common verbs, likes and dislikes
Preparation: none.

Pre-listening: tell pairs of students they have 10 minutes to write down in note form up to 15 things about themselves without telling their partner. Within the 15 statements there must be at least five lies. Discuss with the class and write up some language on the board to help them.

Task: partner A reads statements about him or herself, e.g. *I play tennis with my mum at the weekend; I love chicken, but I hate fish.* Every time partner B thinks they have heard a lie they must interrupt and say *Liar!* in the L2. Partner A either confirms it is a lie or not. After all 15 statements have been made, partner B begins. A variation on this task would be to have students talk in different time frames, e.g. about last weekend or their last holiday.

Post-listening: individual students report what they found out either to the teacher or to a third student. Correction could be given at this stage.

Oral tennis

Level: Intermediate Mid (A2). **Time**: 20 minutes.
Language focus: question forms.
Preparation: print off two sets of about 40 questions (for partner A and partner B). Pitch the questions at an appropriate level for your class. After each question supply the answer for the benefit of the questioner. Below are some which Steve prepared for his French class:

1. *Est-ce qu'un tigre est méchant ou mignon? (méchant)*
2. *Donne une couleur qui commence par M. (marron, mauve)*
3. *Mont Blanc: c'est un fleuve ou une montagne? (montagne)*
4. *Quelle ville est plus grande: Bordeaux ou La Rochelle? (Bordeaux)*
5. *Donne un animal à la maison qui commence par P. (perruche, perroquet, poisson)*
6. *Comment s'appelle le grand stade de football et rugby à Paris? (le stade de France)*
7. *Dans quel magasin est-ce qu'on achète des livres? (une librairie)*
8. *Qui est la mère de ta mère? (grand-mère)*
9. *Où travaille un docteur? (un hôpital)*
10. *Quel moyen de transport est plus rapide: un train ou un avion? (avion)*

Pre-listening: explain the rules of the game in L1. Students work in pairs and each student has a list of questions to ask their partner. They score the activity like tennis. Partner A 'serves' a question and partner B tries to 'return' the answer. If partner B cannot answer the point goes to the server (15.0). If partner B can answer correctly, the returner wins the point (0.15). (Each student has the answers to their questions, so it is easy to keep score.) Advise students to keep a written note of the score. The pairs keep playing until time runs out. Make sure students know how scores are kept in tennis!

Task: students work away as you monitor, checking that students stay in L2. (This is not so hard, as the task mainly consists of reading aloud.)

Post-listening: to bring the class together, ask a selection of the questions to the whole class.

Note: it is important to provide a mixture of questions, some easy, some hard. In general the advantage is with the returner of serve (unlike the real game), because you want students to have success in answering the questions. Only play this game if your class has developed good reading aloud skill.

Yes/no game

Level: Intermediate Mid (A2). **Time**: 20 minutes.
Language focus: using common verbs in present and past with negatives.
Preparation: provide a set of simple questions relating to, for example, personal information likes and dislikes, daily routine or recent activities. The questions should be familiar to the class.

Pre-listening: explain that the game is all about not saying *yes* or *no*. Model an exchange with a chosen student, demonstrating that the most obvious way of answering will usually be to repeat the content of the question, e.g. Question: *Do you go to the cinema every week?* Answer: *I don't go to the cinema every week, I go occasionally*. Encourage students to give some extra detail in their answer where possible. Every time a student says *yes* or *no* by mistake, they lose a point.

Task: students work in pairs; about 15 questions should be enough. High-attaining groups will be able to write or improvise their own questions. Monitor as necessary.

Post-listening: get the students to try and trap you into saying *yes* or *no*.

Word by word

Level: Novice Mid to Intermediate High (A1-B1). **Time**: 20 minutes.
Language focus: building grammatically correct sentences.
Preparation: none.

Pre-listening: model to the class with a volunteer how you can co-construct a simple story, one word at a time. Then work around the class to further model the activity. Each word added by the next person must fit correctly with the previous word or words, respecting rules of gender, agreement, verb agreement and (to an extent) logic. When a sentence reaches a natural end students may say *full stop*.

A sequence in French might go like this:

Samedi – matin – je – vais – au(x) - magasins - avec – mon – ami(e) – (point). Nous – allons – à – la – boulangerie – et – ensuite – nous .....

Higher-proficiency students find ways of extending sentences and making life harder for their partner by choosing challenging words or grammar.

Task : pairs construct narratives word by word. It is suggested that you give students a start to provide a context, e.g. talk about sport, your town, your best friend, etc. After about three minutes get students to restart on a different subject. A variation on the task would be to allow students to do two words at a time.

Post-listening: ask students what they found easy or difficult and point out what skills the activity develops. (Two obvious skills are the use of are collocations and correct grammatical usage.)

Note: this activity is particularly good at getting students to think about lexical choices and grammatical issues such as word order, case, adjective agreement and verb endings.

Rotation

Level: Intermediate Mid (A2). **Time:** 20 minutes.
Language focus: any.
Preparation: prepare a short, highly comprehensible text on your current topic or one done in the past.

Pre-listening: brainstorm some vocabulary from the text, e.g. quickfire translation L2 to L1.

Task:

1. Read the text at near-native speed and ask students to note down the key points in L1.
2. Familiarise students with the text, using a range of activities from your repertoire, e.g. 'find the French/German/Spanish', disappearing text, true/false, correcting false statements and translation of chosen chunks.
3. Divide the class into groups of three and give one student the text they have been working on. In turns, each student has a go at reading the text to the rest of the group while the others take notes in English and/or using pictures or symbols. Then take away the L2 text
4. Each group nominates a scribe and two story-tellers. Based on what they recall, the story-tellers must reconstruct the text in L2 with the help of their L1 notes or pictures.

Post-listening: students reconstruct the text using *Aural gap-fill*.

Read and look up

Level: Novice Mid to High (A1). **Time**: 10 minutes.
Language focus: any.
Pre-listening: explain the point of the task, namely holding in memory chunks of language which can later be used more spontaneously

Preparation: prepare two sets of 10-15 sentences related to your current topic or language focus. Students work in pairs. Give each partner one of the two sets of sentences.

Task:

Students take turns speaking and listening. The speaker looks at a sentence from their list, tries to remember it, then looks away from the text before saying it to their partner. This technique forces the speaker to rely on memory, rehearsing the sentence 'in their head'. The other partner writes down an L1 translation of the sentence. With some classes the partner can simply transcribe the L2 sentence.

> **INFOBOX 17 Should I correct students' errors?**
>
> Much research has been carried on *corrective feedback* (CF). The balance of this research suggests correction, or *negative feedback* (explicit correction), is useful (Long, 1996). On the other hand, you can *recast* students' utterances (repeat the utterance in its correct form), without pointing out any error, which supplies *positive feedback*. Much depends on the aims of the lesson as to what type of feedback you give, e.g. is the focus more on fluency or accuracy? In addition, as you can imagine, the way you correct is important. Giving negative feedback can be at the expense of student confidence. You need to weigh up the situation, student, class atmosphere and the importance of the error, e.g. is it important for getting across meaning unambiguously? We agree with Ellis (2009) who wrote: "simplistic pedagogical proscriptions and prescriptions cannot reflect the reality of either the process by which CF is enacted or its acquisitional product" (p.16).

6. Obstacles to understanding

In two-way listening situations comprehension is impeded when students cannot understand certain key linguistic elements. Let us focus for a moment on two common areas of misunderstanding: questions and time frames.

6.1 Questions

Questions are a common part of dialogues and are easily misunderstood. This is partly due to the phonological similarities between question words. In French the words *qui, que, comment, combien, quel* and *quand* share the same initial phoneme /k/; in German problems arise distinguishing *wie, wieviel, wer, wo* and *wann* (*wer* is a particular problem because of similarity with the English word *where*); Spanish has *cuánto, cuándo, cómo, qué* and *cuál*. This calls for targeted practice of these words to assist listening comprehension and interaction. Below is a graduated sequence of ways you might do this. Note that with some classes you could model these activities before letting students do them in pairs.

1. **Recognition drills**. Give students a list of question words or phrases and tell them to tick one every time they hear it in a dialogue or a list of questions read aloud.
2. **Gap-fill**. Hand out a list of questions with the question words missing. Read a dialogue in which each question occurs; students mark in the correct question word. Reading skill helps with this, but there is no guarantee in advance what the precise question will be. Alternatively, just read aloud the questions, asking students to mark in the words they hear.

3. **Dictation**. Students transcribe whole questions, possibly the ones they have seen in (1) and (2)
4. **Choose the question**. Give students a set of questions, e.g. the ones used above. Read aloud a set of answers. Students have to match the answer to the question.
5. **Translation**. Students translate questions into L1. This reinforces the L1 to L2 meaning link.
6. **Write the question**. Read aloud answers to questions, one by one. Students say or write a corresponding question, e.g. *I arrive home at 10. (When do you arrive home?)*
7. **How many questions?** Give a sentence to which students must find as many relevant questions as possible, e.g. *I go to the cinema with my friends every week because I love movies. (What do you do every week? Where do you go? Who do you go with? and so on.)*

Parts of the sequence above could be picked up in later lessons since question formation is rarely a quickly acquired skill, partly because students spend more time answering questions than asking them. After very focused controlled activities such as the above, it is sensible to make sure you bring in question use repeatedly in subsequent lessons for recycling and retrieval purposes.

6.2 Time frames

These are a source of confusion since to native English-speaker ears the phonological cues in some other languages seem quite subtle. Compare the phonology of the following French verbs by saying them aloud: *je joue, je jouais, j'ai joué, je jouerai, je jouerais, je vais jouer, j'avais joué, j'aurais joué, en jouant*. The considerable meaning changes are conveyed by verb forms and inflections which native English speakers are not used to and which appear therefore less salient. One school of thought would be not to focus too much on these subtle differences of phonology for fear of creating more confusion, or to concentrate on other contextual elements in a sentence such as time expressions (*last week, yesterday, tomorrow*). We believe, however, that there is useful skill work to be done here, which in the long run will help students recognise time frames in speech. Below is a possible sequence, moving from easier to harder. As with the sequence on questions, these could be done in pairs if you think the class would benefit from this.

1. **Spot the time frame (1).** Read aloud sentences containing a time expression and appropriate verb form, e.g. ***Last week*** *I* went *to the bank*. Ask students to tick off or note down *past*, *present* or *future*.
2. **Spot the time frame (2).** Read aloud sentences with different time frames without using a time expression, e.g. *I'll visit my uncle in Madrid*. Students note down the time frame, getting used to matching time with phonological clues. This focuses students more closely on the verb form than in task (1), since there is no extra clue from the time marker.
3. **Spot the time frame (3)**. Read a paragraph containing a number of sentences using different time frames along with time expressions, e.g. *I **love** going shopping with my friend Jill. **Every Saturday** we **go** to the shopping centre in town, **have** a coffee together, then **wander** around the shops. **Last week** I **bought** some clothes for the summer holiday. **This summer** we're going*

to Barcelona for two weeks. We'll be staying in an Air BnB. Every time students hear a reference to present, past or future they make a note or tick from a list. Incidentally, an exercise like this provides an opportunity to discuss how a verb tense can be used to refer to different time frames, e.g. using the present tense to refer to the future, or the present to refer to the past.

4. **Time matching**. Give students a set of time expressions. Read aloud sentences using different time frames, but not containing time expressions. Students choose a suitable expression to add to the sentence. There could be multiple appropriate answers.
5. **Translation**. Students translate sentences you read containing time expressions and verbs. Mini-whiteboards would work well here.
6. **QA**. Ask a series of questions to which students write down answers, either in note form or in whole sentences. Mix up the time frames from sentence to sentence.

Note that interactive digital activities can reinforce the type of work referred to in this section. Commercially available programmes such as *Textivate, Teachvid, This is Language, The Language Gym* and *languagesonline.org.uk* can be used to enhance skills with questions, time frames and other common sources of difficulty.

Concluding remarks

Developing listening skills takes time and a great deal of input. While specific exercises, tasks and games play an important role in developing listening comprehension, it is the day-to-day interpersonal listening which contributes hugely to developing listening skills and success in listening tests. When teachers ask "How do I get my class to be more confident listeners?" our response would be not only to build the bottom-up processing skills from beginner level, but to incorporate in nearly every lesson, opportunities for interpersonal listening, either led by the teacher or carried out in pairs.

Remember that two-way listening is arguably more demanding than one-way listening since students have to react immediately to input and formulate their own response which needs to be relevant and accurate enough for comprehension. This form of listening requires, therefore, an additional set of skills to one-way listening developed through specific practice. One potential danger which Field (2008) points out is that if you spend a lot of time teaching listening through two-way activities which combine listening with other skills, e.g. reading and writing, you may end up neglecting the type of bottom-up decoding practice described in Chapters 3, 4 and 5. You run the risk of not 'teaching listening' at all.

As is so often the case, a suitable balance needs to be found. This balance will depend on your class, their level of proficiency and your own preferences as a teacher. Our view is that it is advisable to devote enough time to various types of listening activity, with a greater emphasis on bottom-up, micro-listening skills with beginners. The next chapter looks at how listening can be developed in the context of *task-based language teaching*. We shall see that 'tasks' involve a good deal of interpersonal listening, but add a powerful extra element to the process.

Questions to consider

In your classroom what would be the ideal balance between teacher-led and peer-to-peer listening work?

What practical classroom management issues are raised when doing pair or group work?

What would be your ideal balance of L2 and L1 use in the classroom?

How would the age of your students affect the type of listening activity you might do?

One of the strengths of task-based teaching is that the conceptual basis is supported by a strong empirical tradition. This distinguishes it from most methods and approaches to pedagogy, which are relatively data-free.
(David Nunan)

7

TASK-BASED LISTENING

Introduction

A book about teaching listening would not be complete without reference to listening within the context of Task-Based Language Teaching (TBLT). Prabhu (1987) was an early advocate of TBLT, believing that students learn more when they pay attention to meaning through purposeful tasks. In fact, the idea of meaning-focused communicative activities as a source of language acquisition is supported by over 50 years of research. The seminal work on comprehensible input by Krashen (1982), Long's Interaction Hypothesis (1996) and Ellis, Long and VanPatten's support for task-based learning (e.g. Ellis, 2017; Long (2015); VanPatten, 2014) all offer support and research evidence for carrying out communicative tasks. More specifically, research has been carried out which suggests that when students engage in tasks their self-efficacy improves (e.g. Motallebzadeh & Defaei, 2013). Put simply students tend to like and benefit from language learning activities with a real purpose.

> **INFOBOX 18 The Comprehension Hypothesis**
>
> Krashen (1982) argues that comprehensible input is all you need for second-language acquisition. We acquire languages by using innate mechanisms to understand messages, just as a young child learns their first language. Krashen also believes that input should not be grammatically sequenced, claiming that such sequencing, as found in language classrooms, may even be harmful. While he does not specify any way of teaching, he believes that if you provide 'compelling' input, nature will take its course.
>
> This claim that *only* input matters in second-language acquisition has been contradicted by more recent research. For example, students enrolled in French immersion programmes in Canada still produced non-native-like grammar when they spoke, even though they had years of meaning-focused lessons and their listening skills were like those of a native (Swain and Lapkin, 1989). Output appears to play an important role, helping provide students with feedback, concentrate on the form of what they are saying and automatise their language knowledge.

> **INFOBOX 19 The Interaction Hypothesis**
>
> According to Long's interaction hypothesis (Long, 1996) the conditions for acquisition are especially good when interacting in L2, e.g. when a breakdown in communication occurs and students must 'negotiate for meaning'. The modifications to speech stemming from interactions like this help make input more comprehensible, provide feedback to students, and push them to modify their speech. Think for a moment how much young children interact with their caregivers, e.g. when stories are being read together.

1. What is a *task*?

There have been numerous definitions, e.g. Willis (1996); Richards and Rogers (2001); Nunan (2004). This a summary based on Ellis (2017):

1. The primary focus is on meaning, not linguistic form.
2. An information gap is needed, creating a need to communicate.
3. Students mainly rely on their existing linguistic knowledge, although they may get input from the task materials.
4. There is a clearly defined outcome to the task, a goal to be achieved.

It could involve, for example, achieving a specific outcome or creating a final product. Examples might include compiling a list of reasons, carrying out an opinion survey, jotting down a set of instructions, completing an information grid, finding the differences between two texts or finding the route on a map based on spoken instructions. Long (1985) distinguishes between two types of task:

- *Target tasks*: tasks that people do in everyday life, such as listening to a message on the phone and jotting down notes.
- *Pedagogical tasks*: simpler versions of target tasks that language learners can work on in class.

VanPatten (2014) argues that tasks should resemble real life activities for best motivational effect, but a looser definition may be more appropriate since the main criteria for tasks should be how enjoyable they are and what linguistic benefit they bring. Some real-life tasks, e.g. form-filling, do not make for much fun in the language classroom!

Willis describes a possible framework for running task-based lessons (Willis, 1998) which is summarised here:

Table 7.1 Planning and running a task (based on J. Willis)

INTRODUCTION	TASK	PLANNING	REPORT
1. Explore the topic with the class. Dictate key words and chunks related to the topic to help them prepare for and carry out their task.	**2.** Students do the task individually, in pairs or small groups. Monitor from a distance, encouraging all attempts at communication. Do not focus on errors.	**3.** Students prepare to report to the whole class, orally or in writing how they did the task and what they discovered. Stand by to help with advice on accuracy at this stage.	**4.** Individuals, pairs or groups report to the class or exchange written reports. Act as a chairperson, commenting on the information and recasting language where useful.

2. Example tasks with a focus on listening

The tasks below generally follow the Willis model described in **Table 7.1** and meet the requirements of Ellis's (2017) definition of a task (see above). Most are appropriate for students with at least three years of language learning behind them and depend on good prior knowledge and a well-ordered classroom. While the skills of speaking, reading and writing may be involved during or after each task, listening is at the heart of them all.

Find out about your teacher

Level: Intermediate Mid to High (A2/B1). **Time:** 40 minutes.
Language focus: personal information present and past tenses.
Preparation: think through or write down your talk. If you write it you are more likely to be thorough in recycling your chosen structures and phrases.

Students are usually interested in teacher-told stories and like to hear about their personal lives. In this case the task is to complete a magazine feature or blog about the teacher by asking questions like a journalist.

Task:

1. Introduce the task and dictate some key language which the students can transcribe. This might include (depending on the level of the class):
   favourite pastimes   in the past   when I was young   my favourite holiday   I go to the cinema   my job   our house   I love my job   I got married   I went to university   my best friend

   Then reveal the language on the board and (optionally) get students to repeat chorally and individually.

2. Talk for between two and three minutes about yourself. Make sure you include the language you prepared earlier. Make the talk more engaging and accessible by displaying photos as you talk. These could be your own (best), or generic photos which support the meaning of your talk. Build in a good degree of repetition of frequent words and phrases, use your 'making language comprehensible' techniques, paraphrase, gesture and facial expression to make the talk as interesting as possible. One possible twist, by the way, is to warn the class that they have to find two deliberate factual errors you will make when talking. These can be as absurd and obvious, or as subtle as you want, depending on the class.

   As you talk students take notes in L1 or L2. Note-taking in L1 has the advantage that the task is strongly focused on meaning while using L2 encourages transcription and a greater focus on written accuracy.

   Give the talk a second or even third time. In pairs students compare the notes they have taken and begin to plan how they are going to report back in L2. Tell them they will have to use the second person of the verb when reporting (*You...*). This is, in fact, a rare opportunity to use this part of the verb, lessons being usually dominated by the first and third person. They may have questions for you at this stage. Help them with language and factual details.

3. A spokesperson from a pair reports back orally. Note their information on the board. At this stage students start to see a written version of your talk and they can adjust or add to their own notes. Elicit further information from other students and add it to the board. When you have all the information covered, summarise it again yourself quickly, then tell students they should read off information, putting it this time into the third person.

4. At this stage students should be ready to produce their final product, a written article about you. Perhaps you can find a way of sharing a photo with the class digitally for them to use. An alternative final product would be for the students to record from their notes a spoken report about you. This could be uploaded to a digital platform if you use one.

Notes

You may have noticed here that, although listening is the prime component of this task, it is used alongside the other three skills. In addition, by thoroughly preparing the task and building in a good deal of modelling, repetition and access to the written word you pre-empt error at the final product stage. Students hear repeated models of good spoken language, do some thinking about grammar and produce something they can be pleased with.

Complete a school plan

Level: Intermediate Mid (A2). **Time:** 40 minutes.
Language focus: school vocabulary, prepositions and prepositional phrases.
Preparation: this is would work well in the context of a unit of work about school. Provide students with a partially completed or empty overhead plan of a school. Include corridors, classrooms (with subject names), computer rooms, a gym, offices, cloakrooms, a dining hall, wash rooms, play area, sports field and swimming pool. Students could transcribe the limited information you give them.

Task:

1. Tell students you are going to describe the school to them as if they were a stranger. Students transcribe some key words and chunks, with a focus, in this case, on prepositions.
    *opposite the maths classroom   next to the gym   near the cloakroom   in the playground
    behind the car park   in front of the dining hall   at the other end of the building*
   Then display this language and provide some repetition work as in the previous example.

2. Describe the school to the class including the key language you have prepared. Use it repeatedly, using gesture where it might help (e.g. to denote classroom subjects). Students fill in their plans.

3. Students compare their grids in pairs and prepare how they are going to describe where each room or area is. Display key language on the board to scaffold the task.

4. Elicit oral descriptions of the school with true/false, correcting false statements or QA. This allows students to hear yet again examples of the language. As a final product, students have their completed plans, but you could easily extend the task having them record or write a description.

Notes

This task is easy to scaffold and adapt. With less proficient classes partially complete the plan before you start. With high-achieving students provide them with both a completed plan and an empty one. Explain that the school is going to be reorganised because of a number of problems (you can add as many more as you wish). Dictate them to the class:

- The English teacher is complaining that there is too much noise coming from the language classroom.
- The PE staff say the gym is too small.
- The IT staff say they need an extra room.
- The school has decided to stop teaching Latin.
- The smell from the toilets is coming through the head teacher's window.
- Fewer students are choosing to do history.
- The school has decided to introduce Chinese lessons.

The task then becomes an oral one as pairs of students redesign the school using language chunks you have primed them with, e.g. *we could, we ought to, it would be a great idea if, what if...*

Lecture notes

Level: Intermediate Mid to High (A2/B1). **Time:** 30 minutes.
Language focus: topic-specific vocabulary.
Preparation: in a way this is the simplest task to run, but one which mirrors a very real-life educational activity – taking notes from a lecture. It resembles Dictogloss, described in Chapter 6. This would work with a proficient intermediate class and simply involves choosing a topic of potential interest and delivering a lecture about it while students take notes: possible topics which would not require much low-frequency vocabulary might include: a famous actor, singer or band; an important issue such as the climate crisis, equality or racism; super-hero movies; private schooling.

Task:

1. Display a bilingual glossary of some words and chunks relating to the task. Ask the class what they think you are going to talk about.
2. Deliver the lecture, building in some repetition, pausing and paraphrasing. If facts and figures are involved, make sure you provide enough time and repetition for students to process and note the information. The lecture could be accompanied by slides and might even be on a topic of your own interest.
3. Alone or in pairs students can organise their notes or compare ideas in preparation for reporting back and producing a summary in L1.
4. Elicit information in L1, writing up useful language in L2 on the board for recycling purposes. Then students write a summary in L1 or, with highly proficient classes, in L2.

Notes

With the emphasis in classrooms often on interaction and fun, it may be forgotten how useful a simple 'listening to information' lesson can be. It is a task students are used to in many other lessons and, as we have observed, listening and note-taking is far from a passive activity. Just make sure the talk is highly comprehensible (with some scaffolding) and interesting! If you doubt your class's capacity for note-taking, you could supply gapped notes to complete.

Guest speaker

Level: Intermediate Mid to High (A2/B1). **Time:** 30-40 minutes.
Language focus: personal information.
Preparation: invite an L2 speaker to visit the classroom for a lesson. They could be a fellow L2-speaking teacher, foreign language assistant or L2 speaker from the local community. Give the speaker a list of questions you have prepared, suggesting the type of answers they might give and the level of language appropriate for the class. Brief them thoroughly by rehearsing the questions, in order to help the speaker pitch their language appropriately.

Task:

1. Introduce the visitor. Tell the class they are going to listen to them being interviewed and that they will be taking notes in L1. Some classes will cope with taking L2 notes. Supply a template for this if it seems helpful.
2. Ask the visitor a series of questions. Listen carefully to the answers, rephrasing any when necessary, asking for repetition or clarification. Write up any noteworthy language on the board. As this is happening, students take notes. Take between 15 to 20 minutes over this.
3. Alone or in pairs students then organise their notes or compare ideas in preparation for reporting back and producing a summary in L1. Students may wish to ask questions of their own.
4. Elicit information in L1 or L2, depending on the class, writing up more useful language in L2 on the board for recycling purposes. Then students write a summary in L2, making use of the language they heard and you wrote on the board.

Notes

Briefing the visitor beforehand is most important, especially if the visitor has little experience of working in schools. Be prepared to do plenty of paraphrasing, choosing language your students already know to maximise the amount of comprehensible input.

Talk about grandparents

Level: Intermediate Mid to High (A2/B1). **Time:** 40 minutes.

Language focus: imperfect tense, family, habitual actions in the past.

Preparation: This task, adapted from Willis (2008), has a personal angle to it. Tell the class that they are going to write or record a feature about their grandparents (or other elderly relatives or friends). This time there is something of a grammatical focus in so far as the imperfect ("used to") tense will be used a good deal. The task would make most sense done towards the end of a unit of work based on using the imperfect.

Task:

1. Dictate some words and chunks relating to the task. Focus on the imperfect tense, e.g.
    he used to live   he went to school in   there was no internet   she used to enjoy   ago
    they got married   he was in the army   she used to work in   they had two children

    Do choral and individual repetition. Display the vocabulary and get students to read it aloud from the board.

2. Talk to the class about your own grandparents, if possible, displaying any relevant photos. Authentic photos would add genuine interest in this case. As before, build in repetition and paraphrase. Consider the possibility of getting students to show if they are understanding as you proceed. Tip: you could ask them to show thumbs up for understanding, down for not understanding and level for 'kind of understanding'. Adjust your repetition and paraphrase accordingly. Students take notes as you talk. Talk through the material a second and even third time.

3. Alone or in pairs students can organise their notes or compare ideas in preparation for reporting back and producing their feature.

4. Elicit information, ensuring further recycling of language and memory-building. Write up some information or do a gap-fill task on the board; students expand their notes ready to write up or record a final product about their own grandparents. If students do not have anyone appropriate to refer to reassure them by saying they can refer to imaginary grandparents.

Notes

The final product in this task allows for more creativity on the part of students and potentially more error since they are not simply summarising the information covered in class. This should ensure a higher level of interest and commitment. Provide a frame for the class if you think they need it and strongly urge them to recycle the language used in class. A similar basis for a task like this would be to show the class a picture of yourself when you were young, perhaps with your primary (elementary) school classmates.

Make a recipe

Level: Intermediate Mid to High (A2/B1). **Time**: 30 minutes + time out of class.
Language focus: cooking vocabulary and imperative mood.
Preparation: This one takes some more preparation on your part. Find a short, clear and easy L2 recipe video from the internet. Prepare a rough transcript of the recipe instructions. Produce a gapped version of the same or a version with errors in.

Task:

1. Explain that the students are to watch and listen to a recipe and make the recipe themselves. Do some pre-listening work on key language. This would typically feature imperative forms of verbs and vocabulary such as:

    mix   pour   bake   roll   cut   place   boil   fry   put in the oven   cook for 10 minutes

2. Play the video right through, then in very short sections, pausing and repeating very frequently. (Tip: several replays of a very short chunk can produce a humorous effect.) Students complete their exercise.

3. Individually or in pairs students check their notes and prepare to feed back to you. As they do, write up some of the language produced. Then hand out your original complete transcription to read. Read it aloud and get students to do the same (perhaps with their fingers in their ears so that they can hear their own voice without being distracted by those nearby).

4. Students use the completed L2 recipe to make it at home at the earliest opportunity. If this is impossible you might enlist the help of the food tech department at school for some cross-curricular work. Finally, you can have a tasting in class.

Notes
Choose a simple recipe with ingredients most families will already have. Encourage the students to work with their families and not to cheat by using an L1 recipe of their own!

Map route

Level: Novice High to Intermediate Mid (A1/A2). **Time**: 30 minutes.
Language focus: giving directions.
Preparation: This is adapted from Rost (2015). Make copies of a simple town map with a number of details - simple landmarks, shops, bridges, rivers and so on. On individual cards or slips of paper write the name of several destinations locatable on the map, but not explicitly labelled, e.g. the post-office or fast food restaurant. On other slips of paper write various starting points.

Task:

1. Explain the task in L1 or L2. Give each student a map and two piles of cards, one with destinations, one with starting-points. It is assumed that students have already done practice on giving directions. This task would best be done later in the teaching sequence, or for later review.
2. Students work in pairs choosing various starting points and destinations from their cards. Demonstrate the procedure from the front with a chosen student. Students should alternate between the direction giver and listener.

   Student A: *I'm going to tell you how to get to the post-office. What's your starting point?* Student B chooses a starting point from the pile of starting point cards. Student A gives directions. *Turn left, take the second on the right near the swimming pool*, etc. Student B may ask for clarifications: *Can you repeat please?*

3. Listen back to two or three model dialogues.
4. As a follow-up activity you could ask students what clarification questions they used. Alternatively, with a less proficient class you could supply this before the task begins.

Notes

This task can run as long as you want it to. Quicker students will get through more examples. The task has the advantage of providing very structured, repeated language at a simple level.

Ask and move

This is adapted from Nation and Newton (2009).

Level: Intermediate Mid to High (A2/B1). **Time**: 30 minutes.
Language focus: any.
Preparation: write and print off five short paragraphs on a chosen topic, say, Berlin. Together these five paragraphs form a general description of the city. Secondly, write and print off ten to twelve questions about the topic, e.g. *What is the population of Berlin? What are the most popular places to visit? What is the weather like in winter?* and so on.

Task:

1. Explain the activity in L1. Five volunteers are 'experts' on Berlin. Each expert has one of the five paragraphs you prepared. The remainder of the class works in pairs, with each pair having a set of questions. One partner is a scribe, the other a seeker of information from the experts. The seekers have to obtain answers to their questions from the five experts, then report back to their scribe who notes them down.

2. Monitor as students move around seeking answers to their questions and reporting back to their scribes. It will be a busy and noisy classroom!
3. The pairs discuss the written notes and prepare to feed back. The five experts can join in with various pairs to help.
4. Students write up a description of Berlin using their notes to help. Recall that the experts each only have one part of the information needed.

Notes

You can vary the number of experts or do the task without scribes, but in the latter case your experts may be overrun with questioners if the class is big!

Detectives and informants

This task is similar in format to the previous one, *Ask and move*.

Level: Novice Mid to Intermediate Mid (A1/A2). **Time**: 20 minutes.
Language focus: personal information and family.
Preparation: write five short paragraphs, each of which provides some (but not all) information about a person. When combined, the five paragraphs describe that person. Include name, age, family, likes and dislikes, pastimes, favourite school subjects, family and friends. Hand out a copy of each paragraph to five students ('informants') in the class. To the remaining students ('detectives') hand out the same set of questions to ask, e.g. *What is her name? Does she have brothers and sisters? What are her favourite hobbies? What is her favourite subject?* Make sure the questions correspond to the information contained in the five paragraphs. If necessary, rehearse the pronunciation of the questions.

Pre-listening: explain that detectives have to find all the information they can about the subject and that they can ask the five informants. The detectives should keep a careful note of the answers. You could supply a grid for this purpose.

Task: having placed the five informants strategically around the room, allow the rest of the class to move around, asking them questions. Groups are bound to form around each informant; this is fine as long as everyone is listening. Detectives take notes, preferably in L2. Ensure that they are not just copying from the informants' written texts!

Post-listening: elicit information from the detectives, writing up language on the board which students can copy. This can be the basis of a written composition as a final product.

House buyer

This exploits the narrow listening principle effectively, but through a communicative task.

Level: Novice Mid (A1). **Time**: 20 minutes.
Language focus: house and home vocabulary.
Preparation: write four short paragraphs about a house, including its location and details such as rooms, garden, garage and so on. Each text should share details in common, but have differences in detail, such as *near the railway station, near the hospital, near a school.* Secondly, write in L1 a list of criteria for a potential house buyer. Make sure that one of the four descriptions matches the criteria best.

Pre-listening: explain that the students are going to look at a house for sale. The estate agent is phoning them to give details of four good-looking prospects which might be of interest. Students have to listen to the descriptions and decide which house fits their criteria best. For pairs or small groups provide a list of criteria (in L1, possibly L2) by which students will make a choice of the four houses. Criteria might be *near the shops, large garden, three bedrooms.*

Task: read each of the four texts twice, while students tick off items they hear which correspond to their criteria. When this is complete, students share their answers in preparation for feeding back.

Post-listening: ask students which house they chose, 1, 2, 3 or 4 and why. Students can respond in L1, or better L2 (depending on the class). Write up examples of chunks on the board. Give them the best answer. As a follow-up try a gapped dictation or translation task based on the language you have been using.

The two detectives

Level: Intermediate Mid to High (A2/B1). **Time:** 20 minutes.
Language focus: past tenses, tense manipulation, describing people and actions; seeking clarification during dialogue.
Preparation: students work in pairs. They are each a detective following a suspect in a drugs case. They are working different shifts so have to share their own information over the phone. Provide each partner with some notes they have taken while observing the suspect at different times. Students will also need paper or empty grids to jot down what they hear (see **Figure 7.1).**

1. Explain the task in L1 or L2. Display a few useful verb forms in the perfect (preterite) tense. Point out that students will need to alter the present tense verbs in their notes to the perfect tense. Model questions which partners can use when seeking clarifications: *Can you repeat that please? Did you say...? What colour was...? At what time did...?*

2. Monitor the pairs at work, giving help when requested.
3. Students compare their notes and make any corrections as required.
4. Selected students report back to you. At this stage you can provide corrections and recasts to focus a little on accuracy. Some classes may then want to produce in pairs, or write down a full account of the day's observations and even come up with an explanation of the events. What crime was this man involved in? Or is there an innocent explanation?

Notes

This task is really 50% speaking, 50% listening, but is a fine example of a meaningful, information-gap task which provides all sorts of language learning opportunities: speaking in short sentences and in longer chunks, hearing repeated uses of high frequency language, linking reading with speaking, listening and writing. In addition, students have to meet the challenge of reacting appropriately to information, responding quickly and with appropriate further questions to keep the conversation going. You might like to include props, e.g. hats and phones, or have the students sit back to back.

Table 7.2 Role-play cards for *The two detectives*

	Detective A		Detective B
9.00	Suspect leaves home, wearing suit and tie; gets in car (Ford Focus, blue, reg AZD2192)	16.00	Suspect leaves golf club at high speed; followed
9.30	Followed suspect by car; suspect enters office opposite HSBC bank; goes up to second floor	17.15	Suspect arrives at motorway service area; meets second man (tall, dark, bearded, jeans and sweat shirt); package exchanged
10.10	Leaves office, looks left and right to check if followed; walks down street	17.45	Suspect followed back to his home; opens garage door; takes package from the garage; returns to car
11.40	Followed suspect on foot from 50 metres; suspect buys a burger and drink; eats in McDonalds	18.20	Followed suspect to Italian restaurant (Luigi's, next to cinema); suspect meets a woman (blonde, long hair, sunglasses)
12.00	Suspect leaves; returns to car; suspect makes a phone call	20.10	Waited opposite restaurant; nothing happens
13.15	Followed by car; suspect goes to golf club car park; picks up a small package left behind a bush; leaves	21.30	Eventually entered restaurant; suspect and woman no longer there; notice exit to rear
14.35	Still at golf club; Suspect makes long phone call in his car; looks anxious; smokes a cigarette	23.05	Waited at suspect's home; no sign of suspect

Plan a holiday

Level: Intermediate Mid to High (A2/B1). **Time:** 30 minutes.
Language focus: describing places and giving opinions.
Preparation: this is an example of a listening task whereby, in small groups, each partner listens to a different source before combining their information to achieve a task. The task here is to decide which destination to choose for a holiday together. Prepare three or four separate recordings of holiday destinations. Each recording should last about 90 seconds and be made available digitally for use on devices or in a computer room, for example. Information about the holiday destinations can be made up or adapted from an authentic reading source such as Tripadvisor. An example might look like this:

> *We spent two weeks on a campsite near the Tarn gorges in the south of France. The campsite was amazing. It had a huge heated pool with slides, a games area for children, a takeaway pizza restaurant and a shop where you could get pretty much everything you needed. The mobile homes are a bit old and could do with air conditioning as the weather gets hot in this area. I'd also say that it's a bit noisy for families, so may suit families with older children. It's definitely not a place for those who like peace and quiet. Also, there's a lot to do in the area: canoeing, rafting, walking and sightseeing. There are quite a few castles not far away.*

In addition, each group member should be given a list of things they are looking for when they go on holiday, e.g. name, age, preferred activities, previous holiday experiences. You can make this a little unusual and amusing. Each group member should keep the list to themselves. This is needed for the discussion following the listening.

Task:

1. Explain the task. Display and run through key language if necessary.
2. Students listen to their recording and make notes in L2 if possible. This has the advantage of providing some transcription practice. Allow about 15 minutes for this. In their small groups each student reads out, using their notes, what they have learned about the destination they were listening to. There then follows a short discussion, following which the group agrees on a favourite place. Each group member should bear in mind their own character's notes. Scaffold this part by displaying possible discussion questions or opinion phrases on the board.
3. Elicit feedback from the group and find out which destination was most popular. Recycle common language chunks as far as possible.
4. A follow-up task could be to provide a set of written user comments about holiday destinations, in which you recycle language from the listening task. These could be accompanied by various exercises, including matching, true/false, translation and gap-fill.

Opinion survey

Level: Novice Mid (A1). **Time:** 40 minutes.
Language focus: expressing likes and dislikes
Preparation: prepare a simple grid for each student with a list of school subjects down the left-hand side and spaces to mark ticks alongside. Alternatively students can work with a piece of blank paper with you dictating the subject names to them for extra transcription practice.

Task:

1. Explain the task in L1 or L2. The aim is to find out which school subject the class likes the most.
2. Students walk around the room interviewing their peers, asking the question *What subjects do you prefer?* Students answer by naming their three favourite subjects. (Choosing three rather than one will tend to avoid very one-sided results, e.g. towards a particularly popular teacher or subject.) Monitor so that students remain in L2.
3. Students then work individually making a tally of the number of responses for each subject. Elicit some results from a selection of students, jotting down the summaries on the board while giving a commentary. Arrive at a 'top three'. Avoid focusing on subjects which may appear to be very unpopular; a degree of discretion is needed.
4. Students could create an Excel spreadsheet and graph to depict their results.

Notes
The principle behind this task can be applied to a number of other topics, e.g. favourite pastimes, pets and foods. At higher levels the topics can become more sophisticated, e.g. weekend activities, holidays, environmental actions or future plans. Students enjoy the freedom of wandering around the class and interacting.

Choose a hotel

Level: Intermediate Mid (A2). **Time:** 30 minutes.
Language focus: modal verb (*you can*).
Preparation: Produce a sheet with six short paragraphs describing hotels, Tripadvisor-style. (You could do the same for holiday homes or campsites, for example.) Flood the written input with the structure *you can*.

Task:

1. Explain that you are going to read aloud, and have them read aloud, the six paragraphs. Then they have to, in small groups, choose a hotel they can agree to stay at. Display some useful language they can use in their discussion.
    you can play   there is   there isn't   I agree   I don't agree   in my opinion   I think that

2. Read aloud, do some choral repetition and paired reading aloud so that students are ready to begin their conversation. Then the groups begin their conversation as you monitor and keep them on track.
3. Students give feedback their chosen hotel with reasons. *We chose... because there is... you can... and you can...*, etc. Interact with them to question their choice.
4. Students write their own descriptions of a hotel recycling the language they have been using. This could also be recorded.

Notes
You can complicate the task by giving each student a character role card which indicates what their preferences are. Students in higher-attaining classes could also go and research hotels on a website you choose for them, summarising in writing what they find out.

Which restaurant?

Level: Novice High to Intermediate Mid (A1/A2). **Time:** 20 minutes.
Language focus: food and drink.
Preparation: write three descriptions of imaginary visits to restaurants. Give a name to each restaurant, mention the general type of food, the atmosphere, the quality of service, price and, most importantly, a detailed account of each course and what you thought of it.

Task:

1. Tell the class they will hear three accounts of restaurant experiences. They must decide, based on their own tastes, which restaurant they would like to go to and why.
2. Read aloud each description twice, allowing students time to take notes in L1.
3. Allow time for students to compare their notes and decision, clarifying any points. Ask students in L2 which restaurant they preferred and why.
4. Students could do a number of follow-up tasks, e.g. write a description of a restaurant and a meal they had or complete a gapped transcription of one of your descriptions. Provide any support as appropriate.

Notes
Similar to the *Choose a* hotel task, this one could also be adapted to other scenarios, e.g. choosing between campsites, theme parks, holidays or shopping malls.

Video conversation

Level: Intermediate Mid to High (A2/B1). **Time:** 30 minutes.
Language focus: various.
Preparation: this requires some careful setting-up and access to the necessary technology. All that may be needed is the student's phone and a list of online addresses. As you read this, other platforms may be in more common use. If you can make this work it will no doubt be an extremely useful and motivational task. Establish a link with another school in the L2 country or take advantage of an existing one. Prepare a set of L2 questions which could be asked to a new acquaintance. These could be worked on collaboratively in class. Agree with your colleague in the other country to do the same. Using mobile devices (or in a computer suite) put pairs of students in touch via Skype, Whatsapp or an alternative. Students could do this in class or in their own time, perhaps with parental permission. Practical issues may make it hard to do this during the school day, so it may be preferable to have students work at home. If the organisation is too cumbersome for a large class, small groups of students could take part at different points in the year.

Task:

1. Lay out the task and its aims: to listen to a native speaker, engage in some conversation and learn a little about the L2 culture.
2. The pairs of students converse for however long is required. They take notes in a mixture of L1 and L2 which can be later used as the basis for a summary of answers, either in individual sentence form or as a lengthier account.
3. In class students can share responses by reading them to each other. They can be collected in to allow for some feedback.
4. This type of task is bound to lead to some healthy follow-up discussion, with students keen to share their experiences.

Talk show

Level: Intermediate Mid to High (A2/B1). **Time:** 40 minutes + write-up time.
Language focus: personal information likes and dislikes, personal experiences.
Preparation: invite a 'guest' into the classroom, e.g. a foreign language assistant, another teacher, older student with good L2 skills or invited L2 speaker. Provide them in advance with a list of about ten questions which they should prepare answers for. Make sure they are briefed about the linguistic level of your class andthe range of language they should use. Advise them about pace of delivery and clarity. The questions could include:

- *Tell us about your family.*
- *Tell us about your home town.*
- *What do you do in your spare time?*
- *What foods do you like and dislike?*
- *What TV programmes do you watch?*

Task:
1. Tell the class that their task will be to listen to the interview, take notes (in L1 or L2), ask further questions, then write a blog feature about the guest. Introduce the guest.
2. Conduct the interview in front of the class. Repeat and clarify answers to give students time for note-taking and to make use of language you know they have already encountered. Ask supplementary questions if needed. Write up key words and phrases, or whole sentences with gaps. Take about 30 minutes over this.
3. Allow time for students to compare their notes and clarify any points. Elicit answers, writing up partial information which students can copy. The amount of scaffolding you use at this point depends on the class's skills.
4. Students write up their feature either digitally or in their exercise books. This write-up could be a template for another similar feature they could write about a chosen celebrity.

Notes

This task can be simplified enough for a beginner class. With the guest's permission the students could take a picture of them for their feature. As in other examples of listening, one advantage of this task is that students are naturally interested in learning about other people, so have a good reason to listen. If you cannot get a speaker to come in to the classroom, consider the possibility of an online interview, either live or pre-recorded.

What's the story?

Level: Intermediate Mid to High (A2/B1). **Time:** 40 minutes.
Language focus: narrative and descriptive.
Preparation: prepare two similar narrative passages, each of which contains some illogical or meaningless elements. The aim of the task is for each pair to work out between them what the correct final version of their story should be. Below are two extracts which give you an idea of how this works.

Partner A's version
David Jones was a young man aged 80. He lived in a small village called Berlin, the capital of Australia. One day he decided to go for a walk with his new pet, a tiny elephant called Marmite. As David was walking along the street he bumped into an old friend of his called Marmite. "Hello!" said David. "Nice to see you again! What will you get up to in the future?" After dancing for five minutes, David went on his way...

Partner B's version
David Jones was an old man aged 20. He lived in a huge village called Berlin, the capital of Spain. One day he decided to go for a walk on his bicycle with his new pet, a small dog called Branston. As David was skateboarding along the street he bumped into an old friend of his called Anne. "Goodbye!" shouted Branston. "Terrible to see you again! What have you been doing this year?" After chatting for three hours, David stood there without moving.

Task:

1. Introduce the task and hand out the sheets. Explain that each partner can speak whenever they wish but that they must emerge with an agreed written version by the end.
2. Monitor the task, bearing in mind that there will be some L1 used as the pair negotiate their texts. Encourage each partner to ask for repetition and clarification. Under no circumstance should they look at their partner's text.
3. Listen back to one agreed final version. Other pairs may want to share their more absurd versions.
4. As a follow-up task you can dictate an acceptable version you have prepared for students to write.

Notes
Students generally like tasks with an absurd twist. You can include in your two texts as many or as few differences as you wish.

Recount an anecdote

Level: Intermediate Mid to High (A2/B1). **Time:** 30 minutes.
Language focus: describing a series of events in the past.
Preparation: This simple idea is adapted from Bilbrough (2011). Think of an anecdote from your past which you are happy to share with the class. Write up or display some chunks of language you will use to tell the story.

Task:

1. Write up or display some chunks of language you will use to tell the story. In the example below Steve recalls trying to buy some beef for a barbecue from a Spanish butcher's. The small village meat-purveyor had nothing on display so Steve had to ask for beef without knowing the Spanish word for beef. (This was in the days before mobile phones.) Steve raised his fingers above his head and tried to make the noise of a bull. The butcher retreated to his refrigerated back room and returned with a bag of meat cuts. On getting out the meat that evening Steve noticed that the 'beef' was not very red and tasted a bit more like pork. It

transpired that Steve's animal impression had been inadequate and he had in fact purchased....... goat. So here are some language chunks you could display in this case:

for a barbecue   decided to buy   didn't know the word   went to the butcher's
in a village near Seville   oh no!   when I ate the meat   what a surprise!
pretended to be   what a fool!

Give a moment or two for pairs to guess what the story could be about. Elicit some ideas.

2. Recount the story to the class. The students could take down notes in L1 or L2.

3. Ask the class to recount what happened in L1 as you write up key parts in L2. Before doing this, students could take turns in pairs making statements based on what they heard and noted.

4. Have students write out the events you described, using their notes. Alternatively, students could think of an anecdote from their own lives or the lives of a friend or parent. Keeping the language as simple as possible, they could draft their own account. An open-ended task like this is not easy to scaffold since the students' stories will be so varied, so use this option only if you are confident the class will cope.

Notes

This is another example of engaging students with an insight into the teacher's personal life, providing both language and content which is memorable.

3.   Other task-like activities

Although the examples below do not align with the Ellis and Willis definitions of a task, they are included here for convenience.

3.1   Flipping the listening

One of the best ways to get students to improve their listening is for them to do more of it in their own time. Research shows autonomous listening is vital for the fastest progress. (Just think how well students do after a family exchange or other immersion visit.) Independent listening needs to be monitored, however, since many students may not show the necessary autonomy! As Field (2008) points out one of the best ways to increase the time given to this critical skill is to set listening homework. Either collect your chosen published recordings digitally to be shared (respecting copyright) or select appropriate recordings or videos online. The best recordings are those which do not contain too much new language, but in any case you can scaffold tasks you set with templates, gap-fills and other comprehension or decoding activities.

Some highly motivated students may benefit from doing a weekly or fortnightly video listening task from the internet. At first it would be wise to specify what clips to use, but once the pattern is established students could make their own choices. To make sure the task is done, expect students to produce an outcome, e.g. an A4 sheet with an L1 summary of the content and a list of 15 new words or chunks they learned.

Check this over yourself very quickly (no need to correct or grade it), or get students to summarise orally to a partner or to the class what they heard. The site *lyricstraining.com (referred to in Chapter 9)* is popular with students and teachers; it features pop videos with gapped sub-titles to complete.

Intermediate-level students could also use audio recordings from the site *audio-lingua.eu* or videos from a commercial site such as *This is Language*. Ask students to translate, transcribe or summarise short recordings. Alternatively supply worksheets for completion with activities such as gap-fill, matching or *Spot the error*; in the latter case provide a faulty transcription to correct.

3.2 Using physical response tasks to develop listening skills

When students use bodily movements or gestures it is likely they will find the language associated with these actions more memorable. The term 'enactment effect' has been used to describe the fact that language instructions are memorised better if a learner performs the described action during learning, compared to just hearing the verbal information, or seeing someone else perform the action (Cohen, 1981). One approach is to tell a story which students have to act out physically.

Act out a story

1. Pre-teach some key words on the board and get classes to repeat. Do not reveal why you are doing this. Then tell the class to stand up and make sure they have a little room to work in. They have to act out what you describe in your story. The example below is in English and is taken from teacher Nick Bilborough who demonstrates it with an audience of teachers: https://www.youtube.com/watch?v=hZ5f66qn0kM&t=2876s

2. Students should all stand up. Narrate your account very slowly with exaggerated intonation: *I was walking through a forest.... I saw a box on the ground..... I picked it up.... I slowly opened the lid.... (shriek).... a bird flew out... and hit me in the face... I looked inside... wow!... it was full of treasure... I filled my pockets as fast as I could... oh no... someone was coming.... I turned around and ran...*

   If any students are confused by any information they can 'cheat' by copying others who understand. This is fine, it is part of the learning process.

3. Then repeat the activity, this time narrating more quickly. Then do a third narration, even more quickly. Fun should ensue!

4. Show a gapped transcription on the board. Your focus might be individual letters, word gaps or whole chunk gaps. Elicit answers from the class or have pairs work out gaps between them.

Note: It is a good idea to proceed from easier to harder gap-fills, providing less scaffolding at each stage. Finally, if all goes well, many students will be able to recount the story from memory. You could even do this as a choral task, providing students with starts of words or sentences, e.g. *I was wa... through a f... when I ... a box on the g.....*, etc. (See also *A walk through town* p. 83).

Other familiar body memory activities which enhance listening skills include:
- *Simon Says* - a twist on this is not just to touch parts of the body, but to get students to mime activities (*Jump three times! Cry! Play tennis! make a cup of tea!*);
- Direct a student around the class (*Turn left, turn left, stop!*);
- Sing *Alouette* in French while touching relevant parts of the body;
- Mime as the teacher describes their daily routine;
- Get students into a circle around you, say a word or phrase and the last person to do the action is out. This person then stands behind you and watches for the student who does the action last. Eventually there is only one student left, who is the winner.

Concluding remarks

To supplement the many micro-listening activities and interpersonal listening tasks described earlier in this book, task-based activities provide a great source of meaningful and motivational input. Some of the tasks described here are quite tightly controlled, notably at beginner level, others much looser in structure. Some may have the goal of practising specific grammar and vocabulary, while others allow students to develop their general language acquisition through experimentation, which in turn further develops listening ability. But let us not forget that your own attitude, expertise and enthusiasm affect students' motivation to a huge degree. Consider offering students some input into the setting of goals, e.g. by giving them a choice, presenting stimulating challenges and training them into using appropriate listening strategies.

Questions to consider

What advantages and disadvantages are there to communicative tasks?

What are the organisational challenges involved in running task-based lessons?

Where could tasks fit most suitably in your syllabus?

How much error correction would you do during communicative tasks?

In order to teach listening effectively, it is important for teachers to have a clear picture of the end behaviour they are aiming to achieve in their learners.

(John Field)

8

LAM IN ACTION: THREE SAMPLE TEACHING SEQUENCES

Introduction

Having provided some principles and tasks for a process-focused approach to listening, let us now see what the approach can look like in the classroom over a series of lessons. The lesson sequences in this chapter provide a template which can be used or adapted to your own contexts. They are by no means prescriptive, but assume that a structured approach to incorporating listening in your planning is a good idea.

The chapter contains a walk-through for three teaching sequences of lessons:

1. **Mixing skills**. This places LAM in the context of the lexicogrammar approach and demonstrates how listening can be integrated with the other three language skills of speaking, reading and writing, as you take a class from initial modelling to the final production stage.
2. **Narrow listening**. This demonstrates the use of narrow listening with highly comprehensible texts.
3. **Tougher texts**. This shows how you can teach texts containing more challenging input (e.g. authentic texts) of the sort students may encounter in high-stakes exams such as the GCSE in England and Wales or the International Baccalaureate.

Before presenting in detail the first sequence, a pedagogical framework is outlined which Gianfranco calls MARS-EARS, along with the principles underpinning the teaching of lexicogrammar.

LAM through lexicogrammar

MARS-EARS: a framework for planning a lexicogrammar curriculum

The MARS-EARS acronym refers to eight phases of a pedagogical cycle: *modelling, awareness-raising, receptive processing, structured production, expansion, autonomy, routinisation, spontaneity.*

This framework underpins the teaching of the building blocks of lexicogrammar, i.e. single words, lexical chunks and sentence patterns, moving from a presentational phase gradually towards spontaneous production. Rooted in cognitive theories of language acquisition and the view that classroom language learning is primarily about building communicative competence, it provides a principled and structured approach to short, medium and long-term planning.

Communicative functions

The starting point of the MARS-EARS approach is choosing the communicative goals we want students to achieve. Traditional Communicative Language Teaching (CLT) uses the notion of *Communicative Functions*, i.e. the purpose for our verbal and non-verbal communication. Examples of communicative functions are: *asking questions, describing people, apologising, making excuses, reporting an event in the past, talking about the way one used to be* (Finocchiaro and Brumfit, 1983). The choice of language structures and lexis is based on the principles of high-frequency, learnability and usefulness in real-life communication (see Chapter 4).

The communicative functions we choose can be broken down into sub-functions. The example in **Table 8.2** shows twelve functions and their sub-functions. These could form the basis of a curriculum of about two lessons a week over three years from beginner level. So for instance, the function *Describing and identifying people, including oneself*, is divided into the sub-functions *giving personal information, describing personality, describing physical appearance, expressing likes and dislikes,* etc.

A pedagogical cycle

Table 8.1 illustrates how the MARS-EARS cycle works. The full sequence could last six lessons or more, progressing from modelling and receptive practice to spontaneous production.

Table 8.1 The MARS-EARS pedagogical cycle

1. Modelling	Constructions, chunks and words are presented and modelled aurally using sentence builders displayed on the board. Read out L2 sentences drawn from the sentence builder which students translate into L1 on mini-whiteboards.
2. Awareness-raising	Raise students' awareness of any phonological, grammatical or syntactic issues you want them to notice (pop-up grammar).
3. Receptive processing	Students do LAM and RAM (Reading-as-Modelling) tasks containing 95-98% comprehensible input and input-flooding. The aim is for students to hear multiple occurrences of the target patterns in order to strengthen their receptive learning. Linger on this phase until you are satisfied that students have developed a solid receptive knowledge.
4. Structured production	The receptive knowledge acquired through listening and reading is now converted into productive knowledge through *pushed output*. This means using highly structured tasks which force students to produce orally and in writing every target lexical item multiple times. Such tasks can be (1) gamified pair work translation tasks; (2) picture tasks and any other tasks which elicit retrieval practice.
5. Expansion	Two things happen in this phase: (1) the target patterns/chunks are 'unpacked' in order to help students make sense of them. This resembles a typical grammar lesson, except that it occurs after students have already memorised the chunks and have become aware of the underlying grammar through exposure and use; (2) the chunks are practised with old and new vocabulary and structures over time through systematic recycling (interleaving).
6. Autonomy	The language is practised productively without scaffolding, but still in familiar contexts. This phase continues throughout the remainder of the year and through extensive recycling and interleaving.
7. Routinisation	The focus here is on automaticity, i.e. working on developing fast retrieval (both in the receptive and productive skills). This requires task repetition and performing tasks more and more quickly.
8. Spontaneity	Spontaneity development is about practice in unfamiliar contexts, i.e. requiring students to perform tasks with little or no preparation and in unfamiliar contexts.

Table 8.2 12 communicative functions and their sub-functions

Describing and identifying people, including oneself (providing personal data, describing appearance, describing personality, etc.)

Describing places, objects and natural phenomena (describing location, size, appearance, weather, etc.)

Creating questions (requesting factual information - including directions, making invitations, asking for an opinion, etc.)

Expressing one's feelings (expressing positive and negative emotions, reacting to events, providing reasons for one's emotions/reactions)

Making arrangements (making suggestions, inviting, accepting, refusing, etc.)

Comparing and contrasting (expressing likes and dislikes, supporting an opinion, explaining preferences, talking about the best and the worst of someone or something, etc.)

Describing routine behaviour in the present (talking about what one usually does, indicating time, expressing a purpose, etc.)

Describing routine behaviour in the past (talking about what one used to do, indicating time, expressing a purpose, etc.)

Describing past events (setting the scene, sequencing events, evaluating the consequences of actions and events, etc.)

Making plans for the future (indicating time, making predictions, hypothesising, discussing probabilities, etc.)

Indicating agreement and disagreement (expressing opinions on events and phenomena, explaining why, supporting an argument, providing examples)

Solving problems (describing the problem, providing solutions, discussing possible consequences, arguing for and against)

Table 8.3 lists six sub-functions for the function *Describing past events* alongside constructions chosen to match them. These would be suitable for students in their second year of study.

Table 8.3 Example of sub-functions and related lexicogrammar constructions

\multicolumn{2}{c}{**Describing past events**}	
Sub-function	**Construction**
Where I went	Time marker + pronoun / noun + *went to* + place
How I went there	*I went there by* + noun + *at* + time + *with* + noun
What I did there	Time marker + pronoun / noun + perfect tense + place
How it was	*It was* + adjective + causal connectives + noun + *was* + adjective
What I did afterwards	*After* + past infinitive + pronoun/noun + perfect tense
What the best and worst things were and why	*The best/worst thing was* + *the* + noun + causal connectives +....

You can see that curriculum planning is neither topic nor grammar-driven. Although the communicative functions and their associated language constructions are set within topic areas, the latter are chosen for their suitability for the teaching of the function. For instance, in the case of *Reporting events in the past*, you could choose the topics of *Talking about last weekend*, *Last year's holiday* or *What I did in school yesterday*.

The grammatical content of the curriculum also stems from the choice of communicative functions; you teach the grammar needed to enable students to manipulate the content of sentence builders creatively. What does this mean in practice? Having practised the construction 'Time marker + *I went to* + place + by + means of transport' (*Last weekend I went to London by train*) you may want students to be able to use the same construction with other persons of the verb, or in a different tense, or with a prepositional phrase other than '*by* + noun' (e.g. '*with* + noun'). In other words, the teaching of grammar serves a communicative goal and is driven by lexis.

This implies two things about the teaching of grammar.

1. The grammatical rules governing the chunks are taught *after* the lexical patterns and chunks have been practised through the four language skills.
2. Taking, for example, the teaching of the imperfect tense in Italian, Spanish or French, rather than presenting and practising all parts of the verb and their usages, you would focus exclusively on the rules which serve the acquisition of the construction you want students to acquire. In teaching the Spanish construction 'Time marker + *I* + *went* + *to* + *the* + noun. *I* + *liked it* + *because* + *it was* + adjective' (e.g. *Ayer fui al parque. Me gustó porque hacía buen tiempo*) you would only focus on using the imperfect to describe the weather.

From a student's perspective, the second approach makes the learning of a complex set of rules like the imperfect more relevant to real life, cognitively manageable and enjoyable.

Three teaching sequences

Described below are three sets of lessons and lesson sequences which show how this general approach could be applied. The first one is set within the MARS-EARS framework, the second follows the LAM model, being based on narrow listening texts, while the third lays out how you might go about tackling a harder text, one with less comprehensible language.

1. Teaching sequence 1

This detailed sequence would take eight or more one-hour lessons. The activities below will be explained in detail only if they have not been dealt with in previous chapters. First, a quick reminder of key principles.

1. **95-98 % comprehensible input**. Input should be understandable without resorting to external help.
2. **Input flooding**. Input is enriched with multiple repetition of patterns and chunks.
3. **Thorough processing tasks**. These force students to process each lexical item in detail.
4. **Extensive processing**. Texts are exploited at every level through a range of exercises.
5. **Readiness for output**. Students produce output only after language has been consolidated receptively.

Lesson 1: modelling through a sentence builder.

1. *Faulty echo* and any other phonological awareness activities described in Chapter 3 (e.g. *Spot the silent letter*, *Broken words*, etc.) can be used in order to focus on challenging sounds.
2. *Delayed repetition*. Display a model sentence from the sentence builder containing the challenging sounds. Say it aloud and ask the students to memorise it and hold it their heads for a few seconds. After 8-10 seconds ask them to say it.
3. *Mind-reading* (teacher-led). This is an opportunity to see (1) how students are coping with the pronunciation of the language you have just modelled and (2) which students need more monitoring than others.
4. **Interactive reading-aloud games.** Play two or three with a focus on decoding skills and pronunciation. These include *Mind-reading* (student-led version), *Sentence stealer*, *Find your match* and the *Algo game*.
5. *One pen one dice*. In pairs each partner has the same gapped L2-L1 translation. Partner A starts with the pen, partner B the dice. While the pen-holder starts their written task, the dice holder rolls the dice until they get a 6. When they do so, they use the pen while their partner gets the dice and starts rolling until it is their turn to write again. The winner is the student who finishes the translation first.
6. **Meaning and vocabulary-focused tasks on narrow reading texts**. These can be bad translation, gapped parallel texts, word hunt, 'Who, what, when, where', content re-ordering, etc.
7. **Interactive reading aloud games with a focus on meaning.**

Lesson 2: receptive processing - listening and reading

The sentence builder can be used by students as a scaffold throughout this phase.

1. ***Delayed translation.*** This is similar to *Delayed dictation*, but students translate into L1 instead of transcribing what the teacher says.
2. **Written sentence puzzles**. These are done, perhaps in pairs, as a prelude to the next activity.
3. ***Aural sentence puzzles.***
4. ***Oral ping-pong*** (from L1 to L2). Do as many rounds of this as time allows.
5. ***Running translation.***
6. ***Spot the missing detail.***
7. ***Spot the differences.***
8. ***Bad translation*** **on narrow listening texts**. Note that you can recycle the narrow reading texts used in the previous lesson, making minor alterations.
9. **Semi-structured survey** (see Chapter 7). Students carry out a simple survey of their friends based on the target language items.

Lesson 3: structured production - controlled speaking

1. ***One of three*** (listening). Read aloud three sentences only one of which is correct. Students must choose the correct version. This could be focused on lexical or parsing skills.
2. ***Listening slalom.***
3. ***Listen and recall.*** Recycle one or more of the narrow listening tasks used previously in the sequence, either in their original form or with slight alterations.
4. ***Oral ping pong* (L1 to L2).**
5. ***No snakes no ladders* (L1 to L2).**
6. **Communication drills.** These are mini role-play cards (**Table 8.4**) recycling the target grammar and lexis which students take turns in translating orally into L2. Note that students work in groups of three, two speakers and a listener/referee who has the full L2 translation of the cards.

Table 8.4 Communicative drill cards

Ejemplo	1	2
1. ¿Qué haces en tu tiempo libre? 2. Juego al tenis de vez en cuando y practico escalada una vez por semana.	1. What do you do in your free time? 2. I play football once a week and go to the cinema twice a week.	1. What do you do in your free time? 2. I go to the swimming pool three times a week and go horse riding once a week.
3	**4**	**5**
1. What do you do in your free time? 2. I go to the shopping mall from time to time, I play tennis and watch television.	1. What do you do in your free time? 2. I go to the gym every day and play on the computer.	1. What do you do in your free time? 2. I go to the gym every day and play on the computer from time to time.
6	**7**	**8**
1. What do you do in your free time? 2. I go to yoga club from time to time and I often play badminton.	1. What do you do in your free time? 2. I often go to the shopping mall and I go to the swimming pool from time to time.	1. What do you do in your free time? 2. I read every day, go to the swimming pool sometimes and I play tennis once a week.
9	**10**	**11**
1. What do you do in your free time? 2. I play on the computer every day and I sometimes play badminton.	1. What do you do in your free time? 2. I go to yoga club every week and I play football from time to time.	1. What do you do in your free time? 2. I go to the cinema once a week, go horse riding from time to time and I read every day.

Lesson 4: structured production - controlled writing

1. *Delayed dictation.*
2. *Quickfire translations* (L1 to L2).
3. *Jigsaw listening.*
4. *Dictocomp.*
5. *One pen one dice* **translation** (L1 to L2).
6. **Narrow translation.** This consists of three or more short L1 texts containing very similar chunks and patterns, the differences between them amounting to 10-15% per cent of the text (see **Figure 8.5**). So for instance, if text 1 contains the sentence *I live in a small town by the sea*, text 2 will contain the sentence *I live in a large town by a lake*, text 3 *I live in a small village by a river* and text 4 *I live in a tiny village in the countryside*. Narrow translation texts are short, even shorter when they are meant for classroom use rather than as homework assignments. Because the texts consist of chunks students have thoroughly practised beforehand, they complete them quite quickly and accurately, which gives them a sense of achievement.
7. **Short guided composition.** Students write a paragraph with as much scaffolding as needed.

Table 8.5 L1 to L2 narrow translation texts

Yesterday I went out with my best friends Marc and Alexis. First of all, we went to the shopping centre to have lunch. Then we went to the sports shop. I didn't buy anything, but Marc bought some expensive trainers and Alexis bought a very cool cap. After that, we went to the cinema to watch the latest Bond movie. The film was great, but very long. I loved the action scenes and the special effects (Karim).	Yesterday I went out with my best friends Laetitia and Marine. First of all, we went to the town centre around six to have dinner. Then we went shopping. I didn't buy anything, but Laetitia bought some expensive shoes and Marine bought a very beautiful dress. After that we went to the cinema to watch a romantic comedy. The film was quite boring, but I loved the music. After the movie, we went to our favourite café to have a drink (Suzanne).
Yesterday I went out with my best friends Denis and Mohamed. First of all, we went to the shopping centre around four to have a meal. Then we went shopping. I bought a T-shirt, Denis bought a pair of jeans and Mohamed bought a pair of trainers. After that, we went to the cinema to watch an action movie. The film was exciting and I loved the special effects. After the movie, we went to a restaurant to have dinner (Manu).	Yesterday I went out with my best friends Luc and Sandrine. First of all, we went to the stadium around six to watch our favourite team. Then we went to a restaurant to have dinner. I ate a hamburger, but Luc and Sandrine ate fries and ice-cream. After that we went to Starbucks to have coffee and chat. The coffee shop was crowded and there was too much noise, but we had fun. After that, we went for a walk in the town centre (Victor).

Lesson 5: expansion - explicit work on grammar and generative processing

It is now time to teach students how to expand the generative power of the language patterns. How this phase unfolds and how many lessons it takes depends on the grammar point. For instance, if you want to practise conjugation of a key verb practised so far in only the first person singular, you may need more than one lesson, as you have to provide practice in using that pattern with all the other persons. On the other hand, if your objective is the use of the partitive article (e.g. *du*, *de la* and *des* in French), one lesson may be enough, as the previous phases will have already provided enough receptive and productive practice.

1. *Listen and change*. Make sure to include the mistakes students have typically been making.
2. *Spot the error* (reading).
3. *Spot the error* (listening).
4. **Deductive or inductive teaching of grammar**. This could involve simply working out a rule through a guided-discovery process or teaching new knowledge aimed at expanding the potential of the chunk (e.g. using the pattern with a different person of the main verb or in a different tense).
5. **A mixture of grammar drills through all four skills.** Oral translation games, sentence puzzles, partial dictations, sorting tasks, grammaticality judgment tasks, gap-fills, etc.
6. **Highly-structured and semi-structured role plays.** These can recycle the use of the structures.
7. *Quickfire translation* (L2 to L1 and L1 to L2).

Lesson 6: routinisation – working towards automaticity

By this this stage students should have solid productive knowledge of the target grammatical or lexical structure(s), i.e. they can use them in spoken and/or written ouput without any support, even though they may hesitate, back-track and self-correct. Try any or all of these ideas.

1. *Quickfire translations*.
2. **Fast and furious.** Students work in groups of three: a referee and two players. The players are given a text with gaps for the structures being focused on. Each gap has the L1 translation in brackets alongside or another cue to the missing item. The players take turns reading out the text as fast as they can, filling the gaps with the correct language forms, trying to outperform their opponent in speed and accuracy. The referee, who has the full text with answers, times the players and provides them with feedback.
3. **Fluency cards** (see **Figure 8.1**). Divide the class into speakers and listeners. The latter are given an answer sheet. The speakers quickly translate the images into a narrative following the order on the card. They do this three or four times, each time with a different listener who notes down their time and feeds back on any major omission or mistake. The aim is for the speaker to increase their speed of delivery and accuracy from time 1 to 4.

Figure 8.1 Fluency card on talking about a past holiday (Image: Pixabay)

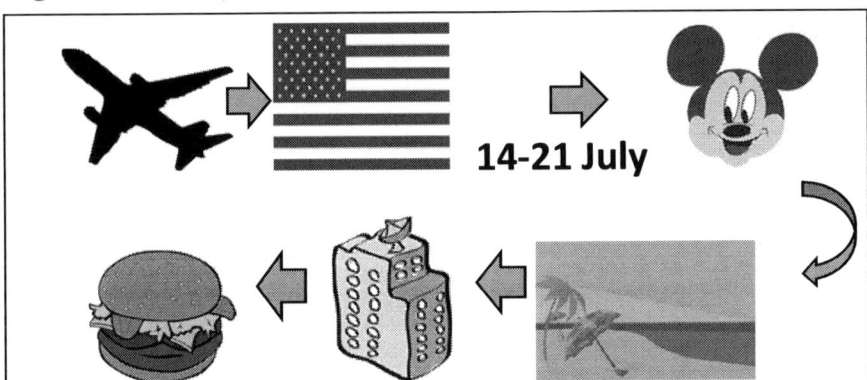

4. **Pyramid translation.** Students work in threes, two players and a referee. Give them a sheet with ten L1 sentences arranged in the form of a pyramid, the sentence at the top being very short and basic in structure, with every other sentence below gradually longer and more complex. As shown in **Figure 8.2**, each sentence contains the previous one plus one or more extra items. Taking turns, the two players, starting from the top, translate each sentence, working their way down the pyramid to a time limit. When a mistake is made, the other player has a go (starting from the top). Whenever a player resumes their turn, they have to start again from the top. Whoever completes the whole translation in the time set without making mistakes is the winner. The role of the referee is to judge when mistakes are made.

Figure 8.2 Pyramid translation

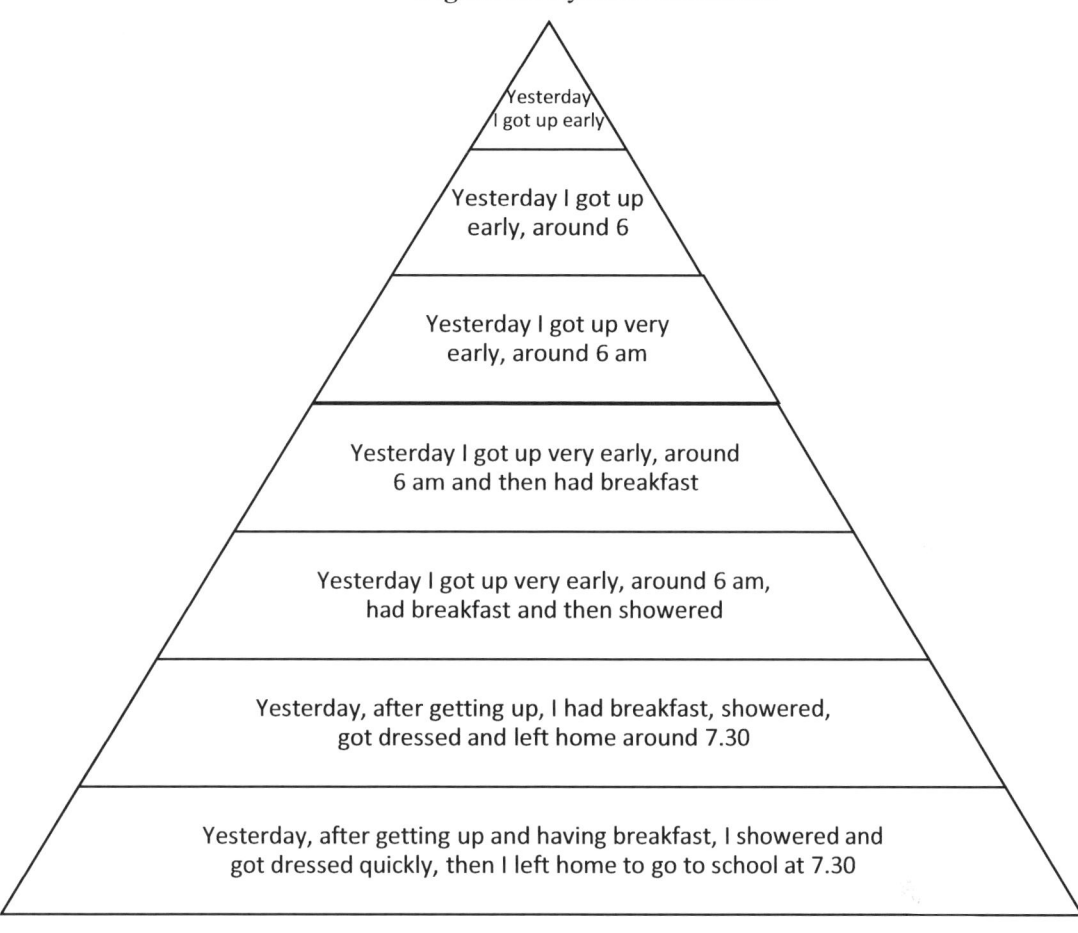

5. **4,3,2 technique**. This is for confident intermediate students working in pairs. Give them a few minutes to prepare a four minute talk on a specific event or topic. (Note: they are not allowed to write anything down). They then deliver the talk to another student in the four minutes originally allocated. Then ask them to give the talk to another student in three minutes, then to another in two minutes. If four minutes is too long to start with, adjust timings to suit the class.

6. **Market place.** Divide students into buyers and sellers. Tell the sellers what they are going to sell (e.g. a car, a house or computer game) and the points they have to include in their sales pitch. Give them time to prepare for the task, while the buyers are given receptive practice in the sort of vocabulary they are likely to hear from the sellers. Give each seller a stall (a table) and the buyers circulate around the marketplace going from seller to seller, listening to the sales talks and jotting down the main points. Buyers report back on which seller they preferred.

7. **Guided composition to a time limit.** Give students a set time to write a short guided composition on the topics and structures practised so far. Make sure that the time given forces them to write faster than usual.

Lesson 7-8: autonomy and spontaneity - semi-structured and unstructured tasks

Students do activities where they mix the language learned so far with previously learned material. These could include interpersonal tasks described in Chapters 6 and 7. Both receptive and productive work at this stage might require students to go slightly beyond their current level of competence, processing and using vocabulary and structures they do not know or have not fully acquired. In carrying out these listening-centred tasks students develop more independence and spontaneity in their language production.

> **INFOBOX 20 Narrow listening**
>
> This term was coined by Krashen (1996) who originally envisaged students obtaining a series of authentic native-speaker recordings on a similar topic. He argued that repeated listening to topics of interest would provide useful comprehensible input which would lead to acquisition. He suggested the same process could also work with reading texts. We are using the term rather differently in the sense that the short listening texts are teacher-written and extremely close in linguistic content, with only a few differences between them. The idea is that by listening to near-identical material numerous times, greater noticing of detail will result in deeper processing.

2. Teaching sequence 2

Exploiting narrow listening texts via thorough and extensive processing

The main rationale for using narrow listening (NL) and narrow reading (NR) texts is that they allow you to flood the input, not just with words, but with chunks and complex sentence patterns (e.g. main clause + one or more subordinates). NL and NR fit well with a lexicogrammar approach, allowing students to encounter target lexis many times over, especially at the early stages of their learning.

NL texts, highly repetitive in their structure (**Table 8.6**), also allow you to interleave target sentences with different vocabulary items. This can be an advantage when compared with exploiting a single text in multiple ways, as is common practice. Beginner-to-intermediate NL texts typically have very high comprehensible input, interleaving the new lexicogrammar with highly familiar items.

Table 8.6 Spanish narrow listening / reading texts

Julio	Marina
En mi tiempo libre hago mucho deporte. Juego al baloncesto tres veces por semana, levanto pesas todos los días y nado el sábado y el domingo. Mi deporte preferido es el baloncesto porque es apasionante y competitivo. Además, lo hago con mis amigos, por lo tanto, es muy divertido. A parte del deporte, leo libros y tebeos, veo la tele, y descargo videos y canciones de internet. También me gusta ver películas de acción e ir de marcha con mis amigos el viernes y el sábado por la noche.	En mi tiempo libre hago mucho deporte. Juego al fútbol cuatro veces por semana, practico escalada casi todos los días y hago footing el sábado y domingo. Mi deporte preferido es el fútbol porque es apasionante y divertido. EL deporte que no me gusta es el cricket porque es aburridísimo. A parte del deporte, navego por internet, escucho música y juego al ajedrez. También me gusta ver películas policiacas e ir de marcha con mis amigos el sábado por la noche.
Miguel	**Marta**
En mi tiempo libre no hago mucho deporte. Levanto pesas dos días por semana y nado el sábado. Mi deporte preferido es la equitación, pero no la practico casi nunca. A parte del deporte, me gusta escuchar música, ir al centro comercial y navegar por internet. También me gusta ver películas cómicas y salir con mis amigos. Por lo general vamos al cine o miramos escaparates en el centro comercial cerca de mi escuela.	En mi tiempo libre hago mucho deporte. Levanto pesas cuatro veces por semana y escaló el sábado. Además, juego al baloncesto en el instituto todos los días con mis amigas. Es muy divertido y apasionante, pero muy agotador también. A parte del deporte, me gusta leer tebeos, ir al centro comercial y chatear por internet. También me gusta ver películas de amor y salir con mis amigas. Por lo general vamos al restaurante de comida rápida o miramos escaparates en el centro comercial cerca de mi casa.

Below is an example of a three-part approach to the exploitation of narrow listening texts where students (1) are prepared linguistically for the texts through a series of exercises; (2) do extensive processing of the texts; (3) consolidate the language through speaking and/or writing.

Pre task(s)

Reading pre-tasks

It has been said that reading exists in space, whereas listening exists in time (Field, 2008). In other words, whilst listening input is fleeting in nature (you hear it, then it is gone), reading matter exists on the page or screen, allowing students to go back to items they do not immediately understand, or use the whole text to make sense of them. To support listening, therefore, one of the best pre-tasks for an NL-based sequence is a series of quick, engaging activities on a set of very similar narrow reading (NR) texts. You can alternate pair-work and individual tasks with whole-class activities to keep up variety and pace.

Example pre narrow listening (NL) tasks

For each example, we indicate in brackets which micro-skill is developed.

- **Vocabulary hunt. Find the French/German/Spanish.** (Processing of words and chunks.) Provide L1 chunks. Students locate and write alongside them their L2 equivalents. Focus on the key patterns, e.g, if using the NL texts in **Table 8.6,** include, in random order: *in my free time, every day, I also like* + verb, *he is, my favourite sport is, because* + clause, etc.
- **Gapped parallel L2 text.** (Processing of words and chunks.) The L1 and L2 versions of one of the NR texts is gapped at key points. Gap whole chunks in order to reinforce the patterns focused on in the previous task, or single words used with those patterns. To increase the challenge, do not provide the blanks, but say that X number of words are missing. Students identify and insert them in L1.
- *Categories.* (Semantic schemata activation, word recognition.) These can refer to parts of speech and/or semantic fields (e.g. family members, hobbies, problems). Students locate L2 words in the NR texts and sort them into those categories, along with their L1 translation.
- *Bad translation.* (Word recognition, meaning building). Give students L1 and L2 versions of a NR text and tell them there are 10 mistakes in the L2 versions which they must identify and correct.
- *Spot the pattern.* (Syntactic processing.) Write two or three key patterns on the board, e.g. *I do/I don't do, apart from, I also like,* and ask students to identify and translate as many as possible in a given amount of time.
- *Jigsaw reading.* (Discourse processing.) Students have to reorder sentences.
- *Content re-ordering.* (Discourse processing.) Students reorder paragraphs.
- *Shadow reading.* (Decoding skills.) Put a text on the classroom screen and read it aloud while the students whisper after you.
- **Traditional reading aloud tasks.** (Decoding skills.) To ensure sustained attention do *Listen-stop-carry on* where you start reading a text then suddenly stop and ask a student to continue where you left off.

Pre-listening tasks

These can be done before a NL sequence and usually involve aural practice with chunks or sentences contained in the texts.

- *Delayed dictation.* (Dual graphological-phonological processing.)
- *Delayed repetition.* (Phonological processing, pronunciation/decoding skills.)
- **L2 to L1 oral ping pong.** (Vocabulary recognition.)
- **Aural L2 to L1** *No snakes, no ladders.* (Vocabulary recognition).
- *Spot the error.* (Parsing.)
- *One of three.* (Vocabulary recognition.) Say three words and student must identify which is correct.
- *Listening slalom.* (Vocabulary recognition.)

- **Aural semantic processing tasks.** (Vocabulary recognition, semantic schema activation.) These include *Odd-one-out*, *Near-synonyms* and sorting activities.
- **Aural sentence puzzles.** (Parsing.)
- **Either…or…** (Parsing.)

While-listening tasks (done as students are listening to a text)

Although the activities below are arranged in chronological order, you can sequence them differently depending on your focus at the time.

1. *Spot the intruder*. (Phonological and graphological processing.)
2. *Partial dictation*. (Phonological and graphological processing, segmenting.)
3. **L1 gapped parallel text**. (Vocabulary recognition.): Students listen and fill gaps.
4. *Jigsaw listening*. (Discourse building.)
5. **Note-taking.** (Meaning building.) Students note down in L1 as many details as they can.
6. **Comprehension**. (Meaning building, discourse building, selective attention.) A classic listening comprehension task.
7. *Syllable completion task*. (Syllable processing.)
8. *Dictogloss or dictocomp*. (All levels of aural processing.)

Post-listening tasks

1. **Gapped L2 text(s)**. Students fill gaps in a text similar to the NL ones. A parallel L1 text may be provided alongside.
2. **L1 to L2 narrow translation.** Using a text similar to the narrow listening ones
3. **Short guided composition**. Designed to elicit content and structures similar to the ones in the NL texts.

3. Teaching sequence 3

Dealing with a less comprehensible text

In text books and when taking exams students frequently have to cope with aural texts which contain below 95% comprehensible vocabulary. In this sequence we describe how a more difficult text of this type could be approached. The teacher-written text in **Figure 8.3** would be appropriate for a class with a minimum of three years of learning. The speaker is describing a film they have seen. Potentially unfamiliar words are marked in bold, but bear in mind that in any class, the degree of comprehensibility depends on individual knowledge and proficiency.

Figure 8.3 Source text for sequence 3: film review

> I watched a great movie last weekend at the new cinema which **has just opened** in the shopping mall. It's called Lion.
>
> The story is **amazing** and it's **absolutely** true. It's about a very **poor** young Indian boy, Saroo, who gets on a train **alone by mistake**. He travels far across India, but can't **find** his mother and brother. He's **picked up** by the police and ends up in an **orphanage** with many other **lost** children.
>
> An Australian **couple agrees to take care of** this little boy. So Saroo goes to live in Australia with his new parents and another Indian **orphan**. When Saroo is an adult he **decides to try** to find his mother and brother in India. He **uses** Google Earth and, after a long **search**, he **manages to identify** the small village where he **was born**.
>
> So at **about** the age of 25 he returns to India and goes to his **native** village. When he arrives in the village he finds his mother, but **unfortunately** his brother died very young. Saroo's mother is very happy of course.
>
> It's a film **based on** a **true story** and **makes you want to cry.** I loved it! **Especially** the two actors who played the role of Saroo when he was young and older.

12-part multi-skill lesson sequence

This might typically take a couple of lessons. Part 12 could be set as a homework task or completed in class.

1. **Pre-listening.** Explain in L1 or L2 that students will hear you describing a film you saw. Tell them that by the end of the activities they will have a very good understanding of what was said and learn some new high-frequency language along the way. They will also be able to talk about a movie and write a short review.

2. **Read the text twice aloud.** Students cannot see the transcript at this stage. Use any techniques you can to make the text more comprehensible (see Chapter 6).

3. **True-false.** Read the text a third time as students do the L2 true-false exercise below on paper or mini-whiteboards. Note that students now begin to see some of the language used in the text in written form, so can make more sound-spelling correspondences.
   a. *The teacher watched the film last weekend.*
   b. *The main character of the film is an Indian boy.*

c. *Saroo's family is quite rich.*
   d. *Saroo gets on a train with his brother.*
   e. *Saroo is lost and has to go to an orphanage.*
   f. *Saroo goes to live in Australia with new parents.*
   g. *He is the only child in his new family.*
   h. *Saroo is trying to find his original family in India.*
   i. *He uses Google Earth to identify the village where he was born.*
   j. *When he returns to India he finds his brother again.*
   k. *Saroo can't find his mother unfortunately.*
   l. *The film is based on a true story.*
   m. *The role of Saroo is played by one actor.*

Check the answers by asking students to put up their hands for true or false after each statement. Give the correct option.

4. **Reading gap-fill**. Hand out the sentences below with options (or without for more proficient classes). Students fill the gaps from memory, as well as using reading cues. They could help each other in pairs. The options focus on verb forms. Display completed answers on the board for students to check.

   a. *The young Indian boy _____ a train.*
   b. *He _____ far across India.*
   c. *But he _____ find his mother and father.*
   d. *He _____ in an orphanage.*
   e. *The Australian couple _____ the little boy.*
   f. *As an older child, Saroo _____ to find his original family.*
   g. *He locates the village where they _____.*
   h. *So he _____ to India and _____ his mother.*
   i. *Unfortunately his brother _____ when he was younger.*
   j. *The teacher _____ the film.*

finds	ends up	looks after	gets on	died	live	can't	travels	tries
returns	loved							

5. **Running dictation**. Reminder: display in various places around the classroom a shortened, simplified version of the text. In pairs, students take turns at fetching chunks or sentences for their partner to transcribe. Do this as a competitive race.
6. **Read aloud**. Display or hand out the original text. In pairs, students take turns at reading aloud. Alternatively, they could read out loud individually with fingers in ears.
7. **Translation**. Students complete a translation into L1 of the original text to a time limit. Listen back to example translations.

8. *Quickfire translation*. Focus on the new language working from L1 into L2, using mini-whiteboards.
9. **Post-listening**. Invite students to ask any more questions.
10. **Whole text gap-fill**. Hand out a gapped transcript of the original text, this time with the more unfamiliar words omitted. Students complete individually or in pairs.
11. **Make a sentence competition**. Without access to the transcript, in pairs students take turns making a statement about the film. The first partner who cannot make a sentence loses. (This simple device motivates students to keep speaking.)
12. **Guided composition**. Students write their own review of a film they have watched. Now, the amount of scaffolding needed for this will depend a great deal on the class. The highest-attaining classes will do very well on this with little extra help, especially if you urge them to recycle language from the source text. Less proficient classes would benefit from having a template to work from, e.g. a table containing example words and chunks they can use and which can be adapted for any film. It would be a good idea to prepare them for the task by modelling some sentences on the board with that age-old advice "use what you know"!

Concluding remarks

Once again, you will have noticed that listening was given pride of place in the context of lessons requiring speaking, reading and writing. It is worth recalling that these other skills all reinforce listening, providing variety to lessons and opportunities for repetition, recycling and interleaving. Keeping students active during listening, both physically (through moving, speaking and writing) and mentally (through concentration) are important factors in making teaching sequences such as the above work for you and your classes. The sequences suggested are all adaptable and can be supplemented by your own ideas or existing practice. As always, context is a key factor in determining what will work.

Questions to consider

For your classes what is the right balance between teacher-led and peer-to-peer activity?

To what extent can you recycle the same activities with different classes to help manage your workload?

To what extent is it wise to alter lesson plans according to circumstances?

What skills do you need if you wish to know if a lesson is going well?

*Words make you think a thought.
Music makes you feel a feeling. A song
makes you feel a thought.*
(E.Y. Harburg, American songwriter)

9

Making the most of songs

Introduction

Most teachers make use of songs in the classroom and it would be remiss not to include this topic in a book about listening. Songs bring a different dimension to the classroom. As well as providing ample opportunities to develop listening skills, they offer insights into the L2 culture. They help students focus on aspects of pronunciation and intonation, the presence of choruses often means that the same language patterns are heard repeatedly, while the use of rhyme can help develop phonological skills. Songs often contain stories while bringing different accents and voices into the classroom. If you can play guitar or keyboard you have an added advantage! We have observed some super lessons with teachers singing and playing.

There is some research evidence on the value of songs. They promote active listening skills and fine discrimination of subtle differences between sounds. Learning to sing folk and pop songs can provide practice with comprehension and pronunciation, which can then transfer to improvements in speaking skills (Spicher and Sweeney, 2007). Songs are also more likely to repeat in the student's mind after a lesson than the same words presented as speech or poetry (Smith Salcedo, 2002).

It has also been suggested that certain properties of songs are especially likely to support verbal learning, e.g. a simple and predictable song structure, such as verse and chorus (Kellaris, 2003); songs or phrases in which the end leads naturally back to the beginning (Kellaris, 2003*)*; a rhyme scheme within the lyrics, since this can facilitate recall (Rubin & Wallace, 1989).

But, as with all authentic resources, finding the right song is not always easy, especially for beginners and intermediate level students. Fortunately, teachers are always happy to share songs they have found beneficial to their classes and songs are very easy to access online. In this chapter a detailed framework is described to exploit a song for maximum linguistic benefit. Songs should normally be used with a very specific purpose in mind – phonological, lexical, grammatical or cultural. Some sources of songs are provided which we have used and which many other teachers have recommended.

A step-by-step framework for the exploitation of a song

The framework below is particularly useful for beginner-to-intermediate students when the focus is on developing listening skills. In reality, few songs will be really suitable for novices. You would probably adopt a different approach when working with advanced learners.

1. Selecting the right song

These are some important principles to bear in mind when selecting a song to achieve the best learning potential.

a. **Comprehensible input**. Choose a song which you believe is linguistically accessible – with some support. If you find you are having to gloss too many new words in the margin, then another song may be better. Tip: glossing in the margin is easier for students than glossing beneath the text.
b. **Flooded input**. Ideally the song will contain repeated occurrences of the linguistic features you want students to hear, e.g. sounds, vocabulary or grammatical structures.
c. **Linguistic relevance**. Select a song which is relevant to the linguistic goals of the curriculum, i.e. which contains lexis and grammar related to the learning outcomes of the lesson, unit or syllabus. Ideally the song will introduce, model, recycle or reinforce linguistic or cultural features you have been teaching or planning to teach. It should not be a 'pedagogical island', as often happens, exposing students to language or other information that is not going to be revisited.
d. **Cultural relevance, sensitivity and style**. 'Cultural' here could mean the culture of the L2 country, or the students' own culture. Some songs may be a poor fit with students' own experience and cultural background. This is significant when working in an international school or other multi-ethnic environments. Do not be frightened to play songs which may sound old-fashioned to teenagers; this may be motivational in itself if they find the style quaint. In any case, using a song in an unfamiliar style may provide insights into the L2 culture.
e. **Surrender value**. The song should ideally contain vocabulary worth learning, including high-frequency vocabulary.

f. **Availability of relevant multimedia resources**. It makes sense to choose a song where the lyrics, L1 translation and video are available online and free. Lyrics online should be checked thoroughly as they often contain spelling errors or small omissions.
g. **Memorability**. The following are factors that usually affect the memorability of a song:

- the lyrics are repetitive and patterned;
- the music is catchy;
- it is packed with features such as alliteration, rhyme or near-rhyme;
- it is distinctive, i.e. there are specific features of the song (and/or in the video that accompanies the song) which make it stand out;
- the speed and enunciation must allow the students to clearly hear the words;
- the song tells a story which is fairly linear and predictable or is not too obscure in terms of message.

2. Pre-listening activities

In order to activate students' prior knowledge and the language related to the themes and semantic areas in the song, you can do a range of tasks which, while recycling vocabulary students have already worked with in previous lessons, make them think about the song's themes. For instance, on a lesson centred on Kenza Farah's French song *Sans jamais se plaindre*, which deals with the theme of parents' daily sacrifices for their children, students might:

- brainstorm in pairs and write down in French five sacrifices parents usually make for their children;
- think about three people in their own families and list the sacrifices they have made in recent years to help them;
- list the qualities of an ideal father, mother and sibling.

At this pre-listening stage you may also want to develop the desire to listen. You could do this by:

- displaying a slideshow featuring photos of the singer and interesting images you have found on the web which relate to the song;
- picking out lines of the song which stand out in some way;
- displaying the most appealing parts of the song's official video without sound;
- relating interesting facts about the singer which may arouse students' curiosity.

Focus on supporting students with their understanding of the text through activities which involve working on key vocabulary from the lyrics, e.g. through split sentence activities, gapped sentences, odd-one-outs, matching exercises, etc.

3. Listening to the song for pleasure

Let students listen to the song for pure enjoyment the first time around before asking them to do any while-listening tasks. Do not show the lyrics at this stage.

4. Recognising and noticing

Get students to listen to the song again. This time ask them to note down any words they recognise and any words they do not know, but they noticed, maybe because they kept recurring; spelling need not matter at this point. After students have jotted down the words, get them to pair up with one or more peers to compare notes. Ask students to tell you these words as you write them on the board, explaining their meaning in L2 or translating them into L1. Finally, ask them what they think the song is about. This can be done in L1.

5. Promoting selective attention and further noticing

Hand out a gapped version of the lyrics, where the missing words or chunks are given as options. Do not overload the students; a gap every two or three lines may be enough. Insert gaps where you want students to pay particular attention, owing to their linguistic, semantic or cultural value.

If you want to emphasise a specific sound pattern, draw students' attention to it by removing words that rhyme, chime or alliterate with others containing that sound. After listening to the song three or four times, show them the complete version of the lyrics on screen and ask them to check and correct, or fill in any missing gaps.

6. Working on specific phonemes

Explicit learning

After students have filled in all the gaps, pick a specific sound you know they struggle with, then play the song again and ask them to highlight the words which contain that sound. Do the same with other key phonemes, making sure they use a different highlighting method for each sound. Then play the song again asking them to focus on the specific letters they highlighted.

Inductive learning

Write on the board two or three combinations of letters (e.g. diphthongs) or syllables which recur a few times. Then ask students, working in pairs, to underline all occurrences of the item. Finally, ask them to listen to the song and work out how those letter combinations or syllables are pronounced.

7. Working on segmentation skills

Tasks described earlier in the book can be used here.

- *Break the flow*. Give students a portion of the song's lyrics (e.g. the first two stanzas) from which you have removed the spaces between words. Students listen to the song and mark with a line the breaks you deleted.
- *Spot the intruder.* Insert as many small function words (e.g. articles and prepositions) as you can between the words in the lyrics and ask the students to delete the ones they do not hear when they listen to the song.
- **Complete the beginnings/endings**. Delete the beginnings and/or the endings of every single word in a section of the song. Students must complete the words.

8. Working on phonics

Do any of the following activities, depending on your focus:

- Remove all consonants or vowels from a few words or even lines of a song.
- Remove specific syllables.
- Jumble up the letters in specific words.
- Split words in half (one or two per line).
- (For French) underline the endings of specific words and ask your students to underline which letters are silent.
- Write a few words on the board and ask students to listen to the song and spot as many words as they can in the song that rhyme with them.

9. Reading comprehension

Lexical level

Work on reading comprehension through deep processing activities such as:

- *Word hunt*. Give students a list of L1 words or chunks. Students find their L2 equivalent in the lyrics;
- *Categories*. Identify the semantic fields the key words in the song refer to, e.g. relationships, weather, time, and ask the students to spot and note down as many words as possible under those headings;
- *Near synonyms/antonyms*. Give students a set of phrases or sentences which are near-synonyms or antonyms of words or phrases from the song and have students match them up.
- **Chronological ordering**. Provide a list of main points from the song in random order and ask students to arrange them in the same order as they occur in the song (jigsaw reading).

Grammatical level

When students know most of the vocabulary and the intended meaning of the song, it is easier for them to process the grammar. At this stage they can:

- identify specific linguistic features. For instance, students have a grid with metalinguistic labels as headings, e.g. adjectives, verbs, nouns, prepositions, connectives, and must find words corresponding to those categories;
- work on grammatical opposites within a specific category: regular versus irregular adjectives, masculine versus feminine nouns, imperfect versus perfect tense. Students should note down items from the song that fall under either category;
- ask metalinguistic questions, e.g. why is such and such a tense used here?
- rewrite a set of sentences lifted from the lyrics incorrectly and containing grammatical mistakes students usually make;
- write the literal L1 translation of a few sentences in the song where the L1 sentence structure is different from the L2's. Students have to notice the differences between the two languages and work out any rule;
- write a sentence structure using shorthand or symbols you have got your students used to, e.g. SVOCA (subject + verb + object + complement + adverbial) or 'Time marker + personal pronoun + verb + preposition + article + noun'. Students have to identify sentences that reflect that structure;
- display a list of subordinate clause types your students are familiar with, e.g. time clauses, final clauses, modal clauses, etc. Then ask the class to identify as many clauses as possible of the same type from the song.

10. Meaning-building and discourse reconstruction tasks

After all the work on vocabulary and grammar, students should be able to approach the meaning level with greater confidence. Meaning-based activities include:

- **Jigsaw reading/listening**. Give students a jigsaw version of the song lyrics and ask them, working in pairs, to rearrange it in the correct order. Then students listen to the song and confirm or rearrange;
- **True or false tasks.**
- **Comprehension questions**.
- **Summarising content in L1 or L2.**
- **Bad translation**. Provide a translation of the lyrics containing a number of obvious mistakes. Students have to spot and correct the mistakes to a time limit.

11. Enjoy the song!

Now that you are confident students really understand the meaning of the song get them to sing along. Some classes do this more readily than others, but they will surely enjoy you singing it!

12. Recycling and consolidating

Below are possible tasks which may suit some classes more than others:

- *Spot the differences*. Edit the lyrics by making a few grammatical or lexical changes to the song and ask students to identify them. Students have no access to the original text.
- **Gapped lyrics**. Students fill the gaps from memory.
- *Disappearing text.* Write a section of the song (or the whole song if it is short) on the board. The text might contain about 50 to 60 words, but this depends on the class. Ask a student or two to read it. Then erase some of the words, e.g. function words like *a, the, in, of, I, he*, etc. at the beginning. Then ask another student to read it aloud supplying the missing words. Then erase some more words and so on.
- *Dictogloss*. Students listen to the song twice, each time noting down as many words as they can. They then pair up with another student to reconstruct the lyrics together.
- **Guided summary**. Give the class a list of words or chunks taken from the lyrics and ask them to write a summary of the song including those items.
- **Substitution tasks**. Underline key items in the song lyrics and ask students to rewrite the song replacing those items creatively, but in a way which is grammatically correct and semantically plausible.
- **Deep processing tasks**. Use vocabulary building tasks requiring deep processing such as odd-one out, categories, find the synonym/antonym, split sentence, ordering, etc.
- **Quizzes**. These reveal how much has been retained in terms of vocabulary, grammar, meaning, etc.
- **Thinking-about-learning tasks**. These may include any of the following:
  - Reflecting on the value of using songs for learning. Ask students to reflect on how songs, based on what you have just done with them, can be valuable for language learning and ask for suggestions on how they could benefit by listening to them independently. You can follow this up by providing them with lists of singers/songs they might enjoy or by giving them the task to find a French/German/Spanish/Italian band or solo artist they like (to share with the rest of the class in the next lesson);
  - Noting down what was challenging about the song and the tasks performed;
  - Making a list of the new items learned and ranking them in order of usefulness for real life communication or reading comprehension purposes.

Finding songs

Beginners (A1)

These cover all kinds of areas of vocabulary and grammar such as numbers, the alphabet, parts of the body, foods, weather, colours, simple verb conjugations. Younger classes are usually keen to sing, but we recommend you insist on accurate pronunciation to get the most out of singalongs for the purpose of developing listening skills. Recall how improving pronunciation also improves listening skills.

At the time of writing we can recommend fun singalong videos in YouTube collections such as:

French: Alain Le Lait, Sylvia Duckworth, Mr Johnson MFL.

German: HooplaKidz Deutsch

Spanish: Basho and Friends, Señor Wooly, Calico Songs, Rockalingua, Songs for Teaching.

Intermediate (A2 to B1)

For intermediate level students, teachers have recommended a number of songs, to which we have added our own choices (**Tables 9.1, 9.2** and **9.3**). The phonological, grammatical or thematic reason for using them are listed. We have listened to them all to check they would work well with intermediate level classes (classes who have been learning the language for at least four years), but what you might like to use is very personal so you may not agree with all our choices! Do not forget that harder songs can be scaffolded by using lyric videos or even parallel translations which could be shown on a first listening with text. You could then remove the parallel translation for further work along the lines described earlier in this chapter.

For French we recommend checking the website by Carmen Vera Pérez which has gap-fill (Hot Potato) exercises on French songs categorised by level.
http://platea.pntic.mec.es/cvera/hotpot/chansons/?fbclid=IwAR0LZrlAkM3EW7TDgiMXIFVem5_o6h9_g5G-c5JH6urT71pRtR5YMg_ie3I
The TES website has links to song resources, some free, categorised by language.
https://www.tes.com/au/articles/mfl-collection-songs-language-learning

For German we recommend having a look at the Goethe Institut's list of songs which come with biographies of artists, lyrics and translations in pdf form.
http://www.goethe.de/ins/us/saf/prj/stg/mus/vid/enindex.htm

For Spanish try the YouTube playlist from Kevin y Karla
https://www.youtube.com/user/kvnvasquez

Table 9.1 Recommended French songs

Artist	Title	Sound/grammar/theme
Zaz	*On ira*	Repeated use of future tense
Kenza Farah	*Sans jamais se plaindre*	Family; present tense; object pronouns
La Grande Sophie	*On savait (devenir grand)*	Imperfect tense
Natasha St Pier	*Tu trouveras*	Silent letters at the ends of words
Christophe	*Aline*	Perfect and imperfect tenses
Francis Cabrel	*Madame X*	Poverty and inequality
Yannick Noah	*On court*	Stress of daily life; good vowel sounds
Zaho	*Je te promets*	Subjunctive
Florent Pagny	*Savoir aimer*	Infinitives
Christophe Maé	*Il est où le bonheur?*	Good clear vowel sounds, including nasals

Table 9.2 Recommended German songs

Artist	Title	Sound/grammar/theme
Die Prinzen	*Millionär*	Conditional
Gerhard Schöne	*Jule wäscht sich nie*	Reflexive verbs
Wise Guys	*Nur für dich*	Perfect tense
Wise Guys	*Mein neues Handy*	Mobile phones
Batomae	*Unvergleichlich*	Eating disorders+ *du* form of verbs
Juli	*Dieses Leben*	*Ich liebe* + inflection with *dies*
Max Giesinger	*80 Millionen*	Relationships + past participles
Luxuslärm	*Leb deine Träume*	*du* form of verbs + imperatives
Alexander Knappe	*Weil ich wieder zu Hause bin*	Use of *weil* (word order)

Table 9.3 Recommended Spanish songs

Artist	Title	Sound/grammar/theme
Marc Anthony	*Vivir mi vida*	Near future of verbs (*voy a* + infinitive)
El Cuarteto de Nos	*Ya no sé qué hacer conmigo*	Perfect tense + Uruguay accent
Lele Pons	*Celoso*	'o' sounds, first person of present tense
Ana y Aitana	*Lo Malo*	*quiero, porque*
Morat	*Amor con hielo*	Object pronouns
Cali y El Dandee	*Sirena*	Future tense
Álvaro Soler	*Ella*	The word *ella* (a lot!)
Álvaro Soler	*Volar*	*quiero*, common infinitives
Banda Machos	*El Bigote*	Adjectives, e.g. colours
Álvaro Soler	*Puebla*	así, plurals: *bailan, les gusta, se pierdan, dicen*, plus infinitives and object pronouns

Concluding remarks

Songs and singing add so much interest and enjoyment to language lessons and there is little doubt they help develop students' listening skills at every level: sound discrimination, lexical growth and parsing. When used effectively and with specific goals in mind they are a valuable addition to a teacher's repertoire. What is more, students who are enthused by a song may well go on to find other L2 songs which will provide more listening opportunities. The response of a class to singing and song will reflect your own enthusiasm for the task.

Questions to consider

How should you weigh up cultural interest against the 'teachability' of a song?

How useful is singing along for the retention of language forms, such as verb conjugations?

When the cook tastes the soup, that's formative assessment; when the customer tastes the soup, that's summative assessment.

(Paul Black)

10

ASSESSING LISTENING

Introduction

Brown and Abeywickrama (2010) point out that a well-constructed test is an instrument which provides an accurate measure of the test-taker's ability within a certain area of knowledge. If only it were that simple! This chapter begins by looking at a few fundamental principles you need for an underlying grasp of this area: formative and summative assessment, practicality, validity, discrete versus mixed skill testing, reliability, the washback effect, test authenticity, and fairness. Some commonly-used question types are then considered, analysing the pros and cons of each type, along with how to help students prepare for tests and the strategies they can use while doing them.

1.   Formative assessment

This is an ongoing process which takes place informally during lessons every time students do a listening task. It could take the form of assessing students' answers to questions during interpersonal listening or their responses to an activity on mini-whiteboards. It might be simply reacting to a response which arose from faulty listening. Formative assessment allows you to constantly weigh up what students know and what they need to do to make further progress. Some now just label it *responsive teaching* (Fletcher-Wood, 2018) to avoid teachers confusing it with summative assessment and to emphasise that formative assessment is built into nearly every classroom interaction.

> **Gianfranco and Steve's tips for formative assessment of listening**
>
> - Use mini-whiteboards to let students show you they are understanding what has been said at any point.
> - Listen and respond to the quality of choral or individual repetition or reading aloud. If the quality of pronunciation is lacking, insist on better performance.
> - Observe who and how many put up their hands and adjust teaching accordingly.
> - Use no hands-up questioning (either random or your choice of student) from time to time to check understanding.
> - Actively walk round and monitor comprehension in paired activities. Intervene as necessary or make a mental note for whole class feedback at a later point in the lesson.
> - Use 'retrospective reports' from students to check for understanding. These are comments written down by students after an activity or lesson(s).
> - Use questionnaires to check students' level of self-efficacy and metacognition (see Chapter 11).
> - Use low-stakes summative tests for formative purposes, e.g. 'end of unit' assessments can inform future teaching.

2. Summative assessment

This is more formal and may be a requirement of your school or exam syllabus. It usually occurs at the end of a unit or course and produces scores or grades, frequently mapped against mark schemes or rubrics, allowing you to see a student's progress at a point in time. Students perceive it as important since it may impact on their future. For many it is a source of extrinsic motivation in itself and teachers are not shy of using upcoming exams to encourage students to work harder.

3. Transfer-appropriate processing (TAP)

As noted in Chapter 4, research demonstrates that learners recall information best in a test when it is presented in the same format and context it was learned in. Expressed a little more technically, the fundamental tenet of TAP is that we can better remember what we have learned if the cognitive processes active during the learning are similar to those which are active during retrieval (Blaxton, 1989; Morris et al., 1977). This has general implications for language learning in classrooms, since TAP suggests that classroom activities should resemble how we use language in 'real life' or whatever context we intend to use the language in. For assessment purposes, the implication is that if we want students to do their best in tests, we should design the tests to resemble the classroom exercises they have done. This is tied up with the issue of washback (see below).

4. Practicality

This is an important consideration when assessing listening. For instance, while it might be desirable for students to be tested using video rather than audio, this may not be possible if the equipment is not available or if the rules of exam awarding bodies prohibit the practice. Ideally it would be desirable for students to listen to audio as many times as they wish, but in formal exam contexts with large numbers of students this may not be authorised or may just be impossible. This does not stop you using video and mobile devices in the classroom if listening skills are enhanced by so doing. Incidentally, research is inconclusive on the merits of using video or audio, with some studies finding an advantage for video in tests, e.g. Wagner (2010); Winiharti and Herlina (2017).

5. Validity

When we talk about a test's validity, we mean does it test what it purports to test? In this case, are we testing listening, or simultaneously some other skill such as reading or writing? It is actually not particularly easy to test listening in isolation, unless you just use pictures or L1 question types such as comprehension questions, true/false and L1 multiple choice. If you wish to minimise the amount of L1 in a test, you may end up assessing other skills such as reading comprehension, speaking or writing. For example, if you use L2 questions students have to decipher the meaning of the written text first, which is a test of reading, not listening. Brown and Abeywickrama (2010) note that a valid test should be: well-constructed, in an expected format with familiar tasks, be feasible in the allotted time limit, be clear and uncomplicated, have crystal-clear instructions, contain tasks which relate to their course and present a reasonable challenge.

6. Discrete skill and mixed skill testing

These terms are applied to two different types of testing which have important implications for both assessment and classroom teaching. A discrete skill test isolates the single skill being assessed, e.g. when assessing listening there is no use of any L2 written material. Mixed-skill, also known as multi-modal or integrative testing, involves more than one skill being used during the assessment process. In the classroom we have encouraged you to use mixed-skill activities, but in many exams listening is tested largely in a discrete fashion. The washback effect (see below) can lead you into questionable classroom practice.

7. Reliability

This term refers to the extent to which the test produces consistent results, irrespective of who grades the test or when the test is taken, for example. In this respect, multiple choice or true/false questions are more objectively reliable than comprehension questions, the answers to which may be open to interpretation. Similarly, if you assess listening through a summarising task in L1 or L2 with a level-based mark scheme consisting of a series of descriptors such as: "The student understands some of the points" or "The student understands most of the points", then different markers will often arrive at different scores. Subjectivity is the enemy of reliability here. This phenomenon is well-attested in the research literature, e.g. Christodoulou (2017). But note that even so-called objective tests such as multi-choice may not be entirely reliable in terms of discriminating between students, e.g. when a question is poorly set and all the students get the right answer with the other options barely being possible.

A further example of where reliability and fairness come into play is when a summative test is too difficult for the students taking the test. If most marks are skewed to the lower end of the range, then firstly and most importantly, students are discouraged and not sufficiently rewarded for what they know. Secondly, the range of marks may not make it easy enough to discriminate between different students. In other words, if the best student gets 25/50 and the weakest gets 15/50, then we cannot be certain that the test has reliably ordered the candidates to reflect their skills.

8. Washback

From what is written previously, for testing to be both valid and reliable, it would seem to be advisable to use objective question types and to eliminate the use of written L2. The problem with this is that, because teachers frequently, for good reasons, use the same sort of assessment in classrooms as used in formal exams ('teaching to the test'), they end up using more L2 than might be desirable. This is known as the washback effect (also known as the backwash effect), where the testing type dictates the activities and assessment style used in lessons. If you are too influenced by exams, you risk neglecting all those more interesting opportunities to engage in listening while acquiring skills, communicating or performing tasks. As Nation and Newton (2009) put it, "A good test sets a good model for what should happen in the classroom" (p.169). On the other hand, washback can be positive, when an informal classroom test provides useful information to students who go on to improve their performance. With TAP in mind (see above) it makes sense for both classroom tasks and tests to be methodologically sound, valid and reliable.

Important to note here is that exams almost always aim to test comprehension, which is understandable, but as we have emphasised in this book, classroom listening tasks may not always be focused on comprehension per se, but the skills which can be built up to make comprehension possible. Dictation is a classic example of a multi-skill activity which can improve listening, but which would be a poor measure of ultimate comprehension. Compare this with a driving test, if you will. The *examiner* wants to see if the person can drive, but the *instructor* taught all the separate skills which made that driving possible.

9. Test authenticity

This refers to factors such as the naturalness of the language being heard and the real-life nature of the context it is used in. You could test students' comprehension of words by simply reading a set of words and asking the class to translate each in turn, but this would lack authenticity, not to mention validity. In reality, the authenticity of text book and exam listening extracts is questionable at best, but at least an effort is made to put listening texts in real-world contexts.

10. Fairness

This can come into play in various ways when assessing listening. Are the listening conditions adequate for the test? Are recordings clear and recorded at a suitable pace? Are students with special needs catered for adequately? Do answers require knowledge beyond the linguistic content, e.g. general knowledge about the topic? Is the test simply too hard, as mentioned above, i.e. does the test material contain too much language students have never encountered? If we believe that in general terms listening texts we use in class should contain at least 95% comprehensible language, is it fair to include too much new language? Against this we need to bear in mind that exam awarding bodies, for their own statistical reasons, need to have a range of grades to be able to fairly discriminate between candidates. (This is why some tests, e.g. the GCSE in England, are thought by many teachers to be too hard and unfair.) Put simply, not every student can get high marks in a high-stakes exam.

11. Implications for teachers

What can we draw from these general points? Firstly, formative assessment is much more useful than summative assessment since the teacher can continually adjust their teaching to students' responses. Constant informal assessment of this sort provides more opportunities for language recycling, as the teacher uses their cognitive empathy, listening and questioning skills to respond to every teaching moment in the classroom. Formal summative tests may be less valid and reliable than you think, so question design takes considerable skill. You may not be able to trust the text book or exam board to get this right every time. When you design a test with the aim of rank-ordering students it is wise to try to ensure that it is neither too easy (with nearly all students getting top marks) or too hard. But bearing in mind how discouraging it can be to get very low marks, it would usually be unwise to design a test for some to get very few or no marks at all.

> **INFOBOX 21 Cognitive empathy**
>
> This is the capacity to understand another person's mental state and perspective. For a teacher it plays a vital role in evaluating at any point in a lesson how the class is thinking and feeling about an activity. For example, cognitive empathy allows you to sense if a task has been pitched at just the right level of challenge and interest. Formative assessment techniques play an important role in helping a teacher develop their cognitive empathy skills.

It is now widely accepted that regular, short-term summative tests or quizzes provide useful retrieval practice, so can be encouraged. You might ask yourself what the difference is between a quiz and simple practice of previously learned language!

The TAP principle referred to above should encourage us to design summative tests to resemble soundly devised classroom activities, so there is no obvious disconnect between teaching and testing. In practice, this could mean redesigning or adapting published assessments or 'unit tests' to make them better reflect what you have been doing in lessons. For instance, you might add a transcription test of some sort to a comprehension-based assessment, or, more radically, throw out the ready-made test completely and start from scratch. Smart assessment design of this type could lead to better student performance and self-efficacy.

Nevertheless, students have to be properly prepared for the requirements of high-stakes exams, so making them familiar with question types, giving them coping strategies and providing ample practice is crucial. Remember that students tend to do better when they are familiar with the question style. Students often approach listening tests with trepidation since they have no control over the input, only a couple of chances to understand and no visual clues to help, so anything we can do to prepare and reassure them is useful.

In essence, we would advocate a balanced approach where the emphasis is on day to day formative assessment and quizzing, keeping the main focus on L2 use, but with rigorous preparation for high stakes tests and exams. The latter requires doing practice tests, especially in the immediate run-up to the big day.

12. Question types

Let us now consider a list of typical question types students encounter when doing listening tests, e.g. in high-stakes public exams. We list the implications of each one in the table below (**Table 10.1**) to help you when designing your own assessments. Non-verbal answers such as box-ticking are less distracting from the actual listening, whereas answers requiring considerable amounts of writing may divide the students' attention and fail to assess their listening skills reliably.

Table 10.1 Question types to use in listening tests

Question type	Comments
True/false/not mentioned	Statistically reliable because there are three options and theoretically objective, but it is notoriously hard to discriminate between false and not mentioned; quick to grade; great care is needed in setting questions; true/false alone may be fine for the classroom, but is statistically unreliable for assessment
Multiple choice in L1	Objective, but the wrong answers ('distractors') need to be 'in play', i.e. be tempting in some way; quick to grade; three choices are as statistically adequate as four; all students need to share the same L1; each option should ideally be of similar length and phrased either all the same or all differently (one answer should not stick out from the others in terms of its grammatical form); they take a long time for teachers to prepare
Multiple choice in L2	Mixed-skill question type, therefore less fair and reliable for testing listening alone; but in classroom teaching terms provides more comprehensible input; same issues as above for question design
Multiple choice with picture options	Objective and reliable as long as pictures are unambiguous, including for those from varied cultural backgrounds.
Comprehension questions in L1	Quite objective; only usable where all the class share the same L1; takes time to write so may distract from listening; heavier memory load; washback effect may encourage teachers to use too much L1 in lessons.
Comprehension questions in L2	Mixed-skill question, therefore less fair and reliable for testing listening alone; in classroom teaching terms the questions themselves provide added comprehensible input; takes time so may distract from listening; heavier working memory load.
Tick off the correct statements	The same points apply in general as for multiple choice questioning; two correct options out of five or three from seven are typical and statistically acceptable.
Note-form answers in L1	Discrete; potentially punitive of students with poor L1 writing skills; often takes the form of completing grids; washback effect may encourage overuse of L1 in lessons
Note-form answers in L2	Potentially punitive of students with poor L2 writing skills; unfair since writing is used as well as listening; washback effect has a positive influence on classroom practice since it encourages greater use of L2 input.
Matching L1 statements with statistical data.	Objective and takes little time.
Sentence completion in L1 (with or without options provided)	Quite objective; takes little time; only suitable where all students share the same L1; where options are available spelling is less of an issue for students.
Sentence completion in L2 (with or without options provided)	Mixed-skill when no options are given since it requires some L2 reading and writing skill; providing options is more reliable, but L2 reading still needed.

13. Preparing students for listening tests

Here is some guidance about steps you can take to help students in advance of important tests.

- Make sure students are familiar with the format of the test and question types, e.g. ensuring that students know when to write answers in L1 or L2. Explain to them that test papers are often structured with easier questions first and occasional easier questions placed between harder ones. The best test papers build in a progression of this type to avoid putting students off.
- Ensure they have had frequent opportunities to practise similar tests.
- Work with transcripts of example tests, highlighting common vocabulary, phrases and, in particular, those which help establish meaning such as *but, on the other hand, I agree, I disagree, it's not true*. Use gap-fill, translation and micro-skills activities to get students to listen intensively.
- Be prepared to adapt existing tests to the level of your class, e.g. by omitting the hardest questions. Although it is true that students need preparation for all eventualities, practising with material which is clearly too hard will discourage them.
- Make tests available for use individually so that students can listen to sections multiple times.
- Suggest online sources of level-appropriate listening to help students tune in their ears. You may be able to find worksheets which support individual listening.
- If possible structure your pre-test listening lessons so that easier material is done first, building up difficulty level.
- Respect the comprehensibility principle by leaving the practice of past papers relatively late if students are not ready for them.

14. Strategies for students to use while doing tests

The list in **Table 10.2** provides strategies students can use when doing a test and ways in which you can help students apply them. A good way to help students develop these strategies is to use the *think-aloud* technique when doing practice tests. For instance, pause a recording at certain points to ask how students are coping with the material and what techniques from the table above they are using to make meaning, e.g. listening out for key vocabulary, tone of voice, verb tenses or prediction. See Chapter 11 in which the whole issue of using strategies is examined in more detail.

Table 10.2 Strategies students can use while doing tests

Strategy	Comments
Read and predict	Train students to read all questions and begin to anticipate what the answers might be, e.g. if the question is about how people help to protect the environment, students can be thinking about what people typically do in their daily lives, e.g. what they recycle.
Never leave a gap	Students often leave answer spaces blank. Ensure they are trained to answer every question with an educated guess at least.
Answer immediately	Suggest that as soon as students hear the answer, they should write it down in the time provided, not wait and risk forgetting what they intended to write.
Double-check hypotheses	If there are two chances to listen, students need to make sure they do not just go with their first hypothesis as they may fall for traps (distractors). However, warn them not to over-think things while being aware there will be distractors.
Does it make sense?	Train students to check any written answers to ensure that what they wrote actually makes sense in L1 or L2.
Focus listening	Train students not to listen generally, but to do so selectively for answers involving specific vocabulary.
Time-frames	Ensure students are prepared to listen out for phonological markers which indicate a change of tense.
Do not give up	Students should keep listening and not panic if they struggled with a question.
Re-read at the end	There is usually time allotted for checking at the end of a test. Ensure students use it.
Tone of voice	Remind students that intonation can give clues to meaning, particularly attitudes and emotions.
Do not panic!	With longer passages to comprehend, students often feel overwhelmed on the first listening. Encourage students to keep a cool head and listen really hard on the second listening.

15. Helping students do well in exams

In languages, as for other subjects, preparation for tests and exams is a key ingredient of success. In many subjects students have a clear idea of what revision means, but in languages students often ask "How do I revise?" In particular, they often ask "How do I revise for listening?" Unfortunately, from some students' point of view, because of the cumulative nature of language learning, it is hard to improve skills overnight, but there are useful general strategies you can employ in the short and longer term which will improve students' performance and, in particular, support struggling listeners.

15.1 Daily exposure to substantial amounts of aural input

Ensure your students practise listening in every lesson. Try the following:
- Increase the amount of L2 use both on your part and on your students'. Some minimal-prep teacher-led activities: every beginning and/or end of the lesson, give sentences for students to translate on the spot; ask the class questions to answer in writing on paper or mini-whiteboards; give them a gapped text and read out to them the full-text version; do very short dictations on mini-whiteboards; increase the number of questions you ask, especially closed questions aimed at modelling, e.g. *Is it X or Y?* Do student-led activities such as surveys, role plays, find-someone-who or speak-and-draw activities; short paired reading-aloud sessions (student A reads a short paragraph while student B translates orally or summarises the gist).
- Plan tasks which teach language through LAM. This means fewer test-like tasks and more tasks of the sort described in previous chapters and below (see points 5 to 10 below) and which focus on developing listening micro-skills.

Varying tasks is important in order not to bore students, but also to allow recycling of L2 vocabulary. Keep tasks brief, with quick and easy feedback.

15.2 A multi-skill approach

Try to ensure listening tasks do not occur randomly in lesson sequences. For instance, before working on an aural text students need to receive plenty of practice in new language through word and pattern recognition tasks. In this way students will approach tasks better prepared and with a greater chance of being successful. Focus students on pattern recognition both at word level (e,g. prefixes and suffixes) and at sentence level (e.g. word order, verb constructions, subordinate clauses), not only through listening, but through other skills, such as reading and grammar exercises.

15.3 Confidence building

To help students succeed and feel confident at listening, scaffold for success in every lesson. Give students opportunities to succeed by letting them listen to texts as often as they request or, after playing the track a couple of times, reading the transcript at a slower speed than in the original recording. In other words, try adapting text book exercises rather than just carrying them out as suggested.

15.4 Phonics

If you take over a struggling class which has never really been taught to listen, be prepared to revisit the most basic listening micro-skills (see Chapter 3). Focus on the sounds that cause the most serious comprehension issues for your students.

15.5 Segmenting the stream of sound

Retrain students in the skill of identifying the boundaries between words and chunks. For instance, take a short text and remove the gaps between the words. Then read each line out to the class, asking them to draw the boundaries between the words. Finally show them the original version for marking or feedback. Alternatively, read or play a text while students have a transcription with a number of different words or chunks. Students underline precisely what is different and, optionally, write in the version they hear.

15.6 Teach vocabulary aurally and in high-frequency chunks

Revise vocabulary aurally/orally via chunks and sentences rather than from word lists or apps. Make sure students hear each word or phrase at least five times. If you do vocabulary mini-quizzes, make sure they involve listening rather than, say, completing written glossaries. The simplest zero preparation revision lesson can involve just reading aloud phrases or sentences for students to translate. Isolated word learning does little to help students specifically recognise vocabulary in the sound stream.

15.7 Focus on parsing skills

Look again at examples of such activities in Chapter 5. Any work you do on grammar, such as drilling, sentence-combining, gap-filling and structured QA will help build listening skills. As always, the more meaningful you can make such work, the better.

15.8 Inference and predictive skills

Inference: try using written texts for training first, then move on to aural sources when you think students are ready. Applying inference strategies to reading comprehension is easier and less threatening. Model the process to the class using the think-aloud technique, showing how you can use morphology, syntax, key words and knowledge of the world to guess meaning. Then provide practice by giving students texts with a number of new words for them to infer the meaning using contextual clues.

Prediction: demonstrate how you can predict the next word or phrase by think-aloud, then give students *Guess what comes next* tasks, i.e. read the beginning of a sentence and students must guess what comes next.

15.9 Short low-stakes assessment

Rather than getting students to sit through a whole past exam paper, try doing only one question at a time with them. If you prepare students thoroughly beforehand so they have a high level of vocabulary knowledge, the input will be largely comprehensible and task success will be greater. Once again, this means you need to consider adapting text book or exam material to scaffold for success. You may be thinking: but the exam will not be like this, so we have to allow them to cope with really difficult material. We suggest that, yes, experience of the 'real thing' is necessary, but it should be a small part of the overall diet. Success is more likely to emerge if you have worked intensively on bottom-up skills over a long period.

15.10 Work with transcripts

Students will gain skills and confidence more quickly if you work with a transcript of the listening text, especially where longer extracts are concerned. It is simple and productive to print off gapped transcripts to complete. Consider carefully where you wish to place the gaps. Is the focus on vocabulary, morphology, verbs, grammatical function words? Seeing text while listening continues to build students' phonics and sound segmentation skills. Consider producing a booklet of listening tasks of this type in the run-up to exams. These could be used regularly in class or taken away for homework if the listening source is available online or digitally.

15.11 Task familiarity and task-specific strategies

Once you have identified the exam tasks your students usually lose the most marks in, spend some time going through the past exam papers and identify their most typical features, such as the format, the register, the typical comprehension questions asked, the kind of vocabulary and grammar structures they contain, the syntax (e.g. Is there a lot of subordination? Are they rich in adjectives, adverbs or idioms you do not normally teach?). Ensure students are very familiar and

practised at doing the required question types. Typical question formats at intermediate level include:
- matching short extracts with a one word or short phrase title, or someone's name;
- multiple-choice with L1 or L2 prompts;
- L1 or L2 sentences to complete (with or without options to choose from);
- questions in L1 or L2;
- note-taking in L1 or L2, e.g. completing a grid;
- choosing correct L1 or L2 statements from a list;
- matching a picture to an extract;
- identifying a general opinion or emotion from a choice of three.

We can teach students how to cope specifically with multiple-choice questions, helping them deal with distractors to avoid falling for obvious traps. These could include words which sound similar and verb tense forms. Low-preparation activities such as getting students to choose a time frame from two or three similar sounding verbs are useful. Incidentally, some research evidence suggests that getting used to hearing verb forms without additional time phrases makes learners more acutely aware of verb morphology and meaning. When the test supplies two listenings of an extract, teach students not to switch off after the first listening. They often come up with a first hypothesis answer which they then fail to test on the second listening. Other students, often higher-attaining ones, can overcomplicate matters by rejecting a first hypothesis which was correct.

15.12 Retrospective reports

At the beginning of your pre-exam listening programme you may want to elicit as much information as possible about the problems your students experience in performing listening tasks. One method that can yield useful data involves retrospective reports carried out immediately after a task has been done. Ask students, as part of a classroom discussion or in writing (e.g. on a Google Doc or similar) to describe what they found difficult about the task. Do this with more than one task, if time allows, in order to get as clear a picture as possible of what gaps you need to address. Your findings can inform your subsequent planning.

15.13 Independent listening

You only have a limited time in the classroom, so get students to seek out online short videos which may correspond with their areas of interest, some of which will be sub-titled. Young children's cartoons such as Peppa Pig are a good source of comprehensible language for many students. Specific sites can be recommended for audio material, such as *audio-lingua.eu* which has easy, short authentic extracts in over a dozen languages. Encourage students to watch easier sub-titled films, for example using Netflix, and to listen to L2 songs, for example using the site *lyricstraining.com*, where students can follow and interact with transcripts of songs as they watch a video. Listening on the bus to school each morning may appeal to some students.

Concluding remarks

This chapter has considered assessment *for* learning and *of* learning, raising a number of significant issues which have a bearing on your pedagogy. A fundamental issue is the disconnect between an approach based on developing listening skills using highly understandable texts and the realities of high-stakes exams, in which source material is designed to be too difficult to fully comprehend. We would urge teachers to stick to sound pedagogical principles and to attempt to design formative and summative tests which echo good practice as far as possible. The following chapter looks in more detail at how teaching cognitive and metacognitive strategies can mitigate the challenges of texts which are hard to understand, and difficult high-stakes exams.

Questions to consider

What constraints do high stakes exams place on your choice of pedagogy?

What are the challenges in isolating the skill of listening for assessment purposes?

What is the value of vocabulary learning and testing for developing listening skills?

The essence of knowledge is self-knowledge.
                    (Plato)

11

COGNITIVE AND METACOGNITIVE STRATEGIES

Introduction

Our main focus in this book has been on improving bottom-up listening skills. But what if these are not enough for students to make sense of texts? Can we teach students specific *compensatory* strategies, 'coping strategies' if you like, to help them improve their performance in listening? How can students make best use of metacognitive techniques alongside their existing linguistic knowledge? This chapter looks at what strategies are, what research supports their use and how you might implement them in your classroom for the benefit of students. A consideration of how to help students prepare for authentic speech is also offered.

1. What are strategies?

1.1 Strategies in general

In the literature they have been described in various ways, but can be seen as thoughts and actions, consciously chosen and used by language learners, to help them perform a range of tasks. The term language *learner* strategies, which incorporates strategies used for language learning and language use, is sometimes used, although the line between the two is a little vague as moments of second language use also provide opportunities for learning (Cohen, 2011; Macaro, 2007). Here is another way of viewing the processes involved in learning strategies (Griffiths, 2008). They are:

- active; they are what students do (both mental and physical behaviour);
- conscious (although they can become automatic, at some level students are partially conscious of them even if not attending to them fully);
- chosen by the student (there needs to be active involvement);
- purposeful (towards the goal of learning the language);
- used by the student to control or regulate their own learning;
- about learning the language more than employing what has been learned.

In the literature strategies are also divided into two types: **cognitive** strategies (using the input itself) and **metacognitive** strategies (planning, monitoring and evaluating the success of the learning). **Table 11.1** summarises the differences between them. In listing some strategies later in the chapter these are combined for the sake of simplicity. In addition, Vandergrift (1997) refers to what he calls socio-affective strategies, such as asking questions for clarification, cooperation and self-encouragement.

Table 11.1 Cognitive and metacognitive strategies summarised (adapted from Vandergrift, 1997).

Cognitive strategies (organisation and use of new material in the input)	**Metacognitive strategies** (planning, monitoring and evaluating success)	
<ul><li>Linguistic inferencing</li><li>Kinesic inferencing (using facial expression, body language, etc)</li><li>Extra-linguistic inferencing (situational clues)</li><li>Between-parts inferencing (using two or more other bits of information from the text to arrive at a third piece of information)</li><li>Summarising</li><li>Grouping</li><li>Resourcing</li><li>Translation</li><li>Transfer</li><li>Deduction</li><li>Induction</li><li>Repetition</li><li>Substitution</li></ul>	Planning	<ul><li>Advance organisation</li><li>Directed attention</li><li>Selective attention</li><li>Goal setting</li></ul>
	Monitoring	<ul><li>Comprehension monitoring</li><li>Double-check monitoring</li><li>Auditory monitoring</li></ul>
	Evaluating	<ul><li>Performance evaluation</li><li>Strategy evaluation</li><li>Problem-identification</li><li>Goal checking</li></ul>

1.2 Listening strategies

With specific regard to listening Michael Rost (2002) came up with a concise definition of strategies He described them as "conscious plans to manage incoming speech" (p.236). A review of research into listening strategies (Macaro, Graham, & Vanderplank, 2007) highlighted four strategies that play an important part in the listening process:
- Making predictions about the likely content of a listening text.
- Selectively attending to certain aspects of the passage, e.g. deciding to listen out for particular words, phrases or ideas.
- Monitoring and evaluating comprehension, i.e. checking that you are in fact understanding or have made the correct interpretation.
- Using a variety of clues (linguistic, contextual, and background knowledge) to infer the meaning of unknown words.

Before looking at strategies in detail, let us consider the general research which supports their use.

2. What does research say about strategies?

2.1 Do strategies work?

Can we be sure that strategies make a difference when it comes to listening? A growing body of research suggests they do. First, there is evidence that skilled L2 listeners use a repertoire of strategies to regulate how they listen. They appear, in particular, to use more metacognitive strategies than less skilled learners. Vandergrift and Tafaghodtari (2010) carried out a study with 106 students studying French as a second language (FSL). They compared two groups taught by the same teacher and found that the group who used metacognitive strategies outperformed the control group in comprehension. In addition, the gains for less able listeners were greater than for skilled listeners – something to bear in mind if you consider implementing a strategies programme.

Graham and Macaro (2008) carried out a study with low-intermediate French students in England. It showed that a programme of listening strategy instruction did somewhat improve performance in listening tests of the students involved. Other research studies have shown mixed results, which is why we believe that, while strategies can bring some gains, they are far less important than other aspects of listening instruction. Graham (2017) claims that the most recent research provides firmer evidence for teaching strategies.

However, the conclusions to be drawn from research are not totally clear-cut. Critics of strategy instruction have pointed out, for instance, that when researchers carry out studies of this type students know they are part of an experiment, so may feel more focused on the tasks they are doing and consequently achieve more highly. This is known as the *Hawthorne effect*. You can imagine how difficult it is to do research comparing groups of students who use learning strategies with other groups who do not, when there are so many variables, as well as the teacher, in play. How can you be sure it is a learning strategy or strategies that have produced a particular outcome? The best language learners may just use successful strategies unconsciously.

Another issue teachers need to keep in mind before embarking on strategy instruction is the fact that strategies are not inherently good or bad. It is how they are used that makes a difference. As Skehan (1989) has pointed out, it is possible that 'good' language learning strategies are also used by bad language learners, but other reasons make them unsuccessful. Hence, strategy instruction requires much more expertise on the part of teachers than identifying the target strategies.

Finally, it should be noted that the failure of many strategy instruction programmes has been pinned down to their short duration (i.e. two or three months). For training in listening strategies to pay significant dividends and have a long-term impact it may have to involve many weeks of extensive reinforcement.

2.2 Strategies and self-efficacy

It is well known that students' beliefs about their own ability to accomplish specific tasks are important. This is referred to as their sense of agency or feeling of self-efficacy (see Chapter 1). Put more simply, when students feel confident about tasks they tend to do them better. Can using strategies build self-efficacy?

Researchers claim that students who attribute the level of their achievement on tasks to factors within their control (e.g. to effort expended or to strategies employed) are likely to have higher levels of self-efficacy and to be motivated to try similar tasks again. Since they can alter the effort or the strategies they use, there is always a possibility of improvement. In contrast, students who attribute their lack of success to factors beyond their control, such as the difficulty of the tasks, or their perception of lack of ability, are likely to have lower levels of self-efficacy and motivation.

Graham (2006) has suggested that self-efficacy beliefs for a skill such as listening comprehension may be particularly important. A study by Graham and Macaro (2008) not only showed gains in comprehension, but also gains in self-efficacy. Why is self-efficacy particularly important for listening? One reason is that students might view the processes involved in listening as relatively uncontrollable. A text is heard two or three times, then they are on their own. Having specific strategies available might play a part in increasing students' sense of personal control. If students can see that their use of a strategy helped them do better they will use it again, consciously or unconsciously, and feel more self-confident as a result.

Furthermore, research confirms what many teachers know, namely that listening is a cause of anxiety for students (e.g. Bekleyen, 2009). Students often worry that they need to understand every word to understand what they hear. Whatever possible gains strategies produce, it is easy to argue that using strategies can reassure students by offering them ways to use their knowledge and compensate for any lack of skill.

3. A pedagogical cycle

One model for incorporating strategies which has been developed over the years is most associated with Larry Vandergrift, e.g. in Vandergrift (2003). You might use it with intermediate-level students when dealing with lengthier, less comprehensible texts. **Table 11.2** explains how it works.

Table 11.2 A pedagogical cycle for implementing strategies

Pedagogical stages	Metacognitive processes
Prelistening: Planning/predicting stage 1. After students have been told about the topic and text type, they predict the types of information and possible words they may hear.	1. Planning and directed attention.
First listen 2. Students verify their initial hypotheses, correct as required, and note additional information understood	2. Selective attention, monitoring and evaluation.
3. Students compare what they have understood or written with peers, modify as required, establish what still needs solving, and decide on the important details that still require attention.	3. Monitoring, evaluation, planning and selective attention.
Second listen 4. Students verify points of earlier disagreement, make corrections, and write down additional details understood.	4. Selective attention, monitoring, evaluation and problem solving.
5. Class discussion in which all class members contribute to the reconstruction of the text's main points and most significant details, interspersed with reflections on how students arrived at the meaning of certain words or parts of the text.	5. Monitoring, evaluation and problem solving.
Third listen 6. Students listen specifically for the information revealed in the class discussion which they were not able to decipher earlier.	6. Selective attention, monitoring and problem solving.
Reflection stage 7. Based on earlier discussions of strategies used to compensate for what was not understood, students write goals for the next listening activity.	7. Evaluation and planning.

4. Examples of listening strategies

So what, in practice, are some of the specific strategies you can teach to students? Here are a number of ways students can make use of both cognitive and metacognitive strategies to help them decipher meaning.

- Work out the type of text (conversation, news, etc.). This can often form part of the pre-listening phase of a listening lesson.
- Figure out the general topic; try to get the gist. It is always worth reminding students that they need not panic if they only pick out small bits of information on first contact with the text and that it will get easier on further listenings. By the way, it is worth being flexible about this. Just because a text book suggests two listenings or playing sections of a certain length, you can always adapt the material to the needs of the class.
- Pay attention to visual clues when working with video, e.g. facial expressions, gesture and visual content in general. This is particularly useful with interpersonal listening when the teacher often uses gesture to signal meaning.
- Think about the tone of voice; what feeling are speakers showing?
- Seek out familiar words and phrases, cognates, suffixes and prefixes.
- Pre-listening: pre-activate students' linguistic and non-linguistic knowledge by providing mind-maps, vocabulary lists, using brainstorming activities related to expected content of what is going to be heard (Graham, 2017).
- Teach students all sorts of background knowledge to help them make sense of texts, e.g. when deciphering a text about the environment it is useful if students have plenty of knowledge about issues such as sustainability, pollution, recycling and global warming. This helps them guess what people might be talking about. If a conversation is taking place about vegetarianism it is useful if students are already well-acquainted with the arguments being discussed. Text books often cover this type of information pretty well.
- Post-listening discussion in pairs or with the teacher. "What did you find hard or easy?"; "What would help you improve in the future?"

5. Raising awareness about strategies

If you wish encourage students to think about strategies, you could give them a questionnaire. An example is the Metacognitive Awareness Listening Questionnaire (MALQ) from Vandergrift et al (2006). The idea is to ask the questions just after an exercise has been carried out. Below are some example statements from the MALQ questionnaire which students answer using a 1-5 scale.

- Before I start to listen I have a plan in my head about how I shall listen.
- I translate in my head when I listen.
- I try to get back on track when I lose concentration.

- As I listen I compare what I am hearing with what I already know about the topic.
- Before listening I think of similar tasks I have done before.
- When I have difficulty understanding, I give up and stop listening.

Questionnaires and other verbal reports bring what is usually automatic behaviour into students' awareness. Handing out a questionnaire may amplify the importance of strategies, as long as the answers are followed up by discussion and 'action points'.

6. An example of modelling strategies

Play an extract to the class and then try the the approach below:

1. Ask students what they did when they failed to understand certain words or phrases. Students discuss this question in pairs.
2. Pairs feed back the things they did when they did not understand as you write them up on the board.
3. Take two of the ideas and, replaying the recording, use 'think aloud' to demonstrate how they could be used, e.g. making use of repetition or cognates to work out meaning.
4. Then model another strategy, such as using nearby words to work out the meaning of an unknown word, e.g. in French: *La plage était très belle et couverte de sable fin (The beach was very beautiful and covered in fine sand)*. The possibly unknown word *sable (sand)* could be inferred from the presence of *plage* and the word *couvert*, which sounds like *cover* in English.
5. Hand out a checklist of strategies. Use another audio passage to try a couple out.
6. After the task students think about which of the strategies seemed to be the most helpful and why, recording their reflections in a log (see Section 7 below).

7. Encouraging self-monitoring

Below is an example of a checklist sheet students can be given to encourage them to reflect on their thinking before and during a listening activity. Students tick and perhaps discuss any strategies they used after the lesson.

Before I listened I...

1. read the exercise carefully, paying attention to the instructions and pictures;
2. thought of possible words, phrases and ideas I might hear;
3. thought about how these words and phrases would be pronounced;
4. thought of the different ways certain phrases could be expressed.

While I listened I paid attention to:

1. repetition or paraphrase;
2. marker phrases;
3. the questions and tasks that go with the passage;
4. all the things I predicted (questions, vocabulary, possible answers).

While I listened I worked out any words I didn't know by:

1. using the words I did understand to get the general meaning of the passage first;
2. listening to words that came before or after the unknown word;
3. using my general knowledge to think about what the unknown word might logically mean;
4. listening to what came later in the passage for further clues, or to check whether the unknown word did in fact mean what I thought it meant;
5. using what I know about sentence structure to work out what kind of word it is (noun, adjective, verb);
6. thinking whether the unknown word is like a word I know in English (or another language), and then checking whether that meaning would make sense.

In future listening tasks I would like to improve
....

I am going to try these strategies (put the strategy number)
....

Teacher's comment:
....

(We are grateful to Suzanne Graham for providing us with the above.)

8. Scaffolding the strategies: an example

In a study by Graham (2007) students were asked to keep a reflective diary or strategy use log over a month, under the headings of *Preparation for Listening*, *Process of Listening*, and *Checking/Monitoring* (based on Vandergrift's (2003) pedagogical cycle (**Table 11.2**). In addition, they were asked to comment on their progress in listening using the following headings:

- What went well? Why?
- What did not go so well? Why?
- How do you feel?
- What next?

The aim was to try to modify the students' metacognitive beliefs about why they were doing well or not so well. Students handed in their logs to the researchers, who then underlined the connection between strategies and outcomes in the feedback they gave to students. When students tried to attribute their learning outcomes to things other than strategies, such as the speed of the recording or the difficulty of the task, the researchers tried to show in their feedback how a different strategy might help them cope with these aspects.

The purpose of this was to draw students' attention to the link between what they did (i.e. the strategies they used) and how well the listening task had gone, and to get them thinking about what strategies they might try out in the future to further improve their learning.

Below is an example of the type of feedback given, which might assist you in developing a similar programme (via Suzanne Graham):

Thank you for writing some interesting comments…Some of the strategies you list as using are helping with this progress—thinking of synonyms for what you might hear is important, as you say, as is making use of how the speaker says things in different ways. When the passage seems fast and fuzzy, try to use some of the strategies we have used to do with intonation—can you try to see where the stress is in the passage, where the speaker has a little pause at the end of sense groupings? You say that you will try to listen out for a phrase at a time—this can be helpful, but don't forget to also take into account what comes before or after the phrase, and don't lose sight of the overall meaning of the passage.

9. Implementing a strategies programme

How might you go about doing this? Working with strategies is firstly about making *explicit* the processes students are already using to help them learn and, secondly, exposing them to a greater range of strategies in order to widen their repertoire and make their learning even more effective. However, it is debatable whether strategies should be taught in dedicated lessons or integrated into normal language learning activities. We favour the laatter, but whichever route you take, it is always worth reminding students to use strategies. It may serve little purpose to tell students once and assume they will always remember what to do. So we are talking here about integrating strategies into the whole formative assessment framework: helping students as often as possible to find the best way of working for themselves to make the maximum progress.

Most research studies have adopted the sequence of steps listed below.

1. Consciousness raising, in which students reflect on their learning and on the strategies they use at present.
2. Modelling of selected strategies by the teacher.

3. Guided and structured practice of the new strategies in the context of normal class activities, with gradually fewer reminders to use appropriate strategies.
4. Action planning, goal setting and evaluation, whereby students identify problem areas, select strategies that might help remedy them and evaluate their success.

To give an example which is quite common in listening assessments, let us say you want to help students recognise opinions given in a text about an issue by getting them to listen out for words and phrases such as *but, on the other hand, however, I agree. I disagree, in my opinion.* Using the above model you would:

1. Ask students what clues they might listen for when trying to work out someone's opinions.
2. Explain that key words and expressions can give a clue about what people think, even if you do not know precisely what they are saying. Tell them what words and expressions to listen out for.
3. Play an audio example, such as from a listening exam, and point out where the key words and phrases are used. Look out for similar examples in the future or build them into your teaching sequence.
4. Ask students to identify obstacles to their comprehension and think of other strategies to help them understand, e.g. using cognates, intonation, or their general knowledge about situations which might help them work out meanings in a text.

Very often you can build strategy instruction organically into your lessons. You can model them by talking them through via think-aloud during an activity, using language such as: "I would listen through once to get the gist, not get hung up on individual words. Do not worry if it seems hard at first; that is normal. Then second time through you can listen out for individual words and understand a bit more," etc. Once strategies have been repeatedly taught or mentioned explicitly there is a chance that they will subsequently be used unconsciously by students.

10. Helping students prepare for language they will hear outside the classroom

We all know how often our students struggle to understand authentic speech when they encounter it for the first time. "It's not like the language we hear in class." "They speak so fast!" "The accent is really weird." "They seem to miss words out."

As you will have gathered, we do not believe in presenting and practising a diet of fast, authentic speech to beginner-to-intermediate students, since this goes against principles of comprehensibility, scaffolding new language, slowing things down to make them easier, moving from easy to harder, avoiding cognitive overload and so on. However, with this approach, it is possible to neglect preparing students for cases where the natural spoken form is unlike the 'correct' grammatical or written form. This typically occurs when speakers elide from one sound or word to the next, drop redundant words or omit some sounds completely. In English, if you say *Do you know what he does for a living?* it might actually sound something like this: *Dje know wha' 'e does fer a livin?* Imagine the difficulties this can create for a novice learner of English. Look what happens to this French sentence: *Tu n'aimes pas ce qu'il a fait il y a deux ans?* (*Don't you like what he did two years ago?*) It would probably sound something like this: *T'aime pa squ'il a fait ya deux ans?* Or how about this example: *Je ne sais pas si tu as fait tes exercices.* (*Chai pas si t'as fait te zercices.*)

This kind of perceptual difficulty confronts students all the time, especially in languages like English and French where there are so many mismatches between sound and spelling, so many mute sounds, liaisons between words, de-stressed words and syllables, and omitted words or sounds.

Here are some specific classroom activities which help students adjust to these problems of perception. The focus here is specifically on French, but think how these would apply to other languages.

1. Dictate short sentences, slowed down or at natural speed, with examples of perceptual difficulty. Students have to write down what they hear using their own phonetic code (assuming you have not taught them the basics of the International Phonetic Alphabet).
2. As above, but ask students to write down correctly spelled versions of the same utterances. Target frequently occurring examples of mismatch between authentic speech and 'correct' forms. For example, in French these could include: omission of *ne*, e.g. *Je sais pas, je pense pas, je crois pas* or before imperatives (*fais pas de bêtises*) and omission (elision) of the /u/ sound before verbs beginning with vowels as in: *t'aimes, t'adores, t'écoutes*.
3. Have students transcribe pairs of sentences with identical meaning, some with phrases or chunks which have optional liaison in French. (Liaison between vowels and consonants is often optional in natural spoken French). Examples:
Vous aimez aller, Venez-ici, Un prix trop élevé, assez intelligent, vous pouvez aller, vous voulez avoir, je vais aller, très habile
4. Teach samples of some common differences in accent in various forms of the L2, e.g. in French alternative pronunciations of the /r/ sound (uvular or other), variations of nasal vowels (including the common addition of the *ng* sounds after nasals in the south of France), the Canadian accent - or at least one form of it, variations in the pronunciation of *ait* (*é* or the more open *ai*).
5. Do choral and individual repetition of all the above to help embed these forms in students' memories. Make it fun!
6. Make occasional use of non-text book authentic audio, e.g. from snippets on *audio-lingua.eu* or authentic videos from a commercial product such as *This is Language* or *TeachVid*. Do targeted gap-fill focusing on 'non-standard' examples of the L2.

7. Be prepared to use natural-sounding L2 in your own speech to help students get up to speed, e.g. when practising likes and dislikes let them hear both *Qu'est-ce que tu aimes faire?* and *Qu'est-ce que t'aimes faire?*
8. Mix up your pace of delivery in teacher-led oral work, e.g. QA or oral drills. Your default should be a bit slower than normal, but not artificially very slow.

Concluding remarks

Macaro (2006), in a review of the literature, reports the following claims about learning strategies on the basis of evidence-based scholarship:

1. Strategy use appears to correlate with various aspects of language learning success although there is a lack of consensus about whether the range, frequency and/or the nature of strategies or their use is the determinant factor.

2. There are group-level differences (e.g. more proficient and less proficient linguists) as well as individual differences in strategy use.

3. Strategy instruction/training appears to be effective in promoting successful learning if it is carried out over lengthy periods of time and if it includes a focus on meta-cognition, i.e. learning about learning.

Our overall view, as you have probably gathered by now, is that teaching strategies has a useful place. Whether you choose to design a planned, long-term approach to teaching them may well depend on the time you have available. We believe that, in most contexts, building them into to your regular teaching sequences repeatedly and in small doses may be the best approach. With the highest attaining classes where skill and confidence are high, strategy teaching may seem less critical, but with most classes they will bear fruit. In addition, the period in the run-up to high stakes exams, when students may be particularly anxious, may be a good time to place extra emphasis on strategies.

Questions to consider

To what extent do you already use strategy instruction?

How can strategies be incorporated in your curriculum plan?

How can you encourage students to be more autonomous strategy users?

It isn't where you come from, it's where you're going that counts.
        (Ella Fitzgerald)

12

PLANNING FOR IMPROVEMENT

Introduction

In this final chapter we put forward a possible strategic approach language departments or individual teachers might adopt if they wish to see an improvement in student listening performance and exam results. This could form the basis of useful discussions between colleagues as part of their continued professional development.

We know that for students to become good listeners it takes lots of time and practice, so there are no quick fixes. However, we are going to suggest, very concisely, what principles could be the basis of an overall plan of action. These principles would inevitably lead you into general discussions about the nature of second language learning: the importance of micro-skills, modelling, comprehensible input, interaction, explicit attention to grammar and vocabulary, the role of memory, repetition, spaced retrieval and so on. As teachers are loaded down with preparation, marking (grading), administrative duties and exam preparation, the pressures of the school week usually limit opportunities for discussions like this. Meetings often deal with organisational and administrative issues rather than those really interesting discussions about pedagogy.

So one significant course of action for a team would be a decision to commit to conversations about theory and pedagogy. It might be, for example, that one member of the faculty could have a role as a research expert who shares their knowledge with colleagues. On a regular basis departments could focus on aspects of theory and pedagogy, leading to sharing of 'best practice', resource writing or developmental observations (as opposed to inspections for appraisal or performance management reasons). Small scale teacher research projects could be carried out to ascertain if certain interventions such as a programme of listening micro-skill teaching lead to improved outcomes. Gianfranco carried out one such piece of informal research on LAM with his own classes which yielded positive results. You might find it a helpful model for small scale research:

https://gianfrancoconti.wordpress.com/2017/05/06/listening-as-modelling-in-action-a-report-on-a-20-week-experiment-with-my-year-8-french-classes/

Another useful discussion would relate to the extent to which your text book materials, if you use them, reflect effective practice and, if not, how they might be adapted to be more productive. As far as listening is concerned: which texts are fine as they stand? which ones should be rejected? which could be adapted or better read aloud? A decision might be reached, for example, to create digital transcripts of every listening text. These could then be used to produce a range of tasks, such as gap-fill, faulty transcription, word boundary spotting and so on.

In sum, we believe there is a very useful dialogue to be had which would result in an honest and critical evaluation of what you do, or perhaps as an affirmation of your current excellent practice.

Below we present a set of principles which could guide conversations or be the basis for an action plan.

Ten principles for guiding planning

1. Where are we now?

An evaluation of current practice is worth carrying out. To what extent do we understand the rationale and research support for activities we do? What percentage of time is spent on one-way and two way-listening? Where listening is happening, to what extent is it focused on process? How do students respond to listening lessons? Is it worth carrying out a 'student voice' survey, or setting up a focus group, to establish students' perspective on listening? What is our balance of audio, video and teacher voice input? If listening is fundamental to acquisition, are we really placing listening at the core of what we do?

2. Target language

How much L2 are we using in class? To what extent does the Scheme of Work/Learning or Curriculum Plan spell out that L2 use is at the heart of lessons? Is this actually carried out? We would not suggest a specific percentage of L2 use since this is too directive and classes vary, but a conscious decision can be made that L2 is the default position. Most of the listening students do is, as we have noted, interpersonal. So should interactive, communicative lessons be a number one priority - **using the language, not talking about it**? How would L2-based lessons look? We know this is a challenging area for many teachers. Would they include choral repetition, reading aloud, the use of sentence-builder frames, thorough structured drilling and QA interactions, L2 games, less controlled dialogues such as role-play, adapting dialogues, information gap activities and communicative tasks? We know students who receive a consistent diet of meaningful interaction will inevitably become better listeners. Why not share with students the rationale for what you do?

3. It is fine to just listen

With pressure on to ensure students are active and 'having fun', do we avoid long bouts of listening work? We know listening is by no means a passive task, so while lessons usually need to be varied to hold interest, is it fine to plan for quiet, active listening in lessons, alongside a diet of teacher-led and paired oral practice? Is spending 20 minutes working on a gapped transcript or dictation more beneficial than a piece of unstructured role play or producing a digital artefact? Furthermore, importantly, would overworked teachers be justified in seeing the 'listening lesson' as a time to recharge batteries as the class does a calm activity? We are familiar with this feeling!

4. Not just comprehension

Instead of just doing comprehension, how many exercises do we do which develop the micro-skills of listening? Could we weave into lessons activities suggested in Chapters 3, 4 and 5? Do we do enough transcription, dictation, gap-filling and intonation practice? Do we take every opportunity to develop phonological and phonics skills by doing specific pronunciation practice, teaching letter to sound equivalents and talking about phonetics and phonology? Do we ever make do with second-best when it comes to pronunciation? Do we exploit short, comprehensible texts thoroughly, rather than longer, harder to understand texts superficially?

5. Listening for a purpose

We know students enjoy meaning-focused tasks with a purpose, so do we build into the curriculum at all levels specific communicative tasks and games where the focus is on listening? Do we find a suitable balance of process-focused, nitty-gritty listening work with information gaps, whole class tasks and purposeful games, such as those described in Chapters 6 and 7? Do we make listening a social activity whenever we can? Do we have chats at the door when students enter or leave? Do we have register routines incorporating use of L2? Do we start lessons with brief listening and speaking exchanges about likes, dislikes, what students did last weekend, last lesson or last night?

6. Confident listeners

We know that making listening tasks comprehensible and feasible builds self-efficacy and creates confident listeners. Are we using texts and our own input at or just above the students' current level? If we use a more challenging resource, do we scaffold exercises sufficiently, exploiting the material intensively so students feel they have mastered it? Are we flexible in our use of audio material, reading it aloud or giving extra opportunities to listen? Do we also make occasional use of short, authentic material so students get to hear what the real language sounds like? Do we use all our teacher skills to make listening comprehensible: gesture, pictures, facial expression, slowing down and so on. Do we deliberately practise these skills? Do we translate from time to time, paraphrase, repeat and pause? Do we write language up on the board after using it? Do we use formative assessment techniques to check for understanding?

7. Strategies

When comprehension fails, students may have to fall back on compensatory strategies for coping. Do we help students to think of ways they can work out meaning when they do not understand the input: their general knowledge of the world, their knowledge of what they might expect people to say, the intonation of what is said, and other linguistic clues? Do we have techniques for developing these skills, such as modelling, thinking aloud and specific strategy exercises? Do we rely too much on these to compensate for weak decoding skills or an inappropriate choice of text? Have we discussed the role and range of strategies to support listening? Have we considered building these into the curriculum? Do we discuss with students their problems with listening and ways to cope with harder texts? Do we do everything we can to find out what students think about listening? Do we attempt to reduce any anxiety about the process?

8. Vocabulary

If we know that vocabulary knowledge is central to listening skills and language acquisition, how might we improve our approach? Are we doing too much isolated word learning? Could we present and practise words through chunks, sentences and paragraphs? Does our syllabus create opportunities to review vocabulary on a regular basis through tasks and texts? Do we take every opportunity to present vocabulary through the aural medium? Do we keep in mind forgetting rates and the principle of spaced learning?

9. Test and exam preparation

Do we have a planned, agreed approach to the run-up to high stakes exams? Do we match our teaching to the test and vice versa? How influenced are we by washback? Are our students well versed in the question types they will encounter? Are we explicit in telling students what they will be tested on? Are our own tests fair, generating scores which will not discourage students?

10. Sharing good practice

Do we have good systems in place, both formal and informal, for sharing resources and good practice? Do we try to devote departmental meeting time to discussion of pedagogy in addition to administrative matters?

We hope that these questions will help guide any improvement programme you may have. We are sure you will agree that even if our students are already doing very well, we can always perfect our craft.

CONCLUSION

In this book we have made the case for making listening a greater focus of lessons. We have emphasised the idea of concentrating on the *process*: how students listen, rather than the product. On the basis that you get better at what you practise, it should be self-evident that the more listening you do to comprehensible language, the better you will become both at listening and acquiring a language in general. We have also argued that working on the micro-skills of listening will ultimately help produce students who understand more spoken language. Through this approach, teaching listening is much more about *modelling* than testing comprehension. In a nutshell, it is about doing listening intensively, not superficially.

You will have observed that we have made a deliberate effort to obtain a balance between activities which are tightly focused on micro-skills and others which model listening via an approach based on achieving communicative goals. You can decide which are the best fit with the students you teach. We are fully aware that classroom contexts and teachers' tastes vary enormously.

Not every activity we have outlined will be your cup of tea, and some readers may even take issue with some of our basic assumptions, but given the reality that classrooms are inhabited by students of varying abilities and motivations, tasks have been chosen which we believe are research-supported, manageable, structured and engaging, suitable for a full range of attainment. We have also selected activities which in general take little preparation: 'low preparation, high impact', as the saying goes.

One of the pleasures of being a language teacher, and a teacher in general, is the creativity it allows you to exercise when planning a curriculum and individual lessons. As teachers we have enjoyed this aspect of the job greatly over the years and take pleasure in sharing what we have read about, picked up from fellow teachers or invented. In our own classrooms we have applied the principles put forward and used thr activities we have described. We hope our tasks will also inspire you to come up with your own, better ones, with the goal of helping students enjoy language learning to the full. Please let us know about your own ideas via social media.

Gianfranco and Steve

Contact us

Twitter: @gianfrancocont9   @spsmith45

Gianfranco's email: thelanguagegymcpd@gmail.com

Steve's email: spsmith45@aol.com

Further reading

The Language Teacher Toolkit (2016) by Steve Smith and Gianfranco Conti.

Becoming an Outstanding Languages Teacher (2017) by Steve Smith (Routledge).

Gianfranco's blog The Language Gym at gianfrancoconti.wordpress.com.

Steve's blog Language Teacher Toolkit at frenchteachernet.blogspot.com.

Further resources

Gianfranco's resources for French, Italian and Spanish teachers can be found at tes.com

Steve's resources for French teachers can be found at frenchteacher.net.

Gianfranco and Steve also have a TES shop with free and paid-for resources at tes.com.

APPENDIX: LIST OF TASKS

Phonological and phonics tasks (Chapter 3)

Task	Page
Alphabet fun games	52
Battleship phonics	46
Beat the Teacher	53
Break the flow	43
Break the flow with intruder	43
Broken words	41
Catch the first or last letter	42
Contrast response	41
Critical listening	51
Delayed dictation	54
False facts dictation	56
Faulty echo	44
Find someone who (with cards)	49
Find your match	48
Gapped letters	42
Grading dictation	56
Group dictation	56
Inductive listening	52
Letters on the board	46
Listen and rearrange	41
Mad dictation	55
Mind-reading (teacher-led)	47
Mind-reading (student-led)	47
Minimal pairs	39
Multiple options	41
Paired gapped dictation	56
Partial dictation	54
Phonics bingo	39
Read and repeat	45
Repeating long or interesting words	47
Rhyming pairs	41
Running dictation	55
Scaffolded dictation	55
Sentence chaos	49
Sentence hunt	50
Sentence stealer	47
Spot and cross out the intruder	53
Spot the correct transcription	42
Spot the differences	49
Spot the different accent	53
Spot the error	44
Spot the foreign sound	40
Spot the intruder	44
Spot the missing word	45
Spot the mistakes and correct	53
Spot the silent endings	40
Spot the silent letters	40
Spot the wrong sound	42
Syllable anagrams	43
Syllable building blocks	43
Syllabling	54
The 'Algo' game	49
Tongue-twisters	50
Tongue-twister race	51
Track the pitch	52
Track the sound	44
Write it as you hear it	45
Writing unknown words	41

Lexical retrieval tasks (Chapter 4)

Task	Page
A walk through town	83
As many as you can	90
Associations	76
Bad translation	88
Blind mimes	82
Brain teasers	80
Categories	76
Climb the wall	77
Definition chains	78
Detectives	79
Disappearing text	93
Find the near-synonym	76

Gapped parallel texts	87
Gapped sentences	76
Guess how often	90
Guess what comes next	93
Listen and colour in	81
Listening bingo	86
Listening grids	90
Listening slalom	87
Match	78
Multi-choice match	86
Musical chairs	89
Mystery words	80
No snakes, no ladders race	89
Odd one out	76
Oral ping pong	89
Our sitting room	83
Photofit	84
Put in the right order	77
Quickfire translation	87
Re-ordering pictures or words	92
Running translation	88
Same or different?	79
Scenarios	93
Spot the differences (with pictures)	90
Spot the differences (with translation)	91
Spot the missing detail (content words)	85
Spot the nonsense	84
Substitution	91
Work out the word	78

Parsing tasks (Chapter 5)

Aural gap-fill	110
Aural sentence puzzles	108
Categories (for parsing)	110
Collocational grids	117
Collocations ping pong	117
Delayed dictation (for parsing)	111
Delayed dictation with open sentence combining	111
Delayed dictation with a cue for combining sentences	111
Dodgy translation	116
Exploiting a set of pictures	105
Faulty echo (for parsing)	108
Either… or	110
Find the object	112
Guess what comes next (for parsing)	109
Listen and change	110
Listen and correct	113
Minimal pair sentences	114
Morphology chart (with or without translation)	119
Multiple options (for grammatical accuracy judgment)	114
Mystery position	116
Narrow listening	118
Parsing grids	108
Partial dictation (for parsing)	108
Same or different? (for parsing)	116
Sentence breakdown	115
Sentence frames	115
Sorting tasks	
Spot and rewrite the pattern	109
Spot the missing detail (for parsing)	114
Spot the wrong collocation	118
Using sentence builders to model lexicogrammar	106
Word completion	119

Interpersonal listening tasks (Chapter 6)

Alibi	137
Answer-question	127
Choose the question	146
Correct the false statement	129
Correct the grammar	128
Correct the pronunciation	128
Creative storytelling from a picture	138
Describe a memorable event	134
Dictocomp	137

Dictogloss	136
False statement	127
Finish the sentence	127
Gap-fill	145
How many questions?	146
Liar, liar	141
'My house' video	135
Oral tennis	141
Question-answer	123
Read and look up	144
Recognition drills	145
Repeat the last few words	128
Rotation	144
Spot the time frame	146
Start the sentence	128
Talk about your family	135
The Price is Right	133
Time matching	147
Translate into L1	146
What can I take on holiday?	139
Write the question	146
Word by word	143
Yes/no game	142

Task-based listening tasks (Chapter 7)

Act out a story	169
Ask and move	158
Choose a hotel	163
Complete a school plan	153
Detectives and informants	159
Find out about your teacher	152
Guest speaker	155
House buyer	160
Lecture notes	154
Make a recipe	157
Map route	157
Plan a holiday	162
Opinion survey	163
Recount an anecdote	167
Talk about grandparents	156
Talk show	165
The two detectives	160
Video conversation	165
What's the story?	166
Which restaurant?	164

Other tasks (Chapters 8 and 9)

4,3,2 technique	181
Chronological ordering	193
Communication drills	177
Complete the beginnings/endings	193
Content re-ordering	184
Deductive or inductive teaching of grammar	179
Delayed repetition	176
Delayed translation	177
Fast and furious	180
Fluency cards	180
Gapped L2 texts	185
Gapped lyrics	195
Gapped parallel L2 text	184
Guided composition to a time limit	181
Guided summary	195
Jigsaw listening	194
Jigsaw reading	184
Listen and recall	177
Listen-stop carry on	184
Make a sentence competition	188
Market place	181
Narrow translation	178
Near synonyms/antonyms	193
Note-taking	185
One pen, one dice	176
One of three	177
Pyramid translation	180
Reading gap-fill	187
Role plays	179
Shadow reading	184
Spot the pattern	184
Short guided composition	178
Substitution tasks	195
Thinking about learning tasks	195
Vocabulary hunt	184

BIBLIOGRAPHY

Alderson, J. C. (2007). Judging the Frequency of English Words. *Applied Linguistics, 28 (3),* 383-409.

Al-jasser, F. (2008). The effect of teaching English phonotactics on the lexical segmentation of English as a foreign language. *System, 36 (1),* 94-106.

Allwright, D., & Bailey, K. M. (1991). *Focus on the language classroom: an introduction to classroom research for language teachers.* Cambridge: Cambridge University Press.

Alroe, M. J. (2011). Error Correction of L2 Students' Texts - Theory and Pedagogy. *Asian EFL Journal.* Available at: http://asian-efl-journal.com/PTA/February-201--Alroe.pdf.

Altenberg, B. (1998). On the phraseology of spoken English: The evidence of recurrent word combinations, in *Phraseology: Theory, Analysis and Applications* (Cowie, A.P ed.). Oxford: OUP p. 101-124.

Anderson, J.R. (1995). Developing expertise. In J.R. Anderson (Ed.) *Cognitive Psychology and its Implications.* New York; Freeman and Company.

Asher, J. J. (1969). The Total Physical Response Approach to Second Language Learning. *The Modern Language Journal, 53 (1),* 3–17.

Baddeley, A. D. (1999). *Essentials of human memory.* Psychology Press.

Baddeley, A. D. (2003). Working memory and language: an overview. *Journal of Communication Disorders, 36 (3),* 189-208.

Baddeley, A. D. (2010). Working memory. *Current Biology, 20 (4),* R136–R140. Available at: https://doi.org/10.1016/J.CUB.2009.12.014

Baddeley, A. D. Gathercole, S. & Papagno, C. (1998). The phonological loop as a language learning device. *Psychological Review, 105 (1),* 158-173.

Bandura, A. (1997). *Self-efficacy: the exercise of control.* New York, NY, US: W H Freeman/Times Books/ Henry Holt & Co.

Bauckham, A. (2016). Modern Foreign Languages Pedagogy Review (2016). Available at: https://www.tscouncil.org.uk/wp-content/uploads/2016/12/MFL-Pedagogy-Review-Report-2.pdf

Bekleyen, N. (2009). Helping teachers become better English students: Causes, effects, and coping strategies for foreign language listening anxiety. *System, 37 (4),* 664-675.

Biedron, A. & Szczepaniak, A. (2012). Working Memory and Short-Term Memory Abilities in Accomplished Multilinguals. *The Modern Language Journal, 96 (2),* 290-306.

Bilbrough, N. (2011). *Memory activities for language learning.* Cambridge: Cambridge University Press.

Blaxton, T. A. (1989). Investigating dissociations among memory measures: Support for a transfer-appropriate processing framework. *Journal of Experimental Psychology:*

Learning, Memory, and Cognition, 15 (4), 657-668.

Bradley, L. & Bryant, P. E. (1983). Categorizing sounds and learning to read: a causal connection. *Nature, 301 (5899),* 419-421.

Brett, A. Rothlein, L. & Hurley, M. (1996). Vocabulary Acquisition from Listening to Stories and Explanations of Target Words. *The Elementary School Journal.* The University of Chicago Press.

Brieter, L. R. (1971). Research in listening and its importance to literature. In L. Barker (Ed.) *Listening behavior.* Englewood Cliffs N-J: Prentice-Hall.

Brown, H. D. (2000). *Principles of language learning and teaching* (4th ed). White Plains, New York: Longman.

Brown, H. D. & Abeywickrama, P. (2010). *Language assessment: principles and classroom practices.* New York: Pearson Education.

Carpenter, S. K., & Olson, K. M. (2012). Are pictures good for learning new vocabulary in a foreign language? Only if you think they are not. *Journal of Experimental Psychology: Learning, Memory, and Cognition, 38 (1),* 92-101.

Carroll, J.B. (1966). The Contributions of Psychological Theory and Educational Research to the Teaching of Foreign Languages. In A. Valdman (1966) (ed.) *Trends in Language Teaching.* New York: McGraw Hill.

Chambers, G. N. (1996). Listening. Why? How? *The Language Learning Journal, 14 (1),* 23-27.

Christodoulou, D. (2017). *Making good progress? The future of assessment for learning.* Oxford: Oxford University Press.

Cohen, A. (2011). *Strategies in learning and using a second language* (2nd ed.). London: Longman.

Cohen R. L. (1981). On the generality of some memory laws. Scandinavian Journal of Psychology. 22, 267-281.

Conti, G. (2004). Metacognitive enhancement and error correction. Unpublished doctoral thesis, University of Reading, Reading, UK.

Corder, S. P. (1967). The Significance of Learners' Errors. *IRAL - International Review of Applied Linguistics in Language Teaching, 5,* 1-4.

Crystal, D. (2013). *The story of English in 100 words.* Profile Books Ltd.

Daller, H. Milton, J. & Treffers-Daller, J. (2007). *Modelling and assessing vocabulary knowledge.* Cambridge: Cambridge University Press.

De Jong, N. (2005). Can second language grammar be learned through listening? An Experimental Study. *Studies in Second Language Acquisition, 27 (2),* 205-234.

DeKeyser, R. (1998). Beyond focus on form: cognitive perspectives on learning and practicing second language grammar. In C. Doughty & J. Williams (Eds.), *Focus on Form in Classroom Second Language Acquisition.* Cambridge: Cambridge University Press.

Dekeyser, R., & Criado, R. (2012). Automatization, Skill Acquisition, and Practice in Second Language Acquisition. In *The Encyclopedia of Applied Linguistics.* Oxford: Blackwell Publishing Ltd.

Donato, R. & McCormick, D. (1994). A Sociocultural Perspective on Language Learning Strategies: The Role of Mediation. *The Modern Language Journal 78 (4),* 453-464

Doughty, C., & Long, M. H. (2003). *The handbook of second language acquisition.* Wiley-Blackwell.

Ebbinghaus, H. (1885). *Über das Gedächtnis.* Leipzig: Dunker.

Elley, W. B. (1989). Vocabulary Acquisition from Listening to Stories. *Reading Research Quarterly, 24 (2),* 174.

Ellis, N. C. (2005). At the Interface*: Dynamic Interactions of explicit and implicit language knowledge.* Available at: https://deepblue.lib.umich.edu/bitstream/handle/2027.42/139748/AttheInterface.pdf?sequence=1&isAllowed=y

Ellis, N. C. (2002). Frequency Effects in Language Processing: a Review with Implications for Theories of Implicit and Explicit Language Acquisition. *SSLA, 24,* 143-188.

Ellis, N.C. (2007). Implicit and explicit knowledge about language. In J. Cenoz & N. Hornberger (Eds.) *Encyclopedia of language and education.* Second Edition, Vol. 6: Knowledge about language (1-13). Berlin: Springer.

Ellis, N. C. (2015). Implicit and Explicit Language Learning: Their dynamic interface and complexity. Chapter in Patrick Rebuschat (Ed.). (2015). Implicit and explicit learning of languages (pp. 3-23). Amsterdam: John Benjamins.

Ellis, R. (1990). *Instructed second language acquisition: learning in the classroom.* Oxford: Blackwell.

Ellis, R. (2004). The Definition and Measurement of L2 Explicit Knowledge. *Language Learning, 54 (2),* 227-275.

Ellis, R. (2008). *The study of second language acquisition.* Oxford: Oxford University Press.

Ellis, R. (2009). Corrective Feedback and Teacher Development. *L2 Journal, 1,* 3-18. Available at: https://doi.org/10.5070/l2.v1i1.9054

Ellis, R. (2017). Position paper: Moving task-based language teaching forward. *Language Teaching, 50 (4),* 507-526.

Ellis, R., Sheen, Y., Murakami, M., & Takashima, H. (2008). The effects of focused and unfocused written corrective feedback in an English as a foreign language context. *System, 36 (3),* 353-371.

Erler, L. (2004). Near-beginner learners of French are reading at a disability level. *Francophonie* (published by the Association for Language Learning), *30,* 9-15. Available at: http://www.languageswithoutlimits.co.uk/Resources/Erler.pdf

Field, J. (1998). Skills and strategies: Towards a new methodology for listening. *ELT Journal, 52 (2),* 110-118.

Field, J. (2004). *Psycholinguistics: the key concepts.* London: Routledge.

Field, J. (2008). *Listening in the Language Classroom.* Cambridge: Cambridge University Press.

Finocchiaro, M. B., & Brumfit, C. (1983). *The functional-notional approach: from theory to practice.* Oxford: Oxford University Press.

Fletcher-Wood, H. (2018). *Responsive Teaching: Cognitive Science and Formative Assessment in Practice.* London: Routledge.

Forrin, N. D., & MacLeod, C. M. (2018). This time it's personal: the memory benefit of hearing oneself. *Memory, 26 (4),* 574-579.

Gallego, M. (2014). Second language learners' reflections on the effectiveness of dictogloss: A multi-sectional, multi-level analysis. *Studies in Second Language Learning and Teaching, 4 (1),* 33-50.

Gathercole, S. E. (2007). *Working Memory and Language.* Oxford: Oxford University Press.

Glisan, E. W. & Donato, R. (2017). *Enacting the work of language instruction: high-leverage teaching practices.* Alexandria, VA: American Council on the Teaching of Foreign Languages.

Goh, C. C. M. (2018). Listening Activities. In *The TESOL Encyclopedia of English Language Teaching* (1–7). Hoboken, NJ, USA: John Wiley & Sons, Inc.

Graham, S. (2006). Listening comprehension: The learners' perspective. *System, 34,* 165-182.

Graham, S. (2007) Learner strategies and self-efficacy: making the connection. *Language Learning Journal, 35 (1). Available at:* http://centaur.reading.ac.uk/12562/1/Learner_strategies_and_self-efficacy_author_version.pdf

Graham, S. (2017). Research into practice: Listening strategies in an instructed classroom setting. *Language Teaching, 50 (1),* 107-119.

Graham, S. & Macaro, E. (2008). Strategy Instruction in Listening for Lower-Intermediate Learners of French. *Language Learning, 58 (4),* 747-783.

Graham, S., Santos, D. & Francis-Brophy, E. (2014). Teacher beliefs about listening in a foreign language. *Teaching and Teacher Education, 40,* 44-60.

Griffiths, C. (ed.) (2008). *Lessons from Good Language Learners.* Cambridge: Cambridge University Press.

Gu, Y. (2018). Two-Way Listening. Chapter from *The TESOL Encyclopedia of English Language Teaching.* Wiley Blackwell.

Halliday, M. A. K. (1961). Categories of the Theory of Grammar. *Word, 17 (2),* 241-292.

Hasan, A. S. (2000). Learners' Perceptions of Listening Comprehension Problems. *Language, Culture and Curriculum, 13 (2),* 137-153.

Hawkes, R. (2012). Learning to talk and talking to learn: how spontaneous teacher-learner interaction in the secondary foreign languages classroom provides greater opportunities for L2 learning. Unpublished doctoral thesis. Available at: http://www.rachelhawkes.com/RHawkes_FinalThesis.pdf

Huang, X. Kim, N. & Christianson, K. (2019). Gesture and Vocabulary Learning in a Second Language. *Language Learning, 69 (1),* 177-197.

Huo, S., & Wang, S. (2017). The Effectiveness of Phonological-Based Instruction in English As a Foreign Language Students at Primary School Level: A Research Synthesis. *Frontiers in Education*, *2*, 15. Available at: https://doi.org/10.3389/feduc.2017.00015

Hutz, M. (2018). Focus on Form: The Lexico-Grammar Approach. In *Teaching English as a Foreign Language* (pp. 133-158). Stuttgart: J.B. Metzler.

Johnson, K. (1996). *Language teaching and skill learning*. Blackwell.

Jones, T. (Ed.) (2016). *Pronunciation in the classroom: the overlooked essential*. Tesol Press.

Kellaris, J. J. (2003). Dissecting earworms: Further evidence on the 'song-stuck-in-your-head' phenomenon. In C. Page & S. Posavac (Eds.), Proceedings of the Society for Consumer Psychology Winter Conference (pp. 220–222). Potsdam, NY: Society for Consumer Psychology.

Kelly, R. (1991). The Graeco-Latin Vocabulary of Formal English: Some Pedagogical Implications. *RELC Journal, 22 (1),* 69-83.

Krashen, S. D. (1982). *Principles and Practice in Second Language Acquisition*. Oxford: Pergamon. Available at: http://www.sdkrashen.com/content/books/principles_and_practice.pdf

Krashen, S.D. (1996). The case for Narrow Listening. *System 24 (1)* 97-100. Available at: http://sdkrashen.com/content/articles/the_case_for_narrow_listening.pdf

Krashen, S.D. (2001). Does "Pure" Phonemic Awareness Training Affect Reading Comprehension? *Perceptual and Motor Skills*, *93 (2),* 356-358.

Kroll, B. (1990). *Second language writing : research insights for the classroom*. Cambridge: Cambridge University Press.

Kumaravadivelu, B. (2006). *Understanding language teaching: from method to post-method*. Lawrence Erlbaum Associates.

Lantolf, J. P. (2000). *Sociocultural theory and second language learning*. Oxford: Oxford University Press.

Lantolf, J. P., & Pavlenko, A. (1995). Sociocultural Theory and Second Language Acquisition. *Annual Review of Applied Linguistics*, *15*, 108.

Larsen-Freeman, D. & Long, M. H. (1991). *An introduction to second language acquisition research*. London: Longman.

Laufer, B., & Rozovski-Roitblat, B. (2011). Incidental vocabulary acquisition: the effects of task type, word occurrence and their combination. *Language Teaching Research, 15 (4),* 391–411.

Lewis, M. (1993). *The lexical approach: the state of ELT and a way forward*. Language Teaching Publications.

Lichtman, K. (2018). *Teaching Proficiency Through Reading and Storytelling : an Input-Based Approach to Second Language Instruction*. New York: Routledge.

Lightbown, P. M. (2008). Transfer appropriate processing as a model for classroom second language acquisition. In Z. Han (Ed.), *Understanding second language process* (pp. 27-44). Clevedon, UK: Multilingual Matters.

Long, M. H. (1983). Does Second Language Instruction Make a Difference? A Review of Research. *TESOL Quarterly, 17 (3),* 359.

Long, M. H. (1996). The role of the linguistic environment in second language acquisition. In W. C. Ritchie & T. K. Bhatia (Eds.), *Handbook of second language acquisition* (pp. 413-468). San Diego, CA: Academic Press.

Long, M. H. (2015). *Second Language Acquisition and Task-Based Language Teaching.* Wiley-Blackwell.

Long, M. H., & Porter, P. A. (1985). *Group Work, Interlanguage Talk, and Second Language Acquisition.* Tesol Quarterly, *19 (2).* Available at: http://citeseerx.ist.psu.edu/viewdoc/download?doi=10.1.1.498.6985&rep=rep1&type=pdf

Ludke, K. M. (2010). Teaching Foreign Languages through Songs. Available at: https://www.era.lib.ed.ac.uk/bitstream/handle/1842/5500/Ludke%2c%20K.M.pdf?sequence=1&isAllowed=y

Lynch, T. (1998). Theoretical Perspectives on Listening. *Annual Review of Applied Linguistics, 18,* 3-19.

Macaro, E. (2001). *Learning strategies in foreign and second language classrooms.* Continuum.

Macaro, E. (2003). *Teaching and learning a second language: a review of recent research.* Continuum.

Macaro, E. (2006). Strategies for Language Learning and for Language Use: Revising the Theoretical Framework. *Modern Language Journal, 90,* 320-337.

Macaro, E. (2007). Language learner strategies: adhering to a theoretical framework. *Language Learning Journal, 35 (2),* 239-243.

Macaro, E., Graham, S. & Vanderplank, R. (2007). A review of listening strategies: Focus on sources of knowledge and on success. In A. D. Cohen & E. Macaro (eds.), *Language learner strategies: 30 years of research and practice.* Oxford: Oxford University Press, 165-185.

Meara, P. (1996). *The dimensions of lexical competence.* Available at: http://www.lognostics.co.uk/vlibrary/meara1996a.pdf

Milton, J., Wade, J., & Hopkins, N. (2010). Aural Word Recognition and Oral Competence in English as a Foreign Language. In R. Chacón-Beltrán, C. Abello-Contesse, & M. del M. Torreblanca-López (Eds.), *Insights into Non-native Vocabulary Teaching and Learning* (pp. 83-98). Bristol, Blue Ridge Summit: Multilingual Matters.

Morris, D. C., Bransford, J. & Franks, J. (1977). Levels of processing versus transfer appropriate processing. *Journal of Verbal Learning and Verbal Behavior, 16 (5),* 519-533.

Motallebzadeh, K. & Defaei, S. (2013). The Effect of Task-Based Listening Activities on Improvement of Listening Self-Efficacy among Iranian Intermediate EFL Learners. *International Journal of Linguistics, 5 (2),* 24-33.

Muter, V. & Diethelm, K. (2001). The Contribution of Phonological Skills and Letter

Knowledge to Early Reading Development in a Multilingual Population. *Language Learning, 51 (2),* 187-219.

Nabei, T. (1996). Dictogloss: Is It an Effective Language Learning Task? *Working Papers in Educational Linguistics, 12 (1),* 59-74.

Nation, I.S.P. (2007). The Four Strands. *Innovation in Language Learning and Teaching, 1 (1),* 2-13.

Nation, I. S. P. (2013). *Learning Vocabulary in Another Language.* Cambridge: Cambridge University Press.

Nation, I.S.P. and Newton, J. (2009) Teaching ESL/EFL Listening and Speaking. New York: Routledge

Nava, A. & Pedrazzini, L. (2018). *Second Language Acquisition in Action: Principles from Practice.* Bloomsbury Academic.

Nemati, A. (2010). Active and passive vocabulary knowledge: The effect of years of instruction. *Asian EFL Journal, 12,* 30-46.

Nguyen, H. H. (2018). Fostering Positive Listening Habits among EFL Learners through the Application of Listening Strategy and Sub-skill Instructions. *Journal of Language Teaching and Research 9 (2)* 268-279. Available at: https://pdfs.semanticscholar.org/8f50/db4e83a9b51ad3c1f188049bb790a7f7a988.pdf

Norris, J. M., & Ortega, L. (2000). Effectiveness of L2 Instruction: A Research Synthesis and Quantitative Meta-analysis. *Language Learning, 50 (3),* 417-528.

Nunan, D. (1991). Communicative Tasks and the Language Curriculum. *Tesol Quarterly, 25 (2),* 279-295.

Nunan, D. (1997). Listening in Language Learning. *The Language Teacher. The Japan Association of Language Learning. 21 (9),* 47-51.

Nunan, D. (2004). *Task-Based Language Teaching.* Cambridge: Cambridge University Press.

O'Malley, J.M & Chamot, A. U. (1990). *Learning Strategies in Second Language Acquisition.* Cambridge: Cambridge University Press.

Özkan, Y. & Kesen, A. (2009). The third way in grammar instruction. *Procedia - Social and Behavioral Sciences, 1,* 1931-1935.

Pachler, N. (2013). *Learning to teach foreign languages in the secondary school: a companion to school experience.* London: Routledge.

Paivio, A. (1986). *Mental Representations.* New York: Oxford University Press.

Pennebaker, J.W. (2013). *The Secret Life of Pronouns: What Our Words Say About Us.* Bloomsbury Press.

Pica, T., Doughty, C. & Young, R. F. (1987). The Impact of Interaction on Comprehension. *Tesol Quarterly 21.*

Pienemann, M. (1984). Psychological Constraints on the Teachability of Languages. *Studies in Second Language Acquisition, 6 (2),* 186-214.

Prabhu, N. S. (1987). *Second language pedagogy.* Oxford: Oxford University Press.

Qian, D. (1999). Assessing the Roles of Depth and Breadth of Vocabulary Knowledge in

Reading Comprehension. *Canadian Modern Language Review, 56 (2),* 282–308.
Qian, D. D. (2002). Investigating the Relationship Between Vocabulary Knowledge and Academic Reading Performance: An Assessment Perspective. *Language Learning, 52 (3),* 513-536.
Qian, D. D., & Schedl, M. (2004). Evaluation of an in-depth vocabulary knowledge measure for assessing reading performance. *Language Testing, 21 (1),* 28-52.
Read, J. (2000). *Assessing Vocabulary.* Cambridge: Cambridge University Press.
Richards, J. C. (2015). *Key issues in language teaching.* Cambridge: Cambridge University Press.
Richards, J. C. & Rodgers, T. S. (Theodore S. (2001). *Approaches and methods in language teaching.* Cambridge: Cambridge University Press.
Ritchie, W. C., & Bhatia, T. K. (1996). *Handbook of second language acquisition.* Academic Press.
Rost, M. (1990). *Listening in language learning.* London: Longman.
Rost, M. (2002). *Teaching and researching listening.* Harlow: Longman.
Rost, M. (2015). *Applied linguistics in action: teaching and researching listening.* London; Routledge.
Rost, K. (Ed.) (2015). *Listening in Action: 101 Ways to Teach Listening eBook.* Kindle e-book (Amazon).
Rubin, J. (1994). A Review of Second Language Listening Comprehension Research. *The Modern Language Journal, 78 (2),* 199-221.
Rubin, D. C., & Wallace, W. T. (1989). Rhyme and reason: Analyses of dual retrieval cues. *Journal of Experimental Psychology: Learning, Memory, and Cognition, 15 (4),* 698-709.
Schmidt, R. W. (1990). The Role of Consciousness in Second Language Learning1. *Applied Linguistics, 11 (2),* 129-158.
Service, E. (1992). Phonology, Working Memory, and Foreign-Language Learning. *The Quarterly Journal of Experimental Psychology Section A, 45 (1),* 21-50.
Sheen, Y. (2011). The Effect of Focused Written Corrective Feedback and Language Aptitude on ESL Learners' Acquisition of Articles. *Tesol Quarterly, 41 (2)* 255-283.
Sheppard, B. (2015). Balanced Listening Instruction. *TESOL Connections.* Available at: https://www.researchgate.net/publication/328202332_Balanced_Listening_Instruction
Skehan, P. (1989). *Individual differences in second-language learning.* Edward Arnold.
Smith, S. P. (2017). *Becoming an Outstanding Languages Teacher.* London: Routledge.
Smith, S. P. & Conti, G. (2016). *The Language Teacher Toolkit.* Createspace Publishing Platform.
Smith-Salcedo, C. (2002). The effects of songs in the foreign language classroom on text recall and involuntary mental rehearsal. *LSU Doctoral Dissertations.* Available at: https://digitalcommons.lsu.edu/cgi/viewcontent.cgi?article=2457&context=gradschool_dissertations

Soh, K.C. (2010). *Bilingual dual-coding and code-switching: Implications for the L1 in L2. L2 Learning. JLLT (1).* Available at: https://repository.nie.edu.sg/bitstream/10497/6302/1/JLLT-1-2-271.pdf

Spada, N., Lightbown, P. & White, J. (2005). The importance of form/meaning mappings in explicit form-focused instruction. In A. Housen & M. Pierrard (Eds.). *Current issues in instructed second language learning*, (pp. 199-234), Berlin: Mouton de Gruyter.

Spada, N. & Tomita, Y. (2010). Interactions Between Type of Instruction and Type of Language Feature: A Meta-Analysis. *Language Learning, 60 (2),* 263-308.

Spicher, L., & Sweeney, F. (2007). Folk music in the L2 classroom: Development of native-like pronunciation through prosodic engagement strategies. *Connections, 1,* 35-48.

Sprenger-Charolles, L. & Casalis, S. (1995). Reading and spelling acquisition in French first graders: Longitudinal evidence. *Reading and Writing, 7 (1),* 39-63.

Stæhr, L. S. (2009). Vocabulary knowledge and advanced listening comprehension in English as a foreign language. *Studies in Second Language Acquisition.* Cambridge University Press.

Stanovich, K. E. (1980). Toward an Interactive-Compensatory Model of Individual Differences in the Development of Reading Fluency. *Reading Research Quarterly, 16 (1),* 32.

Stanovich, K. E. (1986). Matthew Effects in Reading: Some Consequences of Individual Differences in the Acquisition of Literacy. *Reading Research Quarterly, 21 (4),* 360-407.

Suzuki, Y. & DeKeyser, R. (2017). The Interface of Explicit and Implicit Knowledge in a Second Language: Insights From Individual Differences in Cognitive Aptitudes. *Language Learning, 67 (4),* 747-790.

Swain, M. (1993). The Output Hypothesis: Just Speaking and Writing Aren't Enough. *Canadian Modern Language Review, 50 (1),* 158-164.

Swain, M. (2000). The output hypothesis and beyond: mediating acquisition through collaborative dialogue. In: Lantolf, J. (Ed.), *Sociocultural Theory and Second Language Learning.* Oxford: Oxford University Press, pp. 97-114.

Swain, M. & Lapkin, S. (1989). Canadian Immersion and Adult Second Language Teaching: What's the Connection? *The Modern Language Journal, 73 (2),* 150.

Swan, M. (2011). Using texts constructively 2: intensive input-output work. Teaching English, British Council. Available at: https://www.teachingenglish.org.uk/article/using-texts-constructively-2-intensive-input-output-work

Sweller, J. (2017). Cognitive load theory and teaching English as a second language to adult learners. *Contact (TESL Ontario's magazine).* Available at: http://contact.teslontario.org/cognitive-load-theory-esl/

Taie, M. (2014). Skill Acquisition Theory and Its Important Concepts in SLA. *Theory and Practice in Language Studies, 4 (9).* Available at:

http://www.academypublication.com/issues/past/tpls/vol04/09/30.pdf

Thornbury, S. *Scott Thornbury's 30 language teaching methods*. Cambridge; Cambridge University Press.

Torgerson, C., Brooks, G., & Hall, J. (2006). *A systematic review of the research literature on the use of phonics in the teaching of reading and spelling.* DfES Publications.

Treffers-Daller, J. & Milton, J. (2013). Vocabulary size revisited: The link between vocabulary size and academic achievement. *Applied Linguistics Review, 4 (1),* 151-172.

Uysal, H. H. (2010). The role of grammar and error correction in teaching languages to young learners. Chapter 10 in B. Haznedar & H.H. Uysal (Eds.) *Handbook for teaching foreign languages to young learners in primary schools.* Ankara; Ani Publications. Available at: https://www.academia.edu/6425707/The_role_of_grammar_and_error_correction_in_teaching_languages_to_young_learners

Vafaee, P. (2016). The relative significance of syntactic knowledge and vocabulary knowledge in second language listening comprehension. Unpublished doctoral thesis. Available at: https://drum.lib.umd.edu/bitstream/handle/1903/18320/Vafaee_umd_0117E_17069.pdf?sequence=1&isAllowed=y

Vandergrift, L. (1997). The Comprehension Strategies of Second Language (French) Listeners: A Descriptive Study. *Foreign Language Annals, 30 (3),* 387-409.

Vandergrift, L. (2003). From prediction to reflection: Guiding students through the process of L2 listening. *Canadian Modern Language Review, 59,* 425-440.

Vandergrift, L. (2004). 1. Listening to learn or listening to listen? *Annual Review of Applied Linguistics, 24,* 3-25.

Vandergrift, L., Goh, C.C.M., Mareschal, C.J. & Tafaghodtari, M.H. (2006). The Metacognitive Awareness Listening Questionnaire: Development and Validation. *Language Learning, 56 (3),* 431-462.

Vandergrift, L. & Tafaghodtari, M. H. (2010). Teaching L2 Learners How to Listen Does Make a Difference: An Empirical Study. *Language Learning, 60 (2),* 470-497.

VanPatten, B. (2014). *While We're on the Topic.* American Council on the Teaching of Foreign Languages.

VanPatten, B. & Williams, J. (Eds.) (2014). *Theories in Second language Acquisition.* London: Routledge.

Wagner, E. (2010). The effect of the use of video texts on ESL listening test-taker performance. *Language Testing, 27 (4)* 493-513.

Webb, S. (2007). The Effects of Repetition on Vocabulary Knowledge. *Applied Linguistics, 28 (1),* 46-65.

Weber, A., & Cutler, A. (2006). First-language phonotactics in second-language listening. *The Journal of the Acoustical Society of America, 119 (1),* 597-607.

Werner, E. (1975). A study of communication time. Unpublished Master's thesis. College Park: University of Maryland.
Wilkins, D. A. (1972). *Linguistics in language teaching,* Edward Arnold.
Willis, D. (2003). *Rules, Patterns and Words: Grammar and Lexis in English Language Teaching.* Cambridge: Cambridge University Press.
Willis, J. (undated web page). Criteria for identifying tasks for TBL | Teaching English, British Council, BBC. Available at:
https://www.teachingenglish.org.uk/article/criteria-identifying-tasks-tbl
Willis, J. R. (1996). *A framework for task-based learning.* London: Longman.
Willis, J. (1998). Task-Based Learning: What Kind of Adventure? *JALT Publications. Japan Association for Language Teaching, July.* Available at: https://jalt-publications.org/tlt/articles/2333-task-based-learning-what-kind-adventure
Wilson, J.J. (2008). *How to Teach Listening.* Pearson Education Limited.
Wilson, J.J. (2018). Listening Micro-Skills. Chapter in *The TESOL Encyclopedia of English Language Teaching.* Wiley-Blackwell.
Wilt, M. E. (1950). A study of teacher awareness of listening as a factor in elementary education. *Journal of Educational Research, 43, (8), 626-636.*
Winiharti, M. & Herlina, C. (2017). Audio Only or Video? Multimodality for Listening Comprehension. *Advances in Social Science, Education and Humanities Research, 82. Ninth International Conference on Applied Linguistics*
Winitz, H., (1981) *Native language and foreign language acquisition.* New York Academy of Sciences.
Woo, M. & Price, R. (2015). The pronunciation-reading connection. In T. Jones (ed.) *Integrating Pronunciation with other Skills Areas.* Alexandra, VA: TESOL Press.
Zhang, P. & Graham, S. (2019) Vocabulary learning through listening: comparing L2 explanations, teacher codeswitching, contrastive focus on form and incidental learning. Language Teaching Research. Available at:
http://centaur.reading.ac.uk/81387/

INDEX

Accuracy *37, 51, 145, 151,*
ACTFL *2, 133*
affective filter *131*
anxiety *18, 24, 28, 130-1, 216, 228*
apps *4, 94, 209*
aptitude *16, 19*
assessment *199-212*
    authenticity *203*
    fairness *29, 203*
    formative *98, 131, 199-204*
    question types *204-5*
    reliability *199, 202*
    summative *199, 200, 202-204*
    validity *201*
    washback *202, 205*
assimilation *17*
audio-lingual approach *46, 123*
authentic resources *190*
automatization *5-6, 96*
autonomy *51, 168, 172-3, 182*
back-chaining technique *46-7, 50*
blocking (versus interleaving) *72*
bottom-up processing *2, 9-13, 31, 59, 147*
CEFR *2, 137*
chunking *2, 62, 64-5, 70*
clauses *194, 151, 101-3*
cognates *28-9, 131, 218-219, 222*
cognitive
    empathy *204*
    load theory *73*
    strategies *213-218*
colligations *99-101, 103*
collocations *99-101, 103, 116-8*
communicative
    language teaching *6, 25, 120, 172*
    functions *64, 172-175*
compensatory strategies *11, 213, 228*

comprehensible input *1-2, 6-7, 22-23, 27, 55, 72, 74, 98, 122, 130, 182*
comprehension hypothesis *150*
contextualisation *23*
correction *134, 145*
curriculum planning *175, 225-9*
decoding *31-3, 39, 54-7, 68, 95, 123*
discourse-building *14, 22, 119*
distinctiveness principle *73*
drills *4, 7, 145, 177, 179*
dual coding *72, 74*
examinations *1, 3-4, 26, 201-4, 208*
explicit knowledge *96*
feedback *27, 36, 53, 98, 150, 208-9, 221*
flashcards *45, 66, 105*
flipping listening *168*
fluency *6, 9, 32-3, 61-4, 69-70, 87*
forgetting rates *71, 97, 229*
gestures *27, 35, 53, 82, 131-2, 169*
grammar *95-120*
    knowledge types *96*
    internalised *97*
    pedagogical *97*
    pop-up *105-6, 173*
independent listening *168, 211*
interleaving *32, 34, 71-2, 97, 173, 182, 188*
homework *168, 178*
implicit knowledge *96-7*
incidental (vocabulary learning) *66*
inferencing *75, 78, 80, 214*
information gap activities *141, 228*
input *122*
    enhancement *27, 106*
    flooding *2, 22, 24, 27, 103, 119, 176*
    processing *27*
intake *27, 130*
integration (of skills) *7, 208*

intentional (vocabulary learning) *66*
interaction hypothesis *122, 149-50*
interface *96*
interpersonal listening *121-147*
intonation *11-13, 15, 35, 123, 169, 207, 227*
knowledge
    declarative *96*
    procedural *96*
    productive *63*
    receptive *63*
learnability (of vocabulary) *69, 98, 172*
lesson plans *171-188*
lexical
    chunks *63-64*
    priming *2, 14*
    retrieval *59-94*
lexicogrammar *95-120*
lexis *63*
    content v function words *65*
MARS-EARS *171-3*
matching *31*
memory
    working memory *10*
    long term memory *10, 73*
metacognition *28-9, 32*
metacognitive strategies *113, 213-224*
metalanguage *115, 130*
micro-listening tasks *31*
minimal pairs *36, 38-9*
modelling
    listening as *2-3, 21*
    vocabulary use *74*
morphology *54, 69, 97-8, 108, 119*
morpheme *98*
narrow listening *70, 107, 118-9, 182-5*
narrow reading *106, 118, 176-7, 182-3*
native speakers *35, 102*
noticing *18, 22, 26-7, 53, 192*
oral-situational approach *104, 123*
output *25-26, 106, 173, 176*

parsing *15, 95-120*
patterns *69, 73-4, 101*
pedagogical cycle *173*
phonetics *36, 227*
phonics *32-3, 36-9, 46, 193*
    synthetic *37*
phonological
    loop *10, 66-8*
    memory *67-8*
    short-term memory *37*
phonology *36, 146*
phonotactics *38-9*
pictures *27, 46, 92, 105, 125-6*
planning *225-9*
PowerPoint *105*
PPP *25, 104-5*
processing
    bottom-up *9-12, 31, 59, 147*
    deep *73, 75, 80, 193, 195*
    extensive *22, 26, 119, 182-3*
    receptive *34, 106, 172-3*
    top-down *9-12, 17-8, 101*
    thorough *26, 30, 70, 114, 176*
    transfer-appropriate *60, 200*
process versus product *5, 19, 29, 231*
production effect *37, 73*
pronunciation *17, 32-4, 36, 38-9, 42, 68-9*
pushed output *173*
questions *15, 21, 26, 80*
question-answer *123*
reading aloud *32-33, 45, 51, 68*
realia *27*
recasts *134, 161*
recycling language *25, 34, 97, 164, 173, 203*
repetition
    choral *28, 46, 125-6, 129, 227*
    individual *105, 126, 131, 156, 200, 223*
    spaced *71*
retrieval *87, 173, 204*

routinisation *172-3, 180*
rules (grammar) *175*
scaffolding *6, 27-8, 155, 173, 178, 220*
schemas *11, 73*
schemes of work/learning *23*
segmentation *38-9, 52, 193, 210*
self-efficacy *18-9, 21, 26, 149, 204, 216*
self-monitoring *12, 28, 34, 219*
skill theory *5-6*
subvocalisation *67*
task-based listening *120, 149-170*
testing, discrete/mixed skill *201*
transfer appropriate processing (TAP) *200, 204*
washback (backwash) *199-202, 205, 229*

Printed in Great
Britain
by Amazon